THE HOBBIT
AND
HISTORY

The Hobbit
and
History

EDITED BY
JANICE LIEDL AND NANCY R. REAGIN

This book has not been approved, licensed, or sponsored
by any entity or person involved
in creating or producing *The Hobbit* film or book.

WILEY

John Wiley & Sons, Inc.

Wiley General Trade, an imprint of Turner Publishing Company
424 Church Street • Suite 2240 • Nashville, Tennessee 37219
445 Park Avenue • 9th Floor • New York, New York 10022
www.turnerpublishing.com

Cover design: Susan Olinsky
Book design: Kym Whitley
Front cover photo: © Photos 12 / Alamy

Library of Congress Cataloging-in-Publication Data:
ISBN: 978-1-11816-764-9

Printed in the United States of America

10 9 8 7 6 5 4 3 2 1

For Michael who is "as noble and as fair in face as an elf-lord, as strong as a warrior, as wise as a wizard, as venerable as a king of the dwarves, and as kind as summer."
—*The Hobbit*, 49

Contents

THE HOBBIT

AND

HISTORY

Introduction

Bilbo, the Hands-On Historian

Janice Liedl and Nancy R. Reagin

"This account of the end of the Third Age is drawn mainly from the Red Book of Westmarch . . . in origin Bilbo's private diary which he took with him to Rivendell."

—*The Fellowship of the Ring,* 23[1]

J. R. R. Tolkien's *The Hobbit* is written, so we are told, by Bilbo Baggins as a kind of memoir of his short-lived career as a burglar in Thorin's company. His story forms the first part of the Red Book of Westmarch which is later continued by his nephew and heir, Frodo. At the beginning of his story, Bilbo is bookish and set in his ways, a bit of an amateur scholar. Some of his traits foreshadowed the historian he would become. Of course, most historians don't boast of such hairy feet or keep company with wizards. On the other hand, few historians can boast of the same level of hands-on experience that Bilbo racks up during his adventures. However, if crafting history meant dealing with giant spiders and deadly dragons, there'd be a lot fewer histories being published today! Still, by the time he returns from his adventures, Bilbo has characteristically changed — burglary will do that to you. (Note: no archives were burgled in the production of this volume!) Although he still enjoys the fine food and comfortable domesticity that surrounded him before thirteen adventurers came to visit, all of his neighbors agree he's just a little bit strange since returning to the Shire. The same can be said of many historians, bleary-eyed from spending endless hours in the archives or writing out the analysis of their latest historical discoveries.

Superficially, the story of *The Hobbit* comes from someone just as tweedy and stuffy as Bilbo appeared at the start of his story. J. R. R. Tolkien was a professor of medieval languages and literature at Oxford University when he wrote down his tales of hobbits, dwarves, and wizards in Middle-earth. In some ways, Tolkien was the model for his humble hobbit hero: He was fond of books, smoked his pipe, and enjoyed his homely comforts as much as Bilbo ever did. But underneath that conventionality was a spirit as adventurous as any Took, although after some youthful hikes in the European Alps and time in the trenches of World War I, Tolkien confined his adventures to storytelling with his sons and exploring the Middle Ages with paper and pen. Still, like Bilbo, he was a bit of a rebel. Tolkien won fame for his scholarship on *Beowulf*, a rousing medieval adventure story about a would-be king's rise to greatness fighting dreaded monsters. In his much-admired essay, "On Fairy-Stories," Tolkien heartily defended the realms of fantasy against the claims of "real life." He merged belief and practice when he created one of the greatest works in fantasy, drawing on the stories and histories he knew so well.

This book unlocks those historical parallels between the Middle Ages that Tolkien knew so well as a distinguished scholar of medieval literature, and the intricate cultures of Middle-earth that he created. From the medieval European traditions of war and power and the humble (and sometimes delicious) realities of historic human cultures, to the magical elements of myth and legend, there is a hoard of historical lore laid out in these chapters, and each traces parallels between historical cultures and those of Middle-earth. The riddle game that Bilbo plays with Gollum is modeled on the riddles that Anglo-Saxons told each other, such as those contained in the *Exeter Book*, written more than a thousand years ago, while the weapons and tactics we see used by the dwarves and the Five Armies were known to the Vikings and other medieval warriors. The seed-cakes and scones that hobbits yearned for were also featured in old European cookbooks, which were themselves extensions of the older European traditions of hospitality we see maintained by Elrond at Rivendell. Tolkien was inspired by the wizards like Gandalf, dragons, and monsters that he studied in the myths, epic tales, and legends of medieval Europe. We invite readers willing to follow in the footsteps of Bilbo, Tolkien, and the historians who contributed to this collection to explore these connections. Seeing Middle-earth and its peoples against these historical backdrops shines new light on the richness of Tolkien's world, which is rooted in a knowledge of European cultures as deep as the archive that Gandalf explores in Minas Tirith.

PART ONE

"A Darkness Came on with Dreadful Swiftness":

Middle-earth's Warriors and Worthies

"That would be no good," said the wizard, "not without a mighty Warrior, even a Hero. I tried to find one; but warriors are busy fighting one another in distant lands, and in this neighbourhood heroes are scarce, or simply not to be found."

—*The Hobbit*, 21

The Faces of the Five Armies

Marcus Schulzke

"So began a battle that none had expected; and it was called the Battle of Five Armies, and it was very terrible. Upon one side were the Goblins and the wild Wolves, and upon the other were Elves and Men and Dwarves."
　—*The Hobbit*, 292[1]

Tolkien's descriptions of war and of the warrior cultures of Middle-earth have close parallels to ancient and medieval warfare. This chapter explores the different races and characters of *The Hobbit* as warrior archetypes that correspond to real military forces throughout history. In some cases, the historical references are clearly intentional. Beorn's similarities with Viking berserkers, for example, are too close to be coincidental. Other parallels, like those between the dwarves and mercenaries or the goblins and modern armies, become apparent upon close reading of *The Hobbit* and its historical analogues. Toward the end of the book, we see Middle-earth's different warrior cultures in action when each force takes part in the Battle of the Five Armies.

Bilbo Baggins wasn't a warrior at the start of *The Hobbit*, but he becomes one over the course of the book as Tolkien chronicles the hobbit's initiation into the warrior culture. Tolkien draws on themes and examples from ancient and medieval cultures to lay the foundation for Bilbo's transformation, while also describing that transformation in a way that mirrors the modern process of civilian conscripts becoming soldiers during times of war. Although Bilbo is a reluctant soldier, who always remains a civilian at heart, he proves that he is able to defend himself and his friends when they are threatened. Towards the end of the book, we see Middle-earth's different warrior cultures in action when each force takes part in the Battle of the Five Armies.

Tolkien's ability to create convincing warrior cultures and descriptions of battle was rooted in his extensive academic knowledge of medieval literature, including *Beowulf* and *Sir Gawain and the Green Knight*, and his personal experiences of war. As an officer in the British Expeditionary Force during World War I, Tolkien fought on the Western Front until he contracted trench fever in 1916.[2] His personal experience helped Tolkien understand soldiers' psychology and the realities of war, while his own transition from civilian to soldier closely parallels Bilbo's transformation in his journey to the Lonely Mountain.

"Calculating Folk": Dwarves as Medieval Mercenaries

The twelve dwarves Tolkien introduces early in *The Hobbit* are from a race whose members are trained to fight from birth. They are small, but powerfully built—natural warriors who have an affinity for fighting. Initially, their skill makes them seem like ideal allies. However, Bilbo soon realizes that the dwarves' love of gold and lack of loyalty makes them unpredictable and often clouds their judgment. This combination of excellent fighting abilities, a love of money, and erratic behavior makes the dwarves similar to the *condottieri* (contract soldiers) of medieval Italy. The *condottieri* were military professionals in an age when most soldiers were poorly trained amateurs. As merce-

Last stand: Like Thorin Oakenshield, a medieval king confronts death in battle from a 1489 woodcut

naries, the *condottieri* fought for the highest paying employer, or those that guaranteed future employment. Some, like the famous mercenary captain Sir John Hawkwood, were veterans of the Hundred Years' War, who came to Italy to take part in its constant factional violence. Hawkwood's White Company is a prime example of the *condottieri* way of war—composed of an assortment of English, German, Italian, and Hungarian adventurers, who regularly changed sides and threatened their own employers, yet were also ferocious in battle.[3]

The Renaissance Florentine politician and writer Niccolo Machiavelli was one of the most prominent critics of the mercenaries. In his advicebook, *The Prince*, he argues that they were, despite being professional warriors, unreliable and ineffective. He accuses them of defecting to the enemy for higher pay and refusing to risk their lives in battle.[4] Machiavelli thinks that mercenaries are so corrupt that a ruler who employs them is doomed to failure, regardless of whether the mercenaries win or lose their battles. When mercenaries lose, the state employing them suffers all of the usual problems of military defeat, but when they win, mercenaries can demand more money and threaten to retaliate against their employers. Machiavelli's is among the most influential arguments against the use of mercenaries, and his opinions reflect a long-standing disdain for anyone who fights for money.[5]

Thorin, the leader of the band of dwarves that Bilbo accompanies, embodies the strengths and weaknesses of the mercenaries Machiavelli describes. He is a heroic figure who performs well in battle, but his self-centeredness makes him a poor leader. Thorin cannot make effective plans without Gandalf's help and he fails to inspire his followers as they pass through Mirkwood. He insults Bombur instead of helping him after the stouter dwarf had fallen into an enchanted sleep from which it was difficult to recover, and is quick to assign the most difficult tasks to others. Thorin's weaknesses are made clear as he continually relies on Bilbo, the least experienced member of the group, to find solutions to their problems.

As with medieval mercenaries, the dwarves are professionals who, when properly motivated, can be excellent warriors. However, motivating them can prove difficult because they are only willing to fight for material gain. Their concern for the highest profit and their overwhelming greed causes them to make strategically unsound decisions. The most obvious mistake is their decision to defend the dragon Smaug's treasure against overwhelming odds. This is unjust because the humans of Lake-town have a strong claim to the treasure, and extremely greedy because there is enough treasure to be shared. Moreover, the decision risks initiating a battle that the dwarves cannot win—a costly mistake for even the greatest warriors.

Perhaps their worst characteristic is that the dwarves are disloyal. They do not acknowledge Bilbo's help or come to his aid. They repeatedly abandon the hobbit when they are threatened and show no desire to help him as they escape from the goblins. Even after Bilbo saves the dwarves several times, they seem to have no loyalty toward him. When the group first encounters wolves, Dori grudgingly helps Bilbo climb a tree, thus saving the hobbit, but this is one of the few examples where a dwarf risks himself for something other than material rewards. The narrator is explicit on this point, and even says that "dwarves are not heroes, but calculating folk with a great idea of the value of money; some are tricky and treacherous and pretty bad lots; some are not, but are decent enough people like Thorin and Company, if you don't expect too much" (*Hobbit*, 225).

Beorn the Berserker

Beorn is a character based heavily on medieval Viking berserkers. These were specialized fighters, famous for their ferocity and indifference to pain. Contemporaries believed that they became bearlike or even transformed completely into bears when they went into battle. These sources describe them as shape shifters.[6] The word *berserk*, which means "bear shirt," is a reference to their animalistic qualities. They charged into battle as if they were animals, fighting without armor and without the discipline of the warriors who made up the shield wall that comprised most of the Viking force. "The fast attack with swords, often likened to a storm of fire, suited madly raging warriors best."[7] Historians continue to debate whether berserkers' ferocity was induced by drugs or whether it came from other sources.[8]

Whatever the source of their courage, the berserkers were notoriously difficult to kill, and often sustained multiple serious injuries while continuing to fight. This is also an apt description of Beorn's performance during the Battle of the Five Armies. Beorn perfectly fits the descriptions of the berserker fighting style—charging into battle like an animal and fighting independently:

> In that last hour Beorn himself had appeared—no one knew how or from where. He came alone, and in bear's shape; and he seemed to have grown almost to giant-size in his wrath. The roar of his voice was like drums and guns; and he tossed wolves and goblins from his path like straws and feathers. He fell upon their rear, and broke like a clap of thunder through the ring. (*The Hobbit*, 302)

Other similarities go deeper than this. The Viking warriors took on bear names by attaching "bjorn" or "biorn" to their names. Beorn is one who only has the bear name. Gandalf calls Beorn a "skin-changer," and says that he may be a descendant of the bears that once lived in the mountains. (*Hobbit*, 125) This description characterizes Beorn as being only partly human, just as the Viking berserkers are described in legends.

The berserker initiates deliberately copied the lifestyle and fighting style of the animals they sought to become.[9] Their wildness made it necessary for berserkers to live apart from society during peacetime. They were unpredictable and could even threaten their own allies if their urges were not given some type of violent outlet. Many sagas demonize them and link them to rape and murder. They were especially hated by the Christian chroniclers, who composed the later sagas and stories.[10] This may explain why Beorn lives by himself, has little contact with others, and seems to have difficulty maintaining self-control. However, in Norse literature, berserkers are not solitary figures. They usually appear in groups of twelve and often serve as the bodyguards of kings.[11]

Many historical armies had their own berserkers. Warriors wearing bear furs appear on the Roman emperor Trajan's column as auxiliaries in the Roman army. Some joined the ranks of early medieval armies. There is also evidence of warriors fighting naked and in a frenzy in ancient Assyrian and Hittite armies.[12] This suggests that while the Viking berserkers are the most famous union of human and animal, Beorn represents a style of fighting that was once widespread—a style that shows the close affinity between wild animals and the warrior spirit of ancient cultures.

The Wise Warrior-Elves

The elves of Rivendell help the dwarves discover the identity of the two swords that they took from a group of trolls. The weapons turn out to be Orcrist, the goblin cleaver, and Glamdring, the beater. They are feared by the goblins and considered to have special powers. Named weapons are important in legends and appear repeatedly throughout the book. They are signs of nobility and prestige. Swords like King Arthur's Excalibur, Beowulf's Hrunting and Naegling, and

Charlemagne's Joyeuse have become legendary because they served as marks of royal office and sources of power. During the Middle Ages, good swords were so highly valued that they took on religious significance and were sanctified in a church ceremony when first presented to a knight.[13]

A deep personal attachment to weapons, including naming of them, is common across countless societies. Many types of weapons bear names that are symbolic for the people who use them — names that invoke past victories, cultural values, and aspirations.[14] Glenn Gray, a veteran of World War II and author of one of the classic studies of the soldier on the battlefield, describes the depth of the connection between a soldier and his weapon:

> In less sophisticated natures, this presence of others is projected also into the weapons and instruments of war. They become personalized, and the soldier becomes attached to them as an extension of himself. They afford him a vast comfort in a difficult position as protection and a shield, as a second skin.[15]

The elves of Rivendell help Bilbo and the dwarves discover the nature of the weapons that they have found and provide them with an opportunity to rest and recover before continuing on their journey. The Wood-elves that Bilbo's group encounters later in the book are much less hospitable. They are depicted as honorable and good elves, who are nonetheless suspicious of outsiders. This makes them one of the story's most complex races.

The elves inhabit the forest of Mirkwood, but seem to have little concern for keeping the forest safe, or for the welfare of those traveling through it. They are isolationists, only choosing to fight when it is in their interest to do so. They are much like the warriors of feudal Japan, whose deep respect for tradition led them to resist outside influences that might upset their society.[16] The elves of Mirkwood initially seem like hostile characters because of their suspicion of the dwarves crossing their territory. The elf king's decision to imprison the dwarves, temporarily halting their quest and forcing Bilbo to plot a rescue attempt, makes them antagonists. Yet they have good reason to be suspicious of the greedy dwarves, who refuse to cooperate with the elves and threaten to destroy the elves' peaceful isolation from the outside world.

Throughout Tolkien's works, elves represent a lost way of life. They are an older race than humans and dwarves, and are far more attuned to the natural world. It is fitting that the elves of Rivendell reveal the identity of the Orcrist and Glamdring, as they were the ones who created those weapons long ago and who have tracked their great lineage over thousands of years. The Wood-elves are even closer to nature than the High Elves of Rivendell. They live in the heart of a forest, using caves as homes and the trees to hide themselves from intruders. The narrator describes the Elvenking as having a love of wealth, which explains his desire to claim a share of Smaug's treasure; but he defines wealth differently than the dwarves. His crown is composed of materials drawn from the seasonal vegetation, an indication that gold and jewels cannot match the value of the plants that sustain the elves.

Humble, Honest Humans

Like the elves, the humans of *The Hobbit* are complex figures. Although the Wood-elves and humans of Lake-town are allies, the humans are more distant from nature and less wise. They suffer familiar human shortcomings, but they are also far more generous to Bilbo and the dwarves. Bard is the book's most important human and among its most heroic characters. Bard is a knightly figure who embodies chivalric values. He is courageous, honorable, and fair. He also comes from a noble lineage and serves as the captain of Lake-town's guards. Although he is described as being a grim and pessimistic person, Bard is a competent commander. He leads the humans in their battle against Smaug and manages to kill the dragon while it is in flight with a single well-placed arrow—a shot that provides evidence of Bard's prowess with a bow.

Bard is one of Lake-town's many skilled archers. They are so accurate that the eagles are afraid to fly in the region for fear of the humans shooting at them. These archers are very similar to the

English longbowmen who dominated the battlefields of the Hundred
Years War. They even use yew bows, just as the English archers
did.[17] Historically, archers have occupied a low place on the battlefield, even when they were among the most effective fighters. In the
English armies of the Middle Ages, knights and the men-at-arms held
more prestige than the masses of archers because they constantly
trained for battle and fought the enemy in hand-to-hand combat.
Although they were highly skilled, archers were not professional soldiers. They were drawn from the ranks of civilians only for the dura-
tion of a war.

Bard is a character who draws from both the image of the English
archer and the English knight. He is skilled with a bow, but he is also
a professional soldier with the chivalrous qualities of a knight. Scholar
Lee Rossi argues that Bard "is a reincarnation of the heroic ideal fig-
ured in Beowoulf, valour in battle and generosity to his thains, and a
repudiation of the chamber-of-commerce types who figure so largely
in contemporary politics."[18] Moreover, Bard's high status is marked by
the way he uses his own named weapon. Before firing at Smaug, Bard
speaks to his black arrow and tells its story:

> Black arrow! I have saved you to the last. You have never failed
> and and always have I recovered you. I had you from my
> father and he from of old. If ever you came from the forges of
> the true king under the Mountain, go now and speed well! . . .
> The black arrow sped straight from the string . . . it smote and
> vanished [into Smaug], barb, shaft, and feather, so fierce was
> its flight. With a shriek that deafened men, felled trees and
> split stone, Smaug shot spouting into the air, turned over and
> crashed down from on high in ruin. (*The Hobbit*, 262)

Chivalry was never as perfect as it appears in romantic tales; it
had a dual character. Some knights preyed on those who were weaker
than them, waged war for profit, and took up arms against those to
whom they swore allegiance. Simon IV de Montfort epitomizes the
extremes of knightly behavior. He loyally served King Phillip II of
France during the Third Crusade and vigorously opposed the mis-

treatment of Christian prisoners. Later in life, he slaughtered thousands of unarmed Cathars during the Albigensian Crusade, torturing many to set an example for other heretics.[19]

Knights often celebrated war as a chance to earn wealth and prestige. Nevertheless, prior to the enactment of laws of war, chivalry provided some level of order on the battlefield.[20] It motivated combatants to use minimal force against each other, encouraged capturing and ransoming opponents rather than killing them, imposed rules on the treatment of prisoners, and facilitated the formation of truces. Bard embodies the chivalric ideal because he is constantly prepared to fight and yet still eager to find diplomatic solutions that will allow him to avoid bloodshed. This is evident when he attempts to convince Thorin to divide the treasure and when he decides to mount a nonviolent siege. Bard's behavior makes him chivalric in both senses, as he combines the virtues of a warrior with the reluctance to use force.

"Dread has come upon you all!"

Goblins are recurring enemies in *The Hobbit* and even more dangerous than Smaug. The dwarves, humans, and elves are, despite their differences, united by their common hatred and fear of the goblins, as they were almost destroyed by the goblin horde. Because they are the story's villains, the reader has little sense of the goblins' culture aside from what can be seen from the outsider's perspective. Nevertheless, Tolkien does imbue them with some of the marks of warrior cultures. Goblins present a mix of ancient and modern characteristics. They fight with medieval weapons and resemble cavalry when riding their wargs. However, they also build instruments of destruction capable of producing far more damage than typical medieval weapons. The narrator says that "It is not unlikely that they invented some of the machines that have since troubled the world, especially the ingenious devices for killing large numbers of people at once, for wheels and engines and explosions always delighted them" (*The Hobbit*, 73). This description makes goblins sound like they are armed with the medieval equivalents of modern weapons of mass destruction. The goblins' explosives and wheeled war machines have the same terrifying power as the tanks, long-range artillery, and poison gas that were used in World War I.

Goblins represent the cruelty of war. They are violent without reason and enjoy inflicting pain on their opponents. As the narrator says, "goblins are cruel, wicked, and bad-hearted" (*The Hobbit*, 73). They are terrifying in a much different way than the imposing dragon Smaug. They are warriors of average skill. Because they are easily surprised early in the Battle of the Five Armies, they appear incapable of complex planning and are poorly organized. The goblins carry an array of weapons and armor, and have no standardization of either. However, they are resilient, quickly recovering from their initial losses during the Battle of the Five Armies as they manage to outflank their opponents, surprising them from the rear. They are also able to use their super-weapons to temporarily turn the tide of battle. Bolg's giant goblin guards are among these weapons. These huge figures were capable of resisting Thorin's charge and are far more powerful than anyone on the battlefield aside from Beorn.

In *The Lord of the Rings*, Tolkien usually calls the goblins "orcs." Although their name changes from *The Hobbit*, Tolkien continues to characterize them in a way that links them to the worst qualities of modern war. The orcs are anonymous fighters who, like modern armies, can mobilize in huge numbers and who continually employ powerful weapons of unrestrained destructive power, such as when they attempt to destroy the wall of Helm's Deep with explosives. This makes them the most modern of the warrior cultures that Tolkien describes in The Hobbit, aside from Bilbo, who presents a far more positive image of the modern soldier.

Bilbo: The Citizen Soldier

Hobbits are defined by their love of excess and celebration. They are the epitome of the complacent and "soft" civilian. They are so concerned with maintaining stable lives that one who attempts to find adventure is scorned by others, as Bilbo finds when he returns home at the end of the story. Bilbo starts his quest as a simple, respectable Shire resident who lacks experience in the outside world. He is, like the conscript soldier, a grudging participant in his adventure; he feels little reason to join the quest and shows no enthusiasm for battle. Bilbo places little value on the treasure that the other characters are competing for and is carried along on an adventure that others have imposed on him. His disregard for the treasure and his willingness to give it up to preserve peace and repay his debts shows that his primary concerns are finding a peaceful resolution to problems and protecting his own integrity.

The Hobbit has been called a Bildungsroman (a novel about an educational journey) because it follows Bilbo's transformation and provides some lessons about how he becomes a better hobbit.[21] Early in the journey, Bilbo frequently reflects on how much he misses the comforts of home. Most of all, he misses the wonderful food, which he can eat many times a day. "At the start of the book Bilbo, as befits his bourgeois status and anachronistic nature, is helpless and, if not contemptible, at least open to contempt from those around him."[22] He has the experience of a civilian thrust into an unfamiliar world of discomfort and danger.

Like many conscript soldiers, Bilbo is often treated as cannon fodder. Thorin assigns the toughest jobs to the inexperienced hobbit, and none of the dwarves gives much thought to his welfare. Their lack of concern accelerates Bilbo's development, forcing him to learn how to protect himself and the other members of his group. It is significant that the most important fighting experiences—those that really transform Bilbo—happen while he is alone. In the warrior cultures of feudal Japan, Homeric Greece, and medieval Europe, warriors often fought as individuals, relying on their own skill to win. Individual skill in battle was the true test of a warrior, which is why in The Iliad one finds descriptions of leading men on both sides looking for worthy opponents and challenging them to fight.[23]

Initially, Bilbo does not choose to be a lone warrior. This is forced upon him when he is left alone in the goblins' cave and again when he is attacked by the giant spider. He must adapt quickly to flee from or fight against these dangerous encounters. However, by the time his friends are captured by the Elvenking, Bilbo has found the courage to act independently.

One of Bilbo's most significant transformative moments is his fight with the Mirkwood spider. With the dwarves tied up and helpless, it is up to Bilbo to save the group. He does not run away from the spider, nor does he use the ring to become invisible. Instead, he faces the spider without subterfuge and defeats it in battle. This encounter transforms Bilbo into a warrior:

> Somehow the killing of the giant spider, all alone by himself in the dark without the help of the wizard or the dwarves or of anyone else, made a great difference to Mr. Baggins. He felt a different person, and much fiercer and bolder in spite of an empty stomach, as he wiped his sword on the grass and put it back into his sheath. (*The Hobbit*, 167)

To emphasize this transformation, Bilbo names his sword Sting, describing the sword's power to sting the spider when Bilbo feels like an insect caught in a web. The sword's status changes, becoming like the other named weapons in the story, a mark of nobility and power. Bilbo changes along with the sword, as the one who possesses and wielded it when it earned its name. Bilbo's status as a warrior is confirmed in Smaug's cave when he takes a mail coat made of rare mithril. Special armor is a mark of military skill found across cultures and time periods.[24]

During his journey, Bilbo transforms from a peaceful civilian to a true warrior. Nevertheless, there is a critical difference between Bilbo and the warrior elites of the ancient and medieval world that the other characters in the book resemble. Bilbo is a commoner, not a noble like Thorin or Bard. Rather than acting like a soldier of an ancient or medieval army, Bilbo represents the modern conscript soldier. He is a civilian at heart, whose first loyalty is to his comrades. Bilbo, the most complex of the story's characters, is the ideal citizen soldier, whose development is the most dramatic. His experience parallels Tolkien's own transformation from civilian to soldier when Tolkien entered the trenches of the Western Front in 1916. He underwent the difficult experience of leaving home and facing the horrors of war in a foreign land. Like Bilbo, Tolkien saw close friends killed; he narrowly managed to avoid death and returned home.

The Battle of Five Armies

The Battle of the Five Armies is not only the climax of the adventure but also the moment in the story when each of the warrior groups comes together on the battlefield. When the Wood-elves, dwarves, and humans face the goblin army and the wolves, they quickly overcome their differences and form up to meet the enemy as a united force. This leaves little doubt that, despite the different warrior values each group represents, they are all still fundamentally good. The united armies develop a plan that calls for the elves to stand on one of the mountain's spurs, while the dwarves and humans take position on the other. A small force stands between them to draw the goblins between the armies, exposing their flanks to arrows and attacks from the high ground.

The armies are formed in a way that was common during the Middle Ages. As in medieval armies, each group of soldiers owes their loyalty to a lord, whom they fight alongside in battle. Although they are all part of the same force and share a common enemy, each race fights as a semiautonomous group. These groups are organized into a large formation, but they preserve their independence and are able act on their own initiative, without orders from a commander or other elements of the army.[25] The armies take up positions in a way that allows each group to fight on alone if the others are overwhelmed or defect.

In many ways, the opening of the Battle of the Five Armies resembles the Battle of Agincourt—one of the most important battles of the Hundred Years War. At Agincourt in 1415, the main line of the French army advanced against the dismounted knights in the English center, avoiding the archers guarding the flanks.[26] The French line compressed and became disorganized as it was funneled into a narrow front, just as the first line of goblins was when they attacked between the spurs of the mountains. At Agincourt, the mounted knights were easy targets for the archers, whose arrows could strike the unarmored horses. The English archers devastated the French ranks with volleys of arrows, and once the arrows were exhausted they entered into hand-to-hand combat against the French men-at-arms. The goblins suffer the same fate as the French knights. Many goblins riding wargs are killed by archers during their charge. Then, after the elves and the humans fire their first volley of arrows, they charge into the goblins' flanks:

> Just as the goblins were recovering from the [archers'] onslaught and the elf-charge was halted, there arose from across the valley a deep-throated roar. With cries of "Moria!" and "Dain, Dain!" the dwarves of the Iron Hills plunged in, wielding their mattocks, upon the other side; and beside them came the men of the Lake with long swords. Panic came upon the Goblins; and even as they turned to meet this new attack, the elves charged again with renewed numbers. (*The Hobbit,* 295)

Although Tolkien gives the archers a less important role in his battle than they had at Agincourt, events play out in much the same way, with multiple waves of attackers charging into a V-shaped enemy formation as they are struck first by arrows and then by flank attacks. The goblins even attempt to maneuver around the defenders to attack from the rear, as the French did when they captured Henry V's camp.[27]

Once the armies are locked in combat and unable to maneuver, the Battle of the Five Armies degenerates into a melee. Groups of fighters rally around their commanders who, like the commanders of ancient and medieval armies, play a far more active role in the fighting than modern generals. At this point, the Battle of the Five Armies, like so many other mythical battles, becomes a story about the great deeds of the most skilled warriors. Thorin and his companions are partially redeemed when they leave the safety of their cave and join the battle in time to shift the balance back in favor of the Free Folk. Yet they are unable to reach Bolg, the leader of the goblins. Beorn, taking the form of a large bear, makes the decisive attack, singlehandedly killing Bolg and his guards. He and the eagles finally break the exhausted goblin army and force it into retreat.

"Eyes that Fire and Sword Have Seen"

Tolkien's fantasy world is heavily based on historical referents. As this chapter has shown, this is especially true of his depictions of warrior cultures and battle. Each of the races and major characters he introduces in *The Hobbit* embodies qualities of famous warriors and warrior cultures of the past and present—the *condottieri* of medieval Italy, the common and knightly English soldiers of the Hundred Years War, and more. They illustrate both the noblest elements of chivalric war and the greatest evils of modern mechanized warfare. Tolkien blends past and present, and draws on his own experience of war, to bring these different groups into contact with each other, showing how members of each group might react to those with much different values. Finally, through Bilbo, the reader witnesses the metaphorical transformation of a modern citizen into a soldier, as he interacts with these various warrior groups and develops his own distinctive identity and attitude toward the fighting that he is drawn into. Tolkien's world thus reflects realities that we see throughout our own history: that war can both make and break nations and peoples, while it profoundly transforms those who fight.

Notes

1. All references are from J. R. R. Tolkien, *The Hobbit, or There and Back Again* (Boston: Houghton Mifflin, 1979).

2. Humphrey Carpenter, *Tolkien: A Biography:* (New York: Ballantine, 1977), 96.

3. Barbara Wertheim Tuchman, *A Distant Mirror: The Calamitous 14th Century* (New York: Ballatine, 1978).

4. Niccolo Machiavelli, *Discourses on Livy* (New York: Oxford University Press, 2003); Niccolo Machiavelli, *The Prince* (New York: Barnes and Noble, 2004).

5. Sarah Percy, *Mercenaries: The History of a Norm in International Relations* (New York: Oxford University Press, 2007).

6. Catharina Raudvere, "Popular Religion in the Viking Age" in *The Viking World*, ed. S. Brink, Neil Price (New York: Routledge, 2008): 242.

7. Michael P. Speidel, *Ancient Germanic Warriors: Warrior Styles from Trajan's Column to Icelandic Sagas* (New York: Routledge, 2004): 63.

8. Ian Heath, Angus McBride, *The Vikings* (New York: Osprey, 1985): 45.

9. Mircea Eliade, *Essential Sacred Writings from Around the World* (New York: Harper Row, 1967): 294.

10. Mark Harrison, Gerry Embleton, *Viking Hersir 793-1066 AD* (New York: Osprey, 1993).

11. Ian Heath, Angus McBride, *The Vikings* (New York: Osprey, 1985): 49.

12. Michael P. Speidel, "Berserks: A History of Indo-European 'Mad Warrior'." *Journal of World History* 13(2) (2002): 253-90; Michael P. Speidel, *Ancient Germanic Warriors: Warrior Styles from Trajan's Column to Icelandic Sagas* (New York: Routledge, 2004): 52-53.

13. R. Ewart Oakeshott, *The Archaeology of Weapons: Arms and Armour from Prehistory to the Age of Chivalry* (Mineola, NY: Courier Dover Publications, 1996): 251.

14. Charles Kauffman, "Names and Weapons." *Communication Monographs* 56(3) (1989): 273-85.

15. Glenn J. Gray, *The Warriors: Reflections on Men in Battle* (New York: Harper Row, 1967): 477-78.

16. Stephen R. Turnbull, Angus McBride, *Warriors of Medieval Japan* (New York: Osprey Publishing, 2005).

17. Robert Hardy, *Longbow: A Social and Military History* (Sparkford: Haynes, 2006).

18. Lee D. Rossi, *The Politics of Fantasy, C.S. Lewis and J.R.R. Tolkien* (Ann Arbor, MI: UMI Research Press, 1984): 100.

19. J. R. Maddicott, *Simon de Montfort* (New York: Cambridge University Press, 1994).

20. Matthew Strickland, *War and Chivalry: The Conduct and Perception of War in England and Normandy, 1066-1217* (New York: Cambridge University Press, 1996).

21. William H. Green, *The Hobbit: A Journey into Maturity* (New York: Twayne Publishers, 1995).

22. Tom Shippey, *J.R.R. Tolkien: Author of the Century* (Boston, MA: Mariner Books, 2002): 21.

23. Homer, *The Iliad* (New York: Penguin, 1998).

24. Martin van Creveld, *The Culture of War* (New York: Presidio Press, 2008): 14.

25. Matthew Bennett, Jim Bradbury, Kelly DeVries, Iain Dickie, *Fighting Techniques of the Medieval World: Equipment, Combat Skills and Tactics* (New York: St. Martin's Press, 2005).

26. Juliet Barker, *Agincourt: Henry V and the Battle that Made England* (New York: Little, Brown, and Company, 2005).

27. Barker, 263.

CHAPTER 2

From Oakenshield to Bloodaxe:

The Viking Roots of
Tolkien's Dwarves

Colin Gibbons

"They were in shining armour, and red light leapt from their eye.
In the gloom the great dwarf gleamed like gold in a dying fire."
    —*The Hobbit*, 340-341[1]

W hen people think of Vikings, they often picture a hardy
and warlike culture that bears a striking resemblance to the
dwarves of Tolkien's *The Hobbit* and *The Lord of the Rings*—and for
good reason. The name *Viking* refers to Norsemen or Scandinavian
adventurers who practiced piracy at sea and raided settlements on
land.[2] Vikings were Scandinavian adventurers who flourished from
the eighth through the twelfth centuries. With their sleek ships and
well-armed war bands, Vikings raided settlements from Scotland and
Ireland to France, and even into the Mediterranean. They sought gold

and slaves, wealth and fame. Tolkien's dwarves may not have traveled the seas, but in most other respects, they resembled these fierce Norsemen. The dwarves of *The Hobbit* and medieval Vikings share a similar lust for the acquisition of wealth and territory as well as a desire for adventure. Dwarves and Vikings both sought to maintain family honor, and if their family honor had been tarnished, to exact their revenge on those who did so. The names given to the dwarves in *The Hobbit*, Bifur, Thorin, Kili, Ívarr, Olaf, Hálfdan, often are indistinguishable from some of the most famous Viking warriors, leaders, and kings. Tolkien's dwarves' traits mirror those of many historical and mythological Vikings, ranging from their ways of war, including choices of weapons and armor (although neither wore the infamous horned helmet of popular fiction) to a brutish, uncivilized, and often bearded appearance. However, most important parallels have to do with their culture and attitudes.

Many a Gleaming, Golden Hoard: The Dwarves' Driving Desire

"'They found a good deal of gold and a great many jewels too. Anyway they grew immensely rich.'"

— Thorin Oakenshield, *The Hobbit*, 37

At the start of *The Hobbit*, Thorin, Bilbo and the other adventurous dwarves set off on a quest to reclaim Thorin's stolen family wealth and his kingdom from the dragon Smaug. Dwarves, much like medieval Vikings, had a particular taste for plunder, especially gold, jewels, and wealth, as became evident when Thorin and the others stumble upon swords in the troll's lair: "Two caught their eyes particularly, because of their beautiful scabbards and jeweled hilts" (*The Hobbit*, 60). Tolkien discusses and describes the opulence of the lives of those dwarves under the Mountain at great length. Thorin's ancestors were so wealthy that their halls "became full of armour and jewels and carvings and cups" (*The Hobbit*, 37).It was said that even a fourteenth share of the treasure—fourteen being the number of dwarves plus one hobbit—would bring exceedingly great wealth equal to or greater than many kings of Middle-earth. Thorin himself retained this passion for treasure, as did his band of dwarves. Thorin never forgets the splendor of his ancestors' wealth; he wears a gold chain around his neck as a reminder of his desire to reclaim the stolen treasure of his family. Once he's done so, Thorin is trapped by his gold lust—what is described by others as a dragon sickness. Thorin becomes so obsessed with this reclaimed wealth that he steadfastly refuses any offers to parlay this wealth: "Is there nothing for which you would yield any of your gold?" "Nothing that you or your friends have to offer" (*The Hobbit*, 330). Bilbo expresses intimate knowledge of Thorin's lust for treasure when he says: "However you don't know Thorin Oakenshield as well as I do now. I assure you, he is quite ready to sit on a heap of gold and starve, as long as you sit here" (*The Hobbit*, 325). Even if it means his death, Thorin is willing to defend the treasure he has reclaimed from Smaug.

Not only did the dwarves of *The Hobbit* desire wealth and treasure in the fashion of medieval Vikings, but they were also willing to embark on a dangerous, lengthy, and arduous adventure to reclaim that wealth. Thorin Oakenshield and the dwarves put into place a series of plans to retake the wealth that had been taken from Thorin's ancestors. Under the guidance of Gandalf, Thorin and his band of dwarves discussed their plan, ways, means, policy, and devices for reclaiming what was once theirs, both the treasure and the mountain. (*The Hobbit*, 30) They planned meticulously, using all manner of old maps, including one particularly special map of the Lonely Mountain itself. Thorin was even able to personally recall details about the lands that he and his band were questing to reclaim.

Not unlike the dwarves of Tolkien's *The Hobbit*, Vikings also had a burning desire for wealth, treasures, and territories. Vikings were tireless, just like Tolkien's dwarves, in their conquests of new territories or old ones. Ívarr the Boneless arrived in Ireland in 852 B.C. at the head of an army the Irish dubbed "Dark Foreigners" and began to carve out his conquests from the Irish kingdoms. His first victory came at the battle at Carlingford Lough, and after a ruthless campaign, Ívarr became the Viking King of Ireland.[3] Ívarr's desire for wealth and territory didn't stop with his conquest of Ireland. As documented in *The Anglo-Saxon Chronicle,* monks tell of the fury of the "Great Heathen Army", and its leader, Ívarr the Boneless as England soon succumbed to the powerful onslaught of the Viking invaders. In 865–866 the chroniclers told how "a great heathen raiding-army came to the land of the English and took winter-quarters from the East Anglicans, and were provided with horses there, and they made peace with them."[4] Soon much of England acknowledged Ívarr as king. Ívarr and his army conquered the English states with relative ease and in relative haste; Northumbria fell in 867, East Anglia in 869–870 (in a particularly bloody affair), Mercia in 873, and, although Ívarr himself died in 873, the army continued under the guidance of his brothers Hálfdan and Ubbe, who forced King Alfred of Wessex into hiding in 878.[5] Coins minted in Wessex in 878 bear the name Hálfdan, evidence of Viking conquest as well as a lust for wealth and treasure.[6]

Where Thorin and his associates only sought to oust Smaug and reclaim their home, medieval Vikings often attacked others without provocation. They raided Christian monasteries and laid claim to others' lands. In September 1015, Cnut, or Canute, appeared at Sandwich. His army quickly moved on, ravaging and pillaging Dorset, Wiltshire, and Somerset.[7] By Christmas that same year Cnut was recognized as king in England and given a series of hostages, supplies, and horses. Although these items are not tangible treasure, they represented great wealth and power in the medieval world.[8] Not satisfied with his lot, Cnut went on to assault London, Sherston, and Penselwood to further his expansion into English territory.[9] In an attempt to save their city from further hardships, the Londoners offered Cnut a handsome sum of gold, which he accepted. Immediately following Cnut's successful invasion of England, there is evidence that the aristocratic lands taken from English lords were widely redistributed to Cnut's followers.[10]

The Viking desire for wealth and treasure led them far beyond Ireland and England. During his stay in Constantinople, the chief city of the Byzantine Empire, Viking mercenary Harald Hardrada came into great wealth, which ultimately brought him into conflict with the emperor. Harald was forced to flee the city, but only did so after securing his vast riches, despite his endangerment.[11] Harald later attempted, but failed to conquer England for its vast riches. Other Viking war leaders were more successful: Óláf of Dublin, or Óláf the White, fought alongside Ívarr and then carved out an empire for himself in Ireland and northern Britain, where he became overlord of the Vikings in those lands.[12] One of Óláf's sons supported a church in Norway by running frequent raids on English coasts. These raids were very lucrative, as many of the monasteries there held great wealth in gold and holy relics.[13] Óláf and his kin grew wealthy from conquests and raiding.

Thorin, too, is supported by his relatives: His nephews Fili and Kili follow him on his quest, along with others loyal to his cause. Their devotion to their leader and his cause stands in stark contrast to the individualistic practices of some medieval Vikings such as Swein Asleiffson, a twelfth-century war leader who earned a fortune through piracy and attacks upon his allies and relatives across the northern Scotland.[14] Raiding Vikings received very large individual payouts from plundering. Their desire for wealth and treasure was strong enough that Viking warriors even competed against each other to gain a greater share of the spoils. Before Viking raiders left an area, they would often plunder the region so thoroughly that it would be left devoid of all material wealth. Vikings could become settled, enjoying land by conquest and wealth from plunder. Using this wealth, they would establish a peaceful order so that nobody else could challenge their position. The Vikings developed a lucrative and low-cost practice of extorting extreme wealth from their enemies. Kings and citizens, as well as whole cities and communities, often paid Vikings the Danegeld, or money paid in return for peace from hostile Viking forces. In their relentless pursuit of wealth, some medieval Vikings suffered from the dragon sickness, even though they lived in a world where dragons existed only in legends.[15]

By Wave and Wind, for Revenge

"'We still mean to get it back, and to bring our curses home to
Smaug—if we can.'"

—Thorin Oakenshield, *The Hobbit*, 39

Both the dwarves in *The Hobbit* and Vikings prized family honor, and
when that honor was lost, they sought to restore it, often by means
of revenge—a central component to Thorin Oakenshield's plans. He
often mentions the grandeur of his grandfather's halls and his desire
to reclaim them: "So my grandfather's halls became full of armour
and jewels and carvings and cups, and the toy market of Dale was
the wonder of the North" (*The Hobbit*, 37). When Thorin and his
companions finally set their eyes on the feasting and council hall, the
dwarves are filled with possessiveness and pride.

Thorin's grandfather, Thror, died in the Mines of Moria at the
hands of Azog the Goblin, a fact that never escapes Thorin: He would
finally take his revenge on Azog and his kin in the Battle of the Five
Armies. When Smaug stole the dwarves' great treasure, the survivors,
especially Thorin, wept and cursed Smaug, but more importantly,
swore to reclaim what was once theirs and exact revenge on the dragon:
"'But we have never forgotten our stolen treasure. And even now, when
I will allow we have a good bit laid by and are not so badly off'"—here
Thorin stroked the gold chain round his neck—'we still mean to get it
back, and to bring our curses home to Smaug—if we can'"(*The Hobbit*,
39). In his stories, Thorin retraces the history of his ancestors back to
Thrain the Old, who discovered the Lonely Mountain, and who, along
with Thror, began mining and tunneling the mountain. It is this family
legacy shaped by his family's home and treasure, that Thorin hungers to
restore, and, in the process, take his revenge on Smaug.

Much like Thorin, who sought to restore his family's honor and
wealth by taking his revenge against Smaug, historical Vikings also
adventured and battled to restore their families and take revenge
upon those who wronged them. *The Anglo-Saxon Chronicle* documents the devastation wrought by the "Great Heathen Army" and its
leader, Ívarr the Boneless, in revenge for the English execution of his
father. This attack launched a new era of brutal battle between the

English and the Vikings. During a raid in North Anglia, King Ella of Northumbria captured and brutally killed Ívarr's father, King Ragnar Lodbrok of Sweden and Denmark: "Ella told them to take off his outer garment, and when they had done so the snakes attacked him all over his body."[16] Ragnar's lurid execution inspired Ívarr avenge his father—something Ella must have foreseen as, on his deathbed, the Northumbrian king muttered: "The pigs would grunt now if they knew what the old one is suffering."[17] "The pigs" referred to the three sons of Ragnar, and Ívarr eventually avenged his father, suggesting that Ragnar's sons performed a "blood eagle" on the Northumbrian king, cutting his ribs from his spine and splaying them out as if they were wings.

The cycle didn't end with Ívarr's victory. His retaliatory invasion of East Anglia, to avenge Ragnar's death, launched a new era of war and devastation. Ívarr died in Ireland and left his brother, Hálfdan, to claim kingship of Ireland and much of England, as well as command the "Great Heathen Army" in order to complete their vengeance.[18] Although familial honor was prioritized, wealth also held great significance for Viking leaders. When King Cnut died in 1035, his son, Harold, traveled to Winchester to reclaim his father's best treasures from Queen Emma, unwilling to allow others claim his family's wealth.[19] In the same way, Thorin and his ancestors cursed Smaug and sought revenge on him for the theft of their treasure. Ívarr the Boneless and his brothers, hearing of their father's suffering, conquered much of England and exacted their revenge on King Ella of Northumbria as well as countless other ordinary people of England and Ireland.

What's in a Name from Oaken Shields to Bloody Axes

"This last belonged to Thorin, an enormously important dwarf, in fact no other than the great Thorin Oakenshield."

—*The Hobbit*, 22

Balin, Dwalin, Kili, Fili, Dori, Nori, Ori, Oin, Gloin, Bifur, Bofur, Bombur, and Thorin Oakenshield. Ívarr, Hálfdan, Óláf, and Ubbe. Which list consists of Vikings, and which of Tolkien's dwarves?

Thorin wouldn't have been out of place in medieval Scandinavia, at least as a name. Personal names that incorporated the god "Thor" were popular during the Viking age. Medieval historians see Thorbjoryn, Thorsten, Thorgrim, and Thorgautr along with a host of variants everywhere from Cork to Constantinople.[20] Tolkien places great emphasis on Thorin Oakenshield as the leader of the company of dwarves, much like great emphasis was and is placed on the mighty Viking chieftains, warriors, and kings, from Ívarr to Cnut. Although other members of Thorin's company play an important role in the adventure, they are named more simply as Fili or Dori; they are not privileged with an epic epithet or byname in the style of their leader, Oakenshield. A byname refers to the second name that often distinguished prominent Vikings. Oakenshield is not the only prominent dwarf with an unusually earned byname in *The Hobbit*. Consider Thorin's great ancestor, Thrain the Old, who won renown for his long life. By defending himself in battle with merely a thick piece of oak is both brave and reckless enough that any historical Viking would have understood and admired his epithet.

Countless examples of prominent Vikings with unique and identifying bynames show how Thorin Oakenshield fits the Viking mold. For example, Swein Forkbeard, who died in 1014, was an enormously important Viking king of Denmark and England (who also, obviously, set a fashion trend with his beard styling). The first recorded evidence of Swein's unusual and unique byname is in the Roskilde chronicle. Swein's son, Cnut, was also extremely influential but never earned his own byname; although some history books dubbed him "Cnut the Great." The honourable byname was reserved for his English opponent, the king of Wessex, who was known as Edmund Ironside because of his valor in resisting Cnut's army.

Some Viking bynames seem to be simple artifacts of personal distinction. For example, Thorkill the Tall was likely named for his unusual height. Norwegian chieftains often had a byname that showed their family relation, much like Óláf Haraldsson, king of Norway who was later recognized by the church as St. Olaf. His father was a less impressive king known as Sigurd Sýr (Sigurd the Sow). Óláf's stepbrother was the warlike and adventurous Harald Hardrada, whose byname is best translated "Hard Ruler." He was indeed a hard ruler of Norway, over which he governed from 1046 to 1066, until he died in an attempt to conquer England. (Although he failed, the Normans succeeded).[21]

The most unusual Viking byname is that of Ívarr the Boneless, who avenged his father at the head of the "Great Heathen Army" in the ninth century. Some scholars believe that he may have had cartilage where bones should have been, hence the name "Ívarr the Boneless." A condition that causes this, known as osteogenesis imperfecta, was discovered in three major families of northern Norway who are descendants of Ívarr the Boneless.[22] However, others argue that Ívarr's name comes not from a physical attribute of Ívarr himself, but from the way he lived his life: "If Ívarr . . . was really called the Boneless he may have been complimented in a roundabout way for his furious riding."[23] Ívarr's two younger brothers, Hálfdan and Ubbe, played a significant role in not only aiding Ívarr during his invasion but taking the reins after his death. Hálfdan and Ubbe ruled the kingdom after Ívarr's death, but neither gained an interesting or unique byname like their brother (the Boneless) or father (Lodbrok, which meant "Hairy Britches").

It may seem strange to think that clothing could inspire a name, but that, too, happens in Middle-earth. In The Hobbit, Gandalf the Grey takes his name from his grey clothing rather than from his grey beard. Superficially, Gandalf's name resembles that of the historical Óláf the White, conqueror of Ireland and Northern England. Óláf likely received his name based on an unusual hair or skin characteristic—he was either very pale or had white hair and facial hair.[24] Another Norwegian king, Harald I, became known as Harald Fairhair in the grand sagas written centuries after his reign. However, Gandalf's grey nature seems more to do with his cloak than his complexion or his hair color.

Thorin's closest counterpart in the world of Viking warriors might well be Erik Bloodaxe, who was Harald Fairhair's son and a Viking king of Norway and Northumbria during the tenth century. Icelandic sagas written centuries later documented that Erik earned his byname "because he has reddened his sword in many a land . . . and carried a bloodstained blade."[25] Because the Icelanders were, by this time, fierce enemies of the Norwegians, their claims may not be wholly reliable or accurate. Nevertheless, Erik Bloodaxe enjoyed the most fearsome reputation amongst all the Viking leaders as the ideal example of the ferocious barbarian. Bearded, blunt, and bloody-minded, Erik became not only the model of the medieval Viking, but also that of the dwarves of Middle-earth.

And Ever so Our Foes Shall Fall: Two Warlike Peoples

"You have no business here. We are going on, so make way or we shall fight you!"
—*The Hobbit*, 334

The resemblance between the dwarves in *The Hobbit* and Vikings goes beyond names and motives. The dwarves have a rich and honorable culture and only become wandering warriors after Smaug destroys the kingdom of Erebor. Similarly, the historical people of medieval Scandinavia weren't all bloodthirsty barbarians. Although the term "Viking" literally comes from the expression "to go a Viking," which meant to go raid and pillage, this was only a small part of Norse culture. The Vikings also had extensive trade networks, and many historians consider them primarily as traders with rare sidelines in piracy, rather than exclusively raiders. Although the Vikings' reputation as bloodthirsty raiders is difficult to deny, Jinty Nelson noted that many of today's historians linger on "peculiar traits ranging from a kinship system that was one of large descent-groups rather than families, to distinctively elaborate arrangements for feuds and feuding, to ruthless slave-trading, to a bizarre disposition to atrocity (blood-eagle sacrifices), to exceptionally large bones, and hence, large limbs—a race of giant men, to a diet that resulted in farting on a heroic scale."[26] While feuds and farts make for entertaining history, the Vikings are more accurately viewed as entrepreneurs exploiting resources and opportunities rather than only as ruthless invaders.[27] But these entrepreneurs equipped themselves with axes and long ships and, even without those, they cultivated a fearsome appearance.

Upon first appearance, Englishmen labeled the Viking invaders as uncivilized pagans. From the safety of Emperor Charlemagne's court on the continent, the famous English scholar Alcuin described the Vikings as brutish pagans based on their unkempt hairstyle, which he fervently despised.[28] Alcuin condemned the influence these hairy Vikings had on the appearance and dress of his fellow Englishmen. He rebuked his countrymen for abandoning their ancestral English customs to act like heathens and dressing in a Danish manner. Alcuin described the Danish manner as having a bared neck and blinded eyes, which suggests long bangs in front and hair shaved at the neck.[29] Alcuin depicted the Viking as an exotic warrior whose appeal he desperately condemned. However, for the Vikings, English fashions were unnatural and contrary to their lifestyle. Among the Norse, short hair was a sign of servitude while a full beard was admired, as was the case with the *Eyrbyggja Saga's* description of one great Icelandic chieftain, Thorolf: "a tall, strong, handsome man with a big beard, on account of which he was called Most-Beard. He was the noblest man on the island."[30]

The dwarves of Middle-earth share many physical characteristics with the stereotypical Viking warrior. Many people envision a Viking wearing a long beard, which is also the style that Thorin and his company wear. Thorin is introduced as "a dwarf with a blue beard tucked into a golden belt . . ." (*The Hobbit*, 18). Balin is first described as a very old-looking dwarf with a white beard, and Kili and Fili are described as having yellow beards. Dori, Nori, Ori, Oin, and Gloin are all marked by their fine beards, which seem to be a dwarven trademark. When the host of dwarves led by Dain arrive at the Lonely Mountain, they are likened to many mythic and stereotypical Viking figures, but the most striking similarity is once again their beards: "Their beards were forked and plaited and thrust in their belts"(*The Hobbit*, 333).

The dwarves, like the Vikings, share a common taste in weapons as well as armor that reinforce their reputations as brutish warriors. Unlike the hobbits, who keep their thoughts well away from swords and shields and who only use axes to cut timber, the dwarves carry all of these for combat: "In battle they wield heavy two-handed mat-tocks; but each of them had also a short broad sword at his side and a round-shield slung at his back" (*The Hobbit*, 333). The armor of Dain's dwarves is spectacular. Each is clad in a "hauberk of steel mail that hung to his knees and his legs were covered with hose of a fine and flexible mesh . . ." (*The Hobbit*, 333). Thorin himself, at the Battle of the Five Armies, "wielded his axe with mighty strokes . . ." (*The Hobbit*, 341). Dwarven armor is legendary for its superior crafts-manship and utility. Thorin highlights the finer quality of the armor given to Bilbo by exclaiming "It cannot be pierced by arrows . . ." (*The Hobbit*, 327). But battle can damage even dwarven arms and armor, as we discover after the battle's end: "There indeed lay Thorin Oakenshield, wounded with many wounds, and his rent armour and notched axe were cast upon the floor" (*The Hobbit*, 346).

Although not all Vikings fought with the stereotypical axe, the weapon remained common enough that it instilled fear by its mere mention or depiction. The Viking great axe, the bipennis, or Danish axe, was a fearsome instrument of death and carnage standing at about four feet long with a foot-long blade. The axe was usually swung with both hands and was used wreak havoc on man and mount. Warriors wielding this gruesome weapon formed the front-line of many Viking warlords' armies. The great axe was so effective that the housecarls as foot-soldiers and the mainstay of the English army, adopted it as their weapon of choice.[31] Vikings occasionally battled with a broadsword or a spear—equally terrifying weapons for the foes facing them. Although Tolkien's dwarves lack the stature of the Vikings, they too struck fear in their opponents with their brutal axes and battle-ready attitudes.

English folklore tells of a gigantic Viking berserker at the Battle of Stamford Bridge whose rage and battle lust was so great that it is said he single-handedly held the narrow bridge while wielding a massive two-handed battle axe. *The Anglo-Saxon Chronicle* states that the Viking berserker was able to slay forty Englishmen and was finally defeated only when an English soldier snuck under the bridge, where he thrust his spear up through the planks, fatally wounding the Viking.[32] Thorin, at the Battle of the Five Armies, enters into the fray with red light leaping from his eyes, overwhelmed with battle lust. As Thorin fights with intense rage, Tolkien emphasizes that "nothing seemed to harm him" (*The Hobbit*, 341). Thorin's battle lust and apparent immunity to attack bears a striking resemblance to those infamous Viking berserkers discussed in chapter 10 by Stefan Donecker. These fits of madness have been described by Howard D. Fabing, a neurological specialist, as follows:

> This fury, which was called *berserkergang*, is said to have begun with shivering, chattering of the teeth, and chill in the body, and then the face swelled and changed its colour. With this was connected a great hot-headedness, which at last gave over into a great rage, under which they howled as wild animals, bit the edge of their shields, and cut down everything they met without discriminating between friend or foe.[33]

Berserkers appeared to ignore all pain, much as Thorin's rage seems to put him beyond harm. It is unclear what caused these Viking berserkers to enter such destructive and intense episodes of violent rage and apparent immunity to pain. Fabing argued that berserker rage may have been voluntarily induced with hallucinogenic mushrooms or copious amounts of alcohol, but others believe these fits of rage resulted from epilepsy or other illness or genetics.[34] Whether classified as berserkers or not, Thorin and the dwarves of Erebor make for terrifying opponents when defending their homeland.

The Vikings' reputation as fearsome and barbaric raiders served them well. The Norsemen were feared throughout Ireland, England, Scotland, and Continental Europe as merciless raiders and pirates. Viking warriors had a ruthless reputation as violent and brutish savages who continually attacked, plundered, and ravaged lands across Europe. In his letters describing the sack of Lindisfarne in 793, Alcuin attributes his horror at the raid not only to the brutality of the attackers, but also to their simultaneous high spirits. No one was safe from their attacks, especially not the peaceful men of the medieval church whose wealth and lack of weapons made them easy targets.

Viking raiders in 794 attacked the monastery at Jarrow on the island of Iona, where they plundered and destroyed the monastery itself.[35] This was only the first of a long series of unpredictable and vicious attacks that the Vikings led with merciless ferocity—much like those of dwarven warriors against the orcs and other opponents they face in Middle-earth.

When Viking kings invaded England they often brought with them a period of savagery and, as observed by Englishmen, brutish and barbaric behavior. Ívarr was head of the "Great Heathen Army," and Harold was in charge of a "great host", as described in *The Anglo-Saxon Chronicle*. When Cnut, Viking king of England, first seized control, he sent into permanent exile all but one of the English noblemen who had served the previous king. Within a year of Cnut's accession, the English aristocracy was almost entirely dispossessed and replaced, and Cnut continued to execute his noble English subjects well into his reign.[36] The violence of Cnut's accession between 1010 and 1017 rivals that of the Norman Conquest later in the century, when the Normans, themselves descendants of Vikings, ousted the Anglo-Saxons from the throne and nobility of England.

Viking victors were described by poets as being in "possession of the place of slaughter."[37] War was a rite of passage for young Vikings such as Harald Hardrada, who began his warrior ways as a teenager: "In 1030, at the age of fifteen Harald fought in the battle of Stiklestad, in which his stepbrother was killed and Harald himself was wounded."[38] The Viking reputation for being brutish and warlike shares much with the same brutish reputation of the dwarves. But how much of that brutality was simply doing what had to be done? Thorin and his medieval counterparts have to be tough to succeed. That was proven by Erik Bloodaxe: a ruthless and brutal warrior, but also widely acknowledged as an effective leader. His career is a series of brutal raids and homicides remarkable even among tenth-century Vikings; but he was also memorialized by pagans and Christians whose interests he protected with his bloodstained blade.[39]

Certainly some Vikings went too far and rightly earned the bad reputation they enjoy in history. For example, in *The Anglo-Saxon Chronicle*, Harthacnut ("Tough-knot"), Cnut's son, is condemned for ordering the body of his rival and half-brother, Harold Harefoot, to be disinterred and then thrown into marshes near the Thames, stating Harold did nothing worthy of a king's burial. Harthacnut is also famous for his savage attacks on the English he hoped to rule, burning cities to the ground and stealing anything of value. [40] Understandably, medieval Englishmen viewed the Vikings as lawless and violent intruders in the same way that Bilbo initially views the dwarves. In 884, the *Annals of St-Vaast, Arras* condemned the Vikings with a lurid account of corpses of not only warriors but churchmen: "women, young men and babies lying about . . . 'in every square'". [41] Although the dwarves in *The Hobbit* are not as ruthless as those Vikings, the two groups still share much in common in their warlike ways and their vengeful culture..

Peace Must be Made with Point and Edge, With Grim Battle-Play

"Far over the misty mountains cold
To dungeons deep and caverns old
We must away ere break of day,
To find out long-forgotten gold."
— *The Hobbit*, 26

These words summed up the English viewpoint on the Battle of Maldon, a key turning point in the English conflict with the Vikings. In 991, Swein Forkbeard's Viking army descended upon England and defeated the Saxon defenders. The Saxon leader, Ealdorman Brihtnoth, refused to pay tribute, and the small force he rallied had a lot more in common with their Viking opponents than not, except for sheer numbers. Although Swein's army defeated the English, they lost many men, with too few survivors left to man all the ships for their voyage home. [42] Much like the dwarves in the aftermath of the Battle of the Five Armies, Swein's Vikings sacrificed many men for their conquest. Both the dwarves in *The Hobbit* and historical Vikings sought wealth and territory, often in hopes of restoring stolen or lost property. Dwarves and Vikings placed high value in family honor. Both Ívarr the Boneless, after his father was murdered, and Thorin Oakenshield, after the loss of Erebor and his family with it, exacted revenge on those who had wronged their families. The weapons and ways of Viking warriors had much in common with those practiced by Thorin and his company of dwarves. Even the names and naming practices of Vikings and dwarves are remarkably similar. These resemblances are not coincidence. J. R. R. Tolkien drew upon his own knowledge of the Vikings drawn from sagas, annals and stories when he created their smaller but equally fierce Middle-earth counterparts, the Dwarves.

Notes

1. All references to *The Hobbit* come from J. R. R. Tolkien, *The Hobbit* (Toronto: HarperCollins, 1998).

2. Janet L. Nelson, "Presidential Address: England and the Continent in the Ninth Century: II, the Vikings and Others," *Royal Historical Society* 13 (2003), 3.

3. Clare Downham, *Viking Kings of Britain and Ireland: The Dynasty of Ívarr to A.D. 1014* (Dublin: Dunedin Academic Press Ltd., 2007), 14.

4. Michael James Swanton, ed. and trans., *The Anglo-Saxon Chronicle*, (London: Routledge, 1998), 69.

5. Downham, 63, 65, 66.

6. Marios Costambeys, 'Hálfdan (*d.* 877)', *Oxford Dictionary of National Biography*, ed. Lawrence Goldman (Oxford University Press, 2004), http://www.oxforddnb.com/view/article/49260

7. M. K. Lawson, "Cnut (d. 1035)," Oxford Dictionary of National Biography, ed. Lawrence Goldman (Oxford: Oxford University Press, 2004), http://www.oxforddnb.com/view/article/4579

8. Ibid.

9. Ibid.

10. Katharin Mack, "Changing Thegns: Cnut's Conquest and the English Aristocracy," *Albion* 16:4 (Winter, 1984), 380.

11. Claus Krag, "Harald Hardrada (1015–1066)," *Oxford Dictionary of National Biography*, ed. Lawrence Goldman, (Oxford: Oxford University Press, 2004) http://www.oxforddnb.com/view/article/49272

12. Benjamin T. Hudson, "Óláf the White (*fl.* 853–871)," *Oxford Dictionary of National Biography*, ed. Lawrence Goldman, (Oxford: Oxford University Press, 2004), http://www.oxforddnb.com/view/article/49263

13. William Ian Miller, "Of outlaws, Christians, Horsemeat, and Writing: Uniform Laws and Saga," *Michigan Law Review* Vol. 89, No. 8 (Aug. 1991), 13.

14. James Barrett,"Swein Asleiffson (*d.* 1171?)," *Oxford Dictionary of National Biography*, ed. Lawrence Goldman, (Oxford: Oxford University Press, 2004) http://www.oxforddnb.com/view/article/49359.

15. Peter Kurrild-Klitgaard and Gert Tinggaard Svendsen, "Rational Bandits: Plunder, Public Goods, and the Vikings," *Public Choice* 117, 3-4 (2003), 258, 260, 261.

16. Paul B. Du Chaillu, *The Viking Age: The Early History Manners, and Customs of the Ancestors of the English Speaking-Nations* (New York: AMS Press, 1889), 2: 452.

17. Du Chaillu, 452.

18. Costambeys, 'Hálfdan (*d.* 877)'.

19. Lawson.

20. Eric Christiansen, *The Norsemen in the Viking Age* (Oxford: Blackwell Publishing, 2006), 45.

21. Krag.

22. "Ivar the Boneless," *The British Medical Journal* 1, no. 5028 (1957), 1172.

23. Christiansen, 15.

24. Hudson.

25. Marios Costambeys,"Erik Bloodaxe (*d.* 954)," *Oxford Dictionary of National Biography*, ed. Lawrence Goldman, (Oxford: Oxford University Press, 2004) http://www.oxforddnb.com/view/article/49265.

26. Nelson, 11-12.

27. Kurrild-Klitgaard and Svendsen, 256.

28. Roberta Frank, "Terminally Hip and Incredibly Cool: Carol, Vikings, and Anglo-Scandinavian England," *Representations* 1 (2007), 25.

29. Frank, 25.

30. Angus A. Sommerville and R. Andrew McDonald, eds., *The Viking Age: A Reader* (Toronto: University of Toronto Press, 2010), 341.

31. Edd Wheeler, "The Battle of Hastings: Math, Myth and Melee," *Military Affairs*, Vol. 52, No. 3 (Jul., 1988), 132.

32. Swanton, 198.

33. Howard D. Fabing, "On Going Berserk: A Neurochemical Inquiry," *Scientific Monthly* 83 (November 1956), 234.

34. Fabing, 232. Robert Wernick, *The Vikings* (Alexandria, VA: Time-Life Books, 1979), 285.

35. Peter Brent, The Viking Saga (New York: G. P. Putnam's Sons, 1975), 15.

36. Mack, 377, 379.

37. Wheeler, 132.

38. Krag.

39. Costambeys, ,"Erik Bloodaxe (*d.* 954)."

40. DNB, Harthacnut, M. K. Lawson.

41. Nelson, 9.

42. "The Poem on the Battle of Maldon," *English Historical Documents*, 500-1042, edited by Dorothy Whitelock (London: Routledge, 1996), 319-23.

CHAPTER 3

It Is Good to Be the King:

Monarchs in Middle-earth and the Middle Ages

Mark Sundaram and Aven McMaster

"Here at the Gates the king awaits,
His hands are rich with gems and gold.
The king is come unto his hall
Under the Mountain dark and tall."
— *The Hobbit*, 249[1]

Brave and generous, or noble and kind: what makes a "good king"? Tolkien introduces Thorin, the exiled heir to the King under the Mountain at the beginning of *The Hobbit*. By the end of the book, he has taken his place as king with his subjects and other leaders beside him. Throughout their journey in *The Hobbit*, Bilbo and the dwarves encounter a number of other kinglike figures, both helpful and troublesome: the most notable of these figures are Beorn, Thranduil the

Elvenking, the Master of Lake-town, Bard, and Dain. By writing in these various figures, Tolkien invites readers to compare them, to evaluate and assess their good and bad qualities, and to wonder about the character of Thorin himself, and how he compares to the book's other leaders. Is Thorin a good king? By what standards are he and the other leaders judged? How do the actions and characters of the other king-figures in the book cast light on Thorin's character and role? These questions are important in *The Hobbit,* and become even more crucial in Tolkien's later writings about Middle-earth, with leaders such as Théoden, Elrond, and most notably, Aragorn himself. To answer these questions, this chapter will look at the history of kingship evident in *The Hobbit.*

Reflections in the King's Mirror: Models of Kingship

What historical models of kingship were available to Tolkien when he wrote *The Hobbit?* When Tolkien considered rulers and leaders, even when limiting his view to his native British tradition, he could look at recent monarchs such as Queen Victoria, King Edward VII, or King George V; at previous historical kings such as Henry VIII, William the Conqueror, or Alfred the Great; at chivalric figures such as King Arthur, portrayed in both the late medieval literature and the more recent Romantic retellings; or at early medieval figures such as Beowulf, or the kings in the Icelandic sagas. Some of these rulers were honorable and admirable leaders and others had both respectable and dishonorable qualities, while a few were entirely awful.

Tolkien was a scholar of the Middle Ages, so it is not surprising that he turned to the medieval period for inspiration. Specifically, as an Anglo-Saxonist, Tolkien drew on Old English literature and other early medieval literary models—thus his heroes evoke epic, antique, and early medieval romance rather than the chivalric heroes of the later Middle Ages.[2] Other fantasy novelists frequently drew on chivalric romances, such as those of King Arthur and his knights. The model of kingship in novels by C. S. Lewis—Tolkien's contemporary and friend—reflects the chivalric notion of the ideal Christian monarch, who is an equally moral and military leader for his people, and emphasizes qualities such as justice, mercy, and other elements of chivalric behavior more than the elements characteristic of Germanic heroism.[3] The heroes of chivalric romance are usually shown to undergo tests of their moral strength and a resulting change in character, such as the protagonist in Sir Gawain and the Green Knight, while the heroes of epic and earlier romance have no such emotional journeys, though sometimes they must learn to become good kings.

Modern heroes, such as the typical protagonists of novels, come from the later type of romance hero made familiar in the writing of Sir Walter Scott or the poems of Alfred Lord Tennyson. In recent times, heroes have become less idealized and more human. Thus, Aragorn in the Peter Jackson film adaptations of The Lord of the Rings trilogy is transformed into the self-doubting hero familiar to modern audiences.[4] However, in the books, Tolkien's kings are more like the kings of early medieval literature. In addition to epic heroes like Beowulf, Tolkien may have used the heroes of late antiquity and early medieval romances, such as Apollonius of Tyre, King Horn, and Havelok the Dane as parallels for his characters. In many ways, Tolkien's varied references bridge the gap between epic and romance, and parallel his novel alongside classic literature by featuring dispossessed kings who must regain their kingdoms and demonstrate true kingly behavior.[5]

Let us pause here for a brief note about the medieval texts that we will be drawing on for comparisons in this chapter. The main works that are referenced either deal explicitly with Germanic kingship or contain clear examples of good or bad kings. Toward the fall of the Roman Empire, various German-speaking tribes invaded and settled in Roman territory, including Britain. They became the basis of many early medieval societies, such as Anglo-Saxon England. These Germanic tribes were warrior cultures that valued heroism and glory in battle. The earliest written account of Germanic society is that of the late first century Germania, written by the Roman author Tacitus. He describes the various Germanic tribes known to the Roman Empire, including their customs, beliefs, ways of life, and religions.[6] It should be noted, however, that Tacitus is an outsider imperfectly describing what he understands to be true of a foreign people, and furthermore, his description of the Germanic people is colored by his critical views on his own Roman culture, to which he is drawing an implicit comparison in his work. Nevertheless, much of what is described in the *Germania* agrees with the more literary records of Germanic society.[7]

The most well-known literary text of the Germanic heroic world, which has frequently been understood in the context of Tacitus' description of Germanic society, is the Old English epic poem *Beowulf*, written sometime in the Anglo-Saxon period (from the fifth to eleventh centuries).[8] The poem is a narrative about the Germanic hero Beowulf, who fights monsters and interacts with various kings, only to become a king himself years later. There are also various other Old English texts that touch on issues of kingship, such as the wisdom poetry known as *Maxims I* and *Maxims II*, which contain brief proverbial statements about the world of the Anglo-Saxons.[9]

Outside of Anglo-Saxon England, there are other Germanic heroic poems such as *Waltharius*, a tenth-century Latin poetic version of the story of the Germanic hero Walter of Aquitaine, highly influenced by the Roman poetic tradition of Virgil.[10] Here again, we see heroes and kings in the Germanic mold interacting and implicitly being compared. There is also the extensive Old Norse literary output, in particular the Icelandic sagas. Most interesting for our purposes is the Old Icelandic legendary saga *Hrolfs saga kraka* (or *The Saga of Hrolf Kraki*), likely written in the thirteenth or fourteenth century.[11] This work revisits much of the material in the Old English poem *Beowulf*, including the focus on themes of kingship. It has also been seen as an important source text for several aspects of *The Hobbit*, most notably the character of Beorn, whose forebear appears in *Hrolfs saga kraka*.[12] Finally, there is the Old Norwegian *Konungs skuggsjá* (or *King's Mirror*), a thirteenth-century manual of kingship and the courtly world.[13] Though it is heavily influenced by the later courtly tradition, there are still some elements of the earlier Germanic culture in the advice given by a fictional father to his eager-for-advancement son. It is reasonable to imagine that similar stories were passed down among Tolkien's dwarves in their great halls or even farther afield in Middle-earth.

"That was a good king": Tolkien's Medieval Models

Using literary and historical sources, as well as archaeological and even anthropological information, we can put together a fairly plausible picture of the ideal Germanic king.[14] We should stress these are ideal characteristics, not the actual attributes of any known king.[15] The sources we have, in particular Tacitus' *Germania*, Germanic heroic poetry such as the epic *Beowulf*, and Icelandic sagas, are not trustworthy descriptions of actual kings or accurate histories of real events. Still, by looking at elements common to all of these sources, we can see what the Germanic societies of the second through tenth centuries considered desirable behavior for their kings. To better understand how Tolkien viewed Germanic society, it also helps to consider the state of scholarship during the time of his writing. In the early twentieth century, English philologist and historian H. M. Chadwick argued that there had been a distinct 'heroic age', which was reflected in epic poems such as *Beowulf*, and thus it was common to use the poem as a source for historical information.[16] This trend in scholarship certainly shaped Tolkien's view of Anglo-Saxon and Germanic history; however, Tolkien himself argued that *Beowulf* should be read not only as history but as literature as well, thus liberating the poem from the sole possession of historians and philologists. In fact, Tolkien was one of the most important Anglo-Saxon scholars of the twentieth century, radically changing the course of *Beowulf* scholarship with his academic work.[17] Although Chadwick's notion of the real-life reflection of a heroic age in the somewhat later literary texts is now considered problematic, scholars generally accepted the opinion during Tolkien's writing of *The Hobbit*.

In *The Hobbit*, Tolkien focuses heavily on revealing which qualities make a good king. This specifically reflects one of the main themes of both *Beowulf* and *Hrolfs saga kraka*—the differences between good kings and bad kings, and how each contribute to the narration. The *Beowulf* poet frequently directs the reader to consider and compare the various kings in the poem. The phrase "That was a good king"[18] is repeated three times in the poem in reference to three different kings, whom readers are thus invited to compare. We are also given numerous other examples of kings, both good and bad, to act as foils for the more central kings in the poem, most notably the adventuresome Beowulf himself. Similarly, King Hrolf's qualities as king are tested, and compared with a spectrum of other kings.[19]

Just as these two texts invite the reader to evaluate the main character and his honor in comparison to other kings, Tolkien introduces two central king-figures in *The Hobbit*, Thorin and Bard, whose qualities are tested, and who should be evaluated in comparison to a number of less important king-figures whose appearances act as foils to the main characters. By examining the ways in which both the main and secondary king-figures succeed—or fail—as examples of kingly virtue in the Germanic tradition, we are better able to see how Tolkien's understanding of Germanic history and culture informed and influenced his writing.[20]

"Fair words and true, if proudly and grimly spoken": Grading the Kings in *The Hobbit*

So, how do the king-figures in *The Hobbit* compare to an ideal Germanic king? Thorin, as the most important and fully described king-figure in the book, gives us the greatest scope for comparison (though it is helpful to look at Bard as well). Let us begin with the issue of lineage. When he reveals himself to the men of Lake-town, Thorin announces himself with these words: "'Thorin son of Thrain son of Thror King under the Mountain!'"(*The Hobbit*, 188). This emphasis on his father and grandfather, and their role in legitimizing Thorin's claim to kingship, resembles the emphasis on lineage in Anglo-Saxon society. Although leadership was based partly on merit rather than simply on heredity, genealogy was a very important element in heroic literature as well as in historical texts. Characters were known by their genealogy and were often referred to as "son of" rather than by their given name. Indeed, the epic *Beowulf* begins not with King Hrothgar himself, but with a prologue describing his royal dynasty beginning with his great-grandfather Scyld Scefing.

Lineage is also important for Bard—the hero who kills Smaug and then becomes Lord of Dale. We are told that "he was a descendant in long line of Girion, Lord of Dale, whose wife and child had escaped down the Running River from the ruin long ago" (*The Hobbit*, 237). This lineage not only makes him the rightful leader of the re-established city, but is also a crucial element of his heroism during the battle against the dragon, when the thrush brings him Bilbo's information about Smaug's weak spot: "Marvelling he found he could understand its tongue, for he was of the race of Dale" (*The Hobbit*, 237). Thus his ancestry is the key to both his legitimate inheritance of the position of Lord of Dale, and also to his feat of bravery and skill that proves his worthiness for the title.

We can also see that Thorin's appearance, manners, and style of speaking distinguish him from the other dwarves. Tolkien first introduces Thorin falling onto the doormat of Bilbo's hobbit hole—and acting rather grumpy about it: "Thorin indeed was very haughty, and said nothing about service" (*The Hobbit*, 23). He also believes that he is too important to help clear and clean the table, and instead sits and talks with Gandalf. A king's manners speak much about his character and worth; in *The King's Mirror*, the father tells his son: "there are three things (which are, however, almost the same in reality) which one must observe with care: they are wisdom, good breeding, and courtesy."[21] Thorin's haughtiness is, to some degree, appropriate for his position, but when carried to excess, his behavior reflects poorly on his character. Gandalf chides him for his arrogant and bitter treatment of Bilbo, drawing attention specifically to the unkingliness of his behavior: "You are not making a very splendid figure as King under the Mountain" (*The Hobbit*, 262). Bard, on the other hand, demonstrates his kingliness in his address to Thorin at the gates of the Mountain: "Now these were fair words and true, if proudly and grimly spoken" (*The Hobbit*, 250). The contrast between his speech and Thorin's ungracious reply highlights the difference between their actions, and shows Bard in a better light than Thorin.

A king's ability to speak well and communicate with his followers is equally as important as conduct and good manners. *The King's
Mirror* links speaking with wisdom: "These gifts will accompany
wisdom: elegance in speech, eloquence."[22] In the beginning of *The
Hobbit*, after the evening meal in Bilbo's home, Thorin plays a harp
beautifully and sings the song of the Misty Mountains with the other
dwarves. He then begins a speech about their planned adventure, and
we are told this about his speaking style: "He was an important dwarf.
If he had been allowed, he would probably have gone on like this
until he was out of breath, without telling any one there anything that
was not known already" (*The Hobbit*, 29). A similar comment about
his speaking style is made when Bilbo and the dwarves have opened
the door in the mountain: "You are familiar with Thorin's style on
important occasions, so I will not give you any more of it, though
he went on a good deal longer than this" (*The Hobbit*, 203). While
Thorin's usual style was formal and somewhat self-important, after
the battle, when Thorin realizes that he has acted wrongly and speaks
his final words to Bilbo, the real eloquence and poetry of his words
reflect the truly kingly status he has finally achieved: "There is more
in you of good than you know, child of the kindly West. Some courage
and some wisdom, blended in measure. If more of us valued food and
cheer and song above hoarded gold, it would be a merrier world. But
sad or merry, I must leave it now. Farewell!" (*The Hobbit*, 273).

Speaking well wasn't enough for a king, however; he had to look
the part, too. *The Saga of Hrolf Kraki* contains several episodes that
clearly show the significance of a leader's physical appearance; one of
the ways people are punished or humiliated in the saga is by having
their hair shaved or being disfigured in some way. Thus, when Thorin
reveals himself to the men of Lake-town as the descendant of the King
under the Mountain, his kingliness is evident: "…he looked it, in spite
of his torn clothes and draggled hood. The gold gleamed on his neck
and waist: his eyes were dark and deep" (*The Hobbit*, 188). Again, as he
breaks out of the mountain in the Battle of the Five Armies, he stands
out as a hero and a king: "Out leapt the King under the Mountain, and
his companions followed him. Hood and cloak were gone; they were

in shining armour, and red light leapt from their eyes. In the gloom the great dwarf gleamed like gold in a dying fire" (*The Hobbit*, 269).

As we suggested in reference to his manners, Tolkien reveals throughout *The Hobbit* that pride can be a problem for Thorin. Anglo-Saxon society recognized a certain amount of pride as appropriate for a king, as seen in one of the *Maxims*: "Majesty must go with pride."[23] However, the speaker in *The King's Mirror* also linked pride to arrogance and avarice.[24] Bombur tells us that Thorin "was ever a dwarf with a stiff neck" (*The Hobbit*, 254), and we can see his pride and stubbornness in his arrogant manners. In his case, too, the pride is clearly linked to his greed for gold, and his unwillingness to share any with Bard, or to compromise with the other dwarves at all. This progression from pride to covetousness, and the problems this poses for a king, are clearly illustrated in *Beowulf*, in King Hrothgar's speech of advice to Beowulf. Hrothgar warns Beowulf that as pride grows, kings grow arrogant and stop giving out rings and treasure, and are eventually replaced by more generous kings.[25] We will take a closer look at the importance of generosity in the next section.

Although it is interesting to compare Thorin's behavior to that of other kings of literature, assessing the motivations for his behavior is equally important to understand his character. Revenge is an important motivation for Thorin just as it was for medieval kings. Revenge was a necessity in Germanic society; in *Beowulf* the hero reminds King Hrothgar that "It is always better / to avenge one's friend than to mourn overmuch."[26] The cycle of revenge might have tragic consequences, but to leave the death of a kinsman unavenged was unthinkable.[27] For Thorin, too, Smaug's devastation of his people's kingdom necessitates vengeance, however long it might take. As he tells the story of his people's exile to Bilbo, he explains that Smaug must first be punished: The dwarves "have long ago paid the goblins of Moria" for their killing of Thorin's grandfather. Second to Smaug, they "must give a thought to the Necromancer" (*The Hobbit*, 37) to avenge his father's mistreatment. The theme recurs when Bilbo tells the dragon that the adventurers have come for revenge; Smaug laughs, saying "The King under the Mountain is dead, and where are his kin that dare seek revenge?" (*The Hobbit*, 215), not realizing that those are the very dwarves camped on his doorstep.

Thorin's ability to take revenge depends, in part, on his courage. Likewise, a king's worth in Germanic society depended largely on his bravery and fighting ability. Tacitus described the *comitatus* system of Germanic leadership, in which the king leads from the front line rather than from a place of safety behind the troops. He tells us that "when the battle field is reached it is a reproach for a chief to be surpassed in prowess; a reproach for his retinue not to equal the prowess of its chief."[28] The good Germanic leader was the strongest and the best fighter, and was always the first into battle—exemplified by Beowulf, who frequently went into battle alone, leaving his warriors waiting behind him. Of course, literature also often describes the failure of kings to live up to this ideal. In the epic *Waltharius*, Gunther finally confronts his enemy, Walter, but only after sending his warriors in one by one for slaughter. When he finally takes part in the fighting, he is an inadequate warrior with few men left to fight with him.

All of the king-figures in *The Hobbit* are good and brave warriors, except the Master of Lake-town. In fact, the contrast between him and Bard provides the clearest example of the importance of courage in a leader. When Bard is properly introduced, we are told that he is a man of "worth and courage" (*The Hobbit*, 237). He proves himself a leader of men and a brave fighter in the battle against Smaug; he alone has the foresight to realize the dragon is coming, and he rallies the people to fight back: "No one had dared to give battle to him for many an age; nor would they have dared now, if it had not been for the grim-voiced man (Bard was his name), who ran to and fro cheering on the archers and urging the Master to order them to fight to the last arrow" (*The Hobbit*, 236). Meanwhile, the Master of Lake-town runs away: "The Master himself was turning to his great gilded boat, hoping to row away in the confusion and save himself" (*The Hobbit*, 236). In the Battle of the Five Armies, the Elvenking and Dain are both valiant, while Beorn's attack almost single-handedly turns the tide of battle. Thorin's charge with the other dwarves is described in heroic terms: "Thorin wielded his axe with mighty strokes, and nothing seemed to harm him" (*The Hobbit*, 269). After the battle, Thorin dies like a king and a hero, "wounded with many wounds" (*The Hobbit*, 272), looking forward to the heroic afterlife: "I go now to the halls of waiting to sit beside my fathers, until the world is renewed" (*The Hobbit*, 272).

Dragon-sickness: The Fatal Flaw of Greed

All of the comparisons we have discussed so far demonstrate the close similarity between the medieval Germanic ideal of kingship and Tolkien's conception of leaders and kings in *The Hobbit*. We will now turn to one of the most important aspects of kingship in Germanic society: how a king handles treasure and gold. This is also one of Tolkien's primary themes in *The Hobbit*, and he focuses particularly on greed and generosity as determining how a good king will act when presented with the opportunity for wealth.[29] In a story that centers on a quest for a dragon's hoard, it is not surprising that this issue would arise. A king's greed or generosity is central to the evaluation of a medieval Germanic king. A Germanic king accumulates treasure through war or tribute, and then gives it to his companions and his followers. This attribute was important enough that a standard epithet for a king was "ring-giver" (referring to the golden arm-rings commonly given out to warriors). In heroic texts like *Beowulf*, or in the Norse sagas, we see kings giving their warriors treasure, weapons, and armor while entertaining them in the hall with lavish feasts and drinking. Indeed, the *comitatus* relationship bond is cemented in the hall, where heroes boast about their past deeds and vow future deeds for their king, while drinking and feasting copiously. Whatever treasure a warrior won in battle was given to his king, who would then redistribute treasure to his followers. By showing favor to his followers, a king gained followers and companions and retained their loyalty, as we see in Tacitus' summary of the relationship between king and his *comitatus* (companions): "You cannot keep up a great retinue except by war and violence, for it is from their leader's bounty that they demand that glorious warhorse, and that murderous and masterful spear: banquetings and a certain rude but lavish outfit are equivalent to salary."[30] Again, in Old English wisdom poetry, this idea is common: "Treasure must wait in its hoards—and the gift-throne stand prepared—for when men may share it out. Eager for it is he who receives the gold; the man on the high seat has plenty of it. There must needs be a return, if we do not mean to deceive, to the one who afforded us these favours."[31] Generosity is also a key virtue for kings in *Beowulf*.[32] When King Hrolf Kraki's character is judged, his generosity is considered equally important as his fighting ability.[33]

Although a king's generosity and quest for gold is important for the prosperity of his kingdom, he must maintain a delicate balance between keeping and distributing his wealth. A king must desire and work for gold and treasures to have resources for his kingdom, and to share his wealth, but an excessive love of treasure, or hoarding gold for its own sake rather than for giving gifts, is seen as greed and is greatly censured by early Germanic society. Similarly, in *The King's Mirror*, the son is exhorted to avoid greed: "And to love wealth much, when it seems inclined to turn away from a man and does not return his love, is surely sinful and will lead to grief."[34] And perhaps most significant to understanding *The Hobbit*, in *The Saga of Hrolf Kraki*, King Hrolf is trying to regain the treasure of his birthright from the greedy king Athils, the clear villain. The story also features a precious ring that triggers greedy behavior and family dispute, a possible source for Tolkien's ring, particularly as it appears in *The Lord of the Rings*.

In *The Hobbit* we can see that the issue of treasure arises in connection to all of the king-figures. In particular, both Thorin and Bard are paired with a king-figure who acts as their foil: Thorin is contrasted with Dain, and Bard is contrasted with the Master of Laketown. How do the various kings and king-figures compare to the ideal of the generous king, who wants to acquire treasure for noble reasons, and is not himself greedy? Looking more closely at the various kings, we see that they are less than perfect in this regard.

If we start with Beorn, we can see that he (alone among all the leaders) seems to have no interest in gold. Although he is not greedy, he is initially inhospitable to guests—hospitality is closely connected with generosity, as we can see in Tacitus's comments above. His momentary reluctance to play host to the travelers is soon overcome, however, and in the end he proves to be a great help to them and a good king in his own right: "Beorn indeed became a great chief afterwards in those regions and ruled a wide land between the mountains and the wood" (*The Hobbit*, 278).

Next, we see a glimpse of the Elvenking's character: "If the elf-king had a weakness it was for treasure, especially for silver and white gems; and though his hoard was rich, he was ever eager for more" (*The Hobbit*, 165). His avarice is clearly marked as a weakness, and we also see that he wants treasure simply to hoard it, rather than use it. His march on the Mountain is as much for the sake of the treasure as it is to help the men of Lake-town. Therefore, it is no coincidence that his other character flaw is greed, or a lack of generosity: he captures those passing through his lands, and makes them prisoners rather than offering them hospitality. He holds feasts, but does not invite his prisoners to them. Thorin says of him "We were wrongfully waylaid by the Elvenking and imprisoned without cause" (*The Hobbit*, 190). In fact, at the end of the story, Bilbo gives the Elvenking a gift as "some little return for [his] hospitality" (*The Hobbit*, 277), but this good-mannered gesture on Bilbo's part actually highlights the Elvenking's failure to be hospitable to Bilbo and the dwarves.

Tolkien's portrayal of the Master of Lake-town highlights him as a man of business and not a hero, "giving his mind to trade and tolls, to cargoes and gold, to which habit he owed his position" (*The Hobbit*, 190). He thinks of profit and personal gain, not of glory or of the welfare of his people; even his hospitality and help to the companions on their quest for the dragon's hoard is motivated by fear of his own people, and their enthusiasm for the return of the King under the Mountain, which he does not share. His failure as measured by the standards of Germanic kingship is proven by his demise: "Bard had given him much gold for the help of the Lake-people, but being of the kind that easily catches such disease he fell under the dragon-sickness, and took most of the gold and fled with it, and died of starvation in the Waste, deserted by his companions" (*The Hobbit*, 286). He is a perfect example of how a leader should not act, and as such is contrasted with Bard. Although Bard is interested in the treasure—his confrontation with Thorin arises from his desire to claim some portion of the dragon's hoard—he wants to use it to rebuild Dale and Lake-town. As we have seen, the desire for gold is actually praise-worthy in a Germanic king, as long as he intends to use it in the right way. Bard proves himself an admirable leader when, in the end, he is generous with the treasure: "From that treasure Bard sent much gold to the Master of Lake-town; and he rewarded his followers and friends freely" (*The Hobbit*, 275).

The characters of the two men seem to be linked to the types of leadership they exemplify. After Smaug's death, the people of Lake-town say that the Master is good at business, but does not handle crisis well; However, in contrast, they praise Bard's valor and want to make him king. There follows a debate between the Master on the one side and the people and Bard on the other over what constitutes a good leader of the community and what values are required; this is a debate between heroic ideals and capitalist or oligarchic ideals. The Master says, "In the Lake-town we have always elected masters from among the old and wise, and have not endured the rule of mere fighting men. Let 'King Bard' go back to his own kingdom—Dale is now freed by his valour, and nothing hinders his return. . . . The wise will stay here and hope to rebuild our town, and enjoy again in time its peace and riches." But the people reply, "We have had enough of the old men and the money-counters!" (*The Hobbit*, 239). The value of these two types of leadership is shown by the actions of the two men after the battle with Smaug: Bard "strode off to help in the ordering of the camps and in the care of the sick and the wounded. But the Master scowled at his back as he went, and remained sitting on the ground. He thought much but said little, unless it was to call loudly for men to bring him fire and food" (*The Hobbit*, 240).

Finally, when we turn to the dwarves, Tolkien tells us that, as a race, "Dwarves are not heroes, but calculating folk with a great idea of the value of money; some are tricky and treacherous and pretty bad lots; some are not, but are decent enough people like Thorin and Company, if you don't expect too much" (*The Hobbit*, 204). This focus on wealth is not necessarily a vice; in fact, we can see that when we compare Thorin and Dain's attitudes to the dragon's hoard. From the very beginning of the story, we see that Thorin's primary motivation for the adventure is to recover the gold and treasures that his ancestors owned. Once the dwarves have acquired it, his reaction to the news that the elves and men are coming for a share of the gold shows his avarice: "None of our gold shall thieves take or the violent carry off while we are alive" (*The Hobbit*, 246). Tolkien explicitly says that Thorin's actions are driven by greed and the lust for gold is akin to a dragon's: "[Bilbo] did not reckon with the power that gold has upon which a dragon has long brooded, nor with dwarvish hearts. Long hours in the past days Thorin had spent in the treasury, and the lust of it was heavy on him" (*The Hobbit*, 250). He refuses to acknowledge that any of the gold rightfully belongs to others as well, even though Bard's speech to him at the gate points out that he should be using the gold, not hoarding it: "The wealthy may have pity beyond right on the needy that befriended them when they were in want" (*The Hobbit*, 251). Only after the Battle of the Five Armies, when Thorin speaks his dying words to Bilbo, does he come to realize that he acted wrongly, and rejects his previous greed: "Since I leave now all gold and silver, and go where it is of little worth, I wish to part in friendship from you, and I would take back my words and deeds at the Gate" (*The Hobbit*, 272).

In contrast, although we hear little about Dain, Thorin's successor as King under the Mountain, he seems to act in an exemplary and honorable manner. He comes to Thorin's aid when called on, and while enticed by the treasure, once he is king he acts appropriately and gives Bard his promised share of the hoard. Dain's actions are rewarded by the loyalty and service of Thorin's ten remaining companions: "The others remained with Dain; for Dain dealt his treasure well" (*The Hobbit*, 275). The last description of Dain, that he "dealt his treasure well," is reminiscent of an Anglo-Saxon epithet for a good king, and perfectly sums up the Germanic ideal of kingship.

The Ring's Kings

In *The Lord of the Rings* trilogy, other historical models of kingship become important; in particular, the idea of sacral kingship, in which the king has a religious or mystical connection to the land and the people he rules, akin to the stories that tell of King Arthur's prom-

ised return in England's darkest hour. This type of kingship is only
touched on in *The Hobbit*, in which it is most applicable to Bard,
whose royal lineage is particularly significant. The concept of sacral
kingship is important in early medieval belief, but so are other kingly
virtues such as generosity and bravery. These kingly models found in
The Hobbit are developed and expanded greatly in *The Lord of the
Rings* trilogy, where Aragorn, Denethor, Théoden, and others provide
examples of good and bad kings, and where the question of greed wid-
ens to include the lust for power itself. The foundation for the struggles over the One Ring is laid in *The Hobbit*, with a world in which
the standards of kingship are those by which Beowulf was judged, and
the way a king handles treasure is central to determining his worth.

Notes

1. All references from J. R. R. Tolkien, *The Hobbit, or There and Back Again*, revised edition (New York: Ballantine, 1982).

2. For a good overview of the heroic ethos in Anglo-Saxon literature, see Katherine
O'Brien O'Keeffe, "Heroic values and Christian ethics," in *The Cambridge Companion to Old
English Literature*, ed. Malcolm Godden and Michael Lapidge (Cambridge: CUP, 1986),
107–25, especially the discussions of generosity and loyalty 107–108, 109), glory, fame, and
boasting (108, 114–15), and vengeance (111–12, 116).

3. See, for instance Caroline Monks, "Christianity and Kingship in Tolkien and Lewis,"
Mallorn 19 (1982), 5–7, 28.

4. Judy Ann Ford and Robin Anne Reid, "Councils and Kings: Aragorn's Journey Towards
Kingship in J.R.R. Tolkien's The Lord of the Rings and Peter Jackson's The Lord of the
Rings," *Tolkien Studies* 6 (2009): 71–90.

5. Ford and Reid also discuss the presence of the early Germanic kingship model in
Tolkien's fiction, focusing on the later LOTR trilogy and early Germanic kingship issues
such as sacral kingship and primogeniture, and how Peter Jackson transforms Aragorn into a
modern self-doubting hero in his film adaptations. See also Karen Simpson Nikakis, "Sacral
Kingship: Aragorn as the Rightful and Sacrificial King in The Lord of the Rings," *Mythlore* 26
(2007), 83–90, for a discussion of sacral kingship in Tolkien's fiction.

6. Cornelius Tacitus, "Germania," in *Tacitus I*, Loeb Classical Library, trans. M. Hutton
(Cambridge, MA: Harvard UP, 1970), 119–215.

7. For an account of Tacitus as a source for knowledge of early Germanic customs, see
O'Brien O'Keeffe, "Heroic values and Christian ethics," 113.

8. R. M. Liuzza, trans., *Beowulf* (Peterborough: Broadview, 2000).

9. S. A. J. Bradley, trans., "Maxims I" and "Maxims II" in *Anglo-Saxon Poetry* (Everyman,
1982), 344–50, 512–15.

10. Dennis M. Kratz, ed. and trans., *Waltharius and Ruodlieb* (New York: Garland, 1984).

11. Gwyn Jones, trans. "King Hrolf and his Champions" in *Eirik the Red and other
Icelandic Sagas* (Oxford: OUP, 1961), 221–318.

12. T. A. Shippey, *The Road to Middle-Earth* (London: George Allen & Unwin, 1982), 62.

13. Laurence Marcellus Larson, trans., *The King's Mirror* (New York: The American-Scandinavian Foundation, 1917).

14. For an overview of kingship in Anglo-Saxon England, see Peter Hunter Blair, "Chapter IV Government," in *An Introduction to Anglo-Saxon England* (Cambridge: CUP, 1962), 194–244, and B. A. E. Yorke, "Kings and Kingship," in *The Blackwell Encyclopaedia of Anglo-Saxon England*, ed. Michael Lapidge, John Blair, Simon Keynes, and Donald Scragg (Oxford: Blackwell, 1999), 271–72. A more detailed treatment can be found in J. M. Wallace-Hadrill, *Early Germanic Kingship in England and on the Continent* (Oxford, 1971). For more detailed accounts of Anglo-Saxon history, see James Campbell, ed., *The Anglo-Saxons* (London: Penguin, 1982) and F. M. Stenton, *Anglo-Saxon England*, 3rd ed. (Oxford: OUP, 1971).

15. For a discussion of the problems of extrapolating from literary descriptions of kingship to "reality," see O'Brien O'Keeffe, "Heroic values and Christian ethics," 112–13.

16. See H. M. Chadwick, *The Heroic Age* (Cambridge: CUP, 1912).

17. See Tolkien's influential lecture, "Beowulf: The Monsters and the Critics," *Proceedings of the British Academy* 22 (1936), 245–95.

18. R. M. Liuzza, trans., *Beowulf*, ll. 11. 863, 2390.

19. Hrolf goes on a quest to reclaim his inheritance from the greedy and tyrannical king Athils. Hrolf's own father, Helgi, though treated sympathetically in the text, suffers as a result of his foolish behavior in raping the evil Queen Olof in revenge for her humiliation of him after refusing his proposal of marriage. King Hring, the grandfather of Bothvar Bjarki, one of Hrolf's champions, is a foolish old king who takes an evil witch as his second wife. She then turns her stepson Bjorn into a bear after he refuses her sexual advances, and his son Bothvar Bjarki thus inherits supernatural bearlike strength and the ability to fight in the form of a bear, as Tolkien's Beorn does. Bothvar later avenges his father by killing the evil queen, as his grandfather is too old and foolish to do so, in spite of knowing her treachery.

20. In an alternative view, Caroline Monks, "Christianity and Kingship in Tolkien and Lewis," argues that the model of kingship in the fiction of both Tolkien and C. S. Lewis reflects specifically Christian ideals of kingship, suggesting that the prosperity of the realm is linked to the morals of its king; her argument focuses more on the Lord of the Rings trilogy.

21. Larson, trans., *The King's Mirror*, XL, 227.

22. Ibid, XL, 229.

23. Bradley, trans., "Maxims I," 347, l.60.

24. ". . . there are certain vices which you need especially to guard against: arrogant self-esteem, avarice that yearns for bribes, and forgetful neglect of the needs of men who are less capable than yourself. Keep constantly before your eyes as a warning the misfortunes of those who have fallen into disgrace because of immoderate pride." Larson, trans., *The King's Mirror*, XLI, 234.

25. "At last his portion of pride within him / grows and flourishes, while the guardian sleeps, / the soul's shepherd — that sleep is too sound, / bound with cares, the slayer too close / who, sinful and wicked, shoots from his bow. / Then he is struck in his heart, under his helmet / with a bitter dart — he knows no defense — / the strange, dark demands of evil spirits; / What he has long held seems too little, / angry and greedy, he gives no golden rings / for vaunting boasts, and his final destiny / he neglects and forgets, since God, Ruler of glories, / has given him a portion of honors. / In the end it finally comes about / that the loaned life-dwelling starts to decay / and falls, fated to die; another follows him / who doles out his

riches without regret, / the earl's ancient treasure; he heeds no terror." Liuzza, trans., *Beowulf*, ll. 1740–1757.

26. Ibid, ll. 1384–1385.

27. O'Brien O'Keefe, 111–14.

28. Tacitus, "Germania," 14.

29. See Vincent Ferré "The Rout of the King: Tolkien's Readings on Arthurian Kingship—Farmer Giles of Ham and The Homecoming of Beorhtnoth," in *Tolkien's Shorter Works: Essays of the Jena Conference 2007*, ed. Margaret Hiley and Frank Weinreich (Zollikofen: Walking Tree, 2007), 59–76 for an argument about Tolkien's portrayal of flawed kings in some of Tolkien's shorter fiction, and in Tolkien's literary criticism of medieval texts such as *Beowulf* and *Sir Gawain and the Green Knight*. Ferré identifies greed, excessive pride, and rashness as the recurring flaws found in Tolkien's kings, and generosity, devotion to his knights, and justice as the chief positive qualities. Ferré argues that Tolkien is suggesting an alternate model of kingship based on merit rather than heredity. Shippey also discusses the spectrum of greed vs. generosity in *The Hobbit* in *The Road to Middle-Earth*, 67–69.

30. Tacitus, "Germania," 14.

31. Bradley, trans., "Maxims I," 348, ll. 67b–70.

32. "Thus should a young man bring about good / with pious gifts from his father's possessions, / so that later in life loyal comrades / will stand beside him when war comes, / the people will support him—with praiseworthy deeds / a man will prosper among any people." Liuzza, trans., *Beowulf*, ll. 20–25.

33. "I am told this of king Hrolf . . . that he is liberal and free-handed, trustworthy, and particular as to his friends, so that his equal is not to be found. Nor is he sparing of gold and treasures to wellnigh all who care to receive them. He is not all that to look at, but mighty and enduring under pressure; the handsomest of men, harsh towards the oppressor but kindly and gracious to the needy, as to all those who offer him no resistance; the humblest of men, so that he answers the poor as gently as the rich." Jones, trans. "King Hrolf and his Champions," 258.

34. Larson, trans., *The King's Mirror*, XLI, 232.

CHAPTER 4

"The Last Homely House":

Elf-Lords and the Rules of Medieval Nobility

Janice Liedl

"The feast that they now saw was greater and more magnificent than before; and at the head of a long line of feasters sat a woodland king with a crown of leaves upon his golden hair, very much as Bombur had described the figure in his dream. The elvish folk were passing bowls from hand to hand and across the fires, and some were harping and many were singing."
—*The Hobbit*, 142[1]

Bilbo Baggins is disturbed when he is tricked into hosting a wizard and dwarves at his cozy home in Bag End. However, his attitude changes upon arriving at Rivendell; in fact, he's instantly enchanted by the elves. Rare visitors to the humble world of the Shire, the High Elves of Rivendell are nonetheless familiar and admirable figures to the tired hobbit. Their songs of greeting and merry ways make Bilbo feel immediately welcome, and the great house of Rivendell was a model of hospitality that mirrored his own generosity when Gandalf and the dwarves showed up on his doorstep.

However, not all of the elves in Tolkien's world are so welcoming. When Thorin and the other dwarves meet up with the elves of Mirkwood, hostility trumps hospitality. The Wood-elves are aggressive, stuck-up, and suspicious, or at least that's how they appear to the exhausted and beleaguered party of adventurers. Instead of enjoying friendly songs and fine food, the thirteen become prisoners of the warlike Wood-elves and their dour king.

Although the two communities of Rivendell and Mirkwood may seem like polar opposites, their leaders, Elrond and Thranduil, share a common cause with Gandalf—resisting the evil forces threatening the West: the Necromancer of Dol Guldur (later revealed to be Sauron in disguise) and the hordes of dark creatures his magic summoned to threaten the peaceful elven realms, particularly Thranduil's woodland kingdom. The extreme contrasts in Bilbo's experience of elves in his adventure, sometimes hospitable and sometimes hostile, parallel how medieval commoners related to nobles. Aristocrats were expected to provide hospitality, dispense justice, and wage war. Not all of them lived up to these obligations. For *The Hobbit*, Tolkien referenced the grand traditions of aristocratic courts and the difficult lives of medieval monarchs ruling in treacherous times. Tolkien used these many histories, intertwined with medieval myths of elves, to create the noble and powerful elves of Middle-earth.

"Now Can No Man See Elves No More": Stories of Elves in the Middle Ages

Tolkien's elves are not exclusively based on the elves of medieval European tradition, although they share some similarities. Elves were an integral part of medieval lore, but by the end the Middle Ages, they only appeared in legends. In the fourteenth century, Geoffrey Chaucer's fictional Wife of Bath complained that churches replaced the old places where the elf-queen and her merry company once resided: "now kan no man se none elves mo".[2] What were these lost elves supposed to be like? Isidore of Seville, a seventh-century churchman and author of the first encyclopedia, described elves as something akin to nymphs or tree-spirits. In Scandinavian myths, such as the *Volundarkviða*, the elven hero, Volundr, who appears in English legends as Wayland the Smith, is described as beautiful and pale—a warrior of the *álfar*.[3] Anglo-Saxon nobles incorporated elves into their given names: Alfred (elf-counsel) and Aelfgifu (elf-gift) were popular names among the medieval English aristocrats. After the Norman conquest of England in 1066, French traditions of beautiful fairy women expanded the mythology of elves in English ballads and poetry.

Legends of elves also had darker components: In some English stories, the elves caused illnesses such as epilepsy, strokes, and fever. Afflicted individuals were described as "elf-shot." The *Beowulf* poet counted the uncanny elves among the damned descendants of the Biblical murderer, Cain. Some other medieval traditions, including the thirteenth-century *South England Legendary*, thought that elves were angels who failed to fight for or against God and were therefore banished to Earth. In the ballad *Tam Lin*, the fair queen of Elf-land abducted ordinary mortals to join her court.[4] Before he wrote *The Hobbit*, Tolkien wrote a long poem in Old English, *Ides Ælfscȳene (The Elf-Fair Lady)*. Elrond's ally and the great lady of Lothlorien, Galadriel, has a fair, fearsome beauty which echoes the beautiful and powerful elf-queens of Tolkien's poem and medieval legend.[5]

By the nineteenth century, elves, dwarves, goblins, and other fantastic beings were fodder for the folklorists who collected fairy tales, such as the brothers Jacob and Wilhelm Grimm. The elves of their tales who helped the shoemaker were a far cry from the elves of medieval lore, yet the Grimms preserved a sense of wonder that tied the medieval past to a magical world. For them, the most important element was the setting. The Grimm Brothers rejected the bustling towns and cities that resembled Tolkien's community of the Shire and turned to the forests for their story settings. A letter Jacob wrote to Wilhelm in 1805 explained: "The only time in which it might be possible to allow an idea of the past, an idea of the world of knights, if you will, to blossom anew within us is when it is transformed into a forest in which wild animals roam about."[6] Tolkien's elves are there in Grimm's forest. They inhabit the hidden foothills and lush woodlands of Middle-earth, where they embody many of the virtues—and occasionally, the vices—of the knights of old.

"They Stayed Long in that Good House": Elves and Noble Hospitality

Bilbo and his companions are already weary when they reach the refuge of Rivendell early on in their journey to the Lonely Mountain. The "Last Homely House" is not easy to find, hidden as it is on the "very edge of the Wild" that the party approached on a daunting path past deep gullies, ravines, and bogs. (*The Hobbit*, 44–45) These natural obstacles protect Rivendell much as they secured early medieval British fortresses such as Tintagel in far western Cornwall. There, a narrow peninsula provided the only connection of the cliff-top fortress to the mainland. This provided an excellent natural defense for what some scholars believe was King Arthur's birthplace.[7] Mirkwood, home to the Elvenking and his followers, is even better defended than Tintagel or Rivendell, considering both the forest and the creatures that dwell within it are dangerous to any who dare trespass in Thranduil's realm. Gandalf describes Mirkwood as "The greatest of the forests of the Northern world" (*The Hobbit*, 127). To Bilbo and the dwarves, the heavy canopy of the gnarled trees offers only gloom and catastrophe as they wander for weeks without fresh water and food.

Even though Rivendell is not the best-defended stronghold, it still impresses Bilbo and the gruff dwarves. Rivendell's master is Elrond, an ancient and wise elf. He's seen the rise and fall of great kingdoms as well as the coming of Sauron's evil threats against Middle-earth. *The Hobbit* introduces Elrond as an "elf-friend—one of those people whose fathers came into the strange stories before the beginning of History, the wars of the evil goblins and the elves and the first men in the North" (*The Hobbit*, 48). Tolkien describes him as someone who is as noble as an elf-lord, as wise as a wizard, and as kind as summer.

It is this kindness that exemplifies the first important parallel between medieval ideas of nobility and the elves of Tolkien's world.

Elrond's kindness is particularly evident in his hospitality to Bilbo and company. Hospitality and generosity were important virtues for medieval nobles and rulers. Great kings in the age of *Beowulf* were renowned for the gifts of gold, weapons, and jewelry they gave to heir followers, as Mark Sundaram and Aven McMaster note in chapter 3 of this book. Medieval aristocrats also offered humble hospitality of food and shelter. A lord's fortified manor or a monastery might offer the only safe haven for weary travelers crossing the countryside where bandits and wild animals lurked. However, travelers were a rare occurrence in most wealthy homes. The most frequent visitors were relatives, friends, business acquaintances, tradesfolk, and the poor. The aristocratic Petre family hosted mostly friends and local paupers at Ingatestone Hall in Essex during the sixteenth century. Rarely true strangers were included, as in the account for April 24, 1552, when "ii wayfaring men" were among the guests. Usually the food served to ordinary folks and the poor wasn't on a par with that served to truly noble guests. Herring, salt fish, beer, and coarse, cheap bread were what the poor could expect from the charity of fourteenth- and fifteenth-century English aristocrats such as Dame Catherine de Norwich or Elizabeth de Burgh, Lady of Clare.[8] Unlike the pantry-emptying party Bilbo hosted, medieval travelers dining in noble households made do with common fare.

The food might be different, but the people who served it filled similar roles in medieval Europe and Middle-earth. There were butlers and guards working for the elves of Middle-earth and the aristocrats of medieval Europe. A medieval noble's "household" referred to the people who served the lord or lady; almost everyone had a different duty. Aristocrats often owned many properties, so that a mix of permanent and traveling employees made up their households. The average noble household of the fourteenth or fifteenth century numbered nearly 100 members, and most were employed in rather humble jobs working in the stables, the laundry, and the kitchens, or as attendants for the lord and lady. A great nobleman such as the Duke of Norfolk or the Earl of Warwick might have as many as 500 servants in his household, to appear important and enjoy his lavish lifestyle.[9] Elrond and Thranduil, as lords of kingly establishments, probably employed at least that many and in very similar style. For instance, we know that the job of the Elvenking's butler is different than the modern butler's duties to greet visitors and manage his master's house. His duties are more akin to the work of butlers in the Middle Ages. Butlers back then were responsible for storing bottles and casks of wine, also known as butts, hence the job title "butt-ler." This was a position of great responsibility because wine was both valuable and prone to theft; Thranduil's butler is sadly negligent, sharing large flagons of the king's private stores of strong wine with his friend, the chief of the guards. The two servants' dishonesty gives Bilbo all he needs to free his friends from the Elvenking's captivity:

> Then Bilbo heard the king's butler bidding the chief of the guards good-night.
> "Now come with me," he said, "and taste the new wine that has just come in. I shall be hard at work tonight clearing the cellar of the empty wood, so let us have a drink first to help the labour."
> "Very good," laughed the chief of the guards. "I'll taste with you and see if it is fit for the king's table. There is a feast tonight and it would not do to send up poor stuff."
> (*The Hobbit*, 163-164)

Kings, aristocrats, and great churchmen provided essential hospitality to their friends, relatives, servants, and the needy as well as travelers. Great households had to stockpile impressive quantities of food and drink to provide for all of their dependents and guests. Vast cellars and larders were stocked with a variety of goods, many of them produced by skilled servants, but others purchased from local grocers, brewers, and bakers. A good host provided his guests with more than the minimum: shelter, food, and liquor. The fifteenth-century Archbishop of York, Henry Bowet, was famed for his lavish hospitality and had the receipts to prove it. His busy household ran through 80 tuns, or 640 barrels, of wine in a year, not to mention the quantities of ale he provided for servants and the poor.[10] The many empty barrels that Bilbo uses to smuggle his friends out of Mirkwood show that Thranduil and his household are as fond of wine and food as the Archbishop and his guests.

The elves of Rivendell probably enjoyed their wine as much as those of Mirkwood, although Bilbo remarks more upon the food, singing, and general pleasantries of life in Elrond's wonderful house, where the adventurers rested for two full weeks. Their clothes are mended, their provisions replenished, and their spirits refreshed by Elrond's hospitality. From the point of view of weary guests, Elrond's house is, indeed, as Tolkien termed it, "perfect" (*The Hobbit*, 49). Medieval aristocrats strove to be generous in their hospitality, inspired by Biblical exhortations to charity and literary models of open-handed giving.

Not every guest benefited equally, nor would that have been the host's goal. In fourteenth-century Lorraine, laws of hospitality required hosts to provide appropriate food for guests of different ranks. Bread was guaranteed to laborers, along with fish, soup, and occasionally wine. White bread, wine, and at least three dishes suitable for a gentleman were prescribed by law for guests of higher rank.[11] Of course, many hosts paid the highest attention to their friends, relatives, and social superiors, whereas ideal hospitality offered equal if not more attention to the poor and needy. Stefano Guazzo scolded wealthy noblemen and church leaders in his 1574 courtesy book, *La civil conversation*, for failing to open their houses to the truly needy, whether foreigners or poor, virtuous citizens of their own territories.[12] When the elves of Mirkwood hold Thorin and the other dwarves prisoner, they behave worse than the status-conscious hosts that Guazzo condemned. Of course, noble hosts in the Middle Ages would have expected their guests to be open and honest about their travels and purposes—something that Thorin wouldn't risk. So the Wood-elves' lack of hospitality was somewhat excusable.

According to medieval expectations of hospitality, a host's generosity should extend beyond offers of food, shelter, and entertainment. For example, the lord of Rivendell shares his wisdom and knowledge with his guests, as well as his goods. Elrond provides important assistance to the expedition when he reads the runic script on each of the swords and decodes the hidden moon-letters on Thorin's map. Although reading and writing exotic languages wasn't a strong point for medieval nobility, some aristocrats might have sounded as alien to the ordinary people around them as Elrond's reading of the runes did to Bilbo's ears. After William the Conqueror led the Norman conquest of England in 1066, the noble courts and even the law courts started communicating only in the imported Norman French language. The gap between medieval nobles and ordinary people grew when they not only lived apart but also spoke different languages. By the end of the Middle Ages, aristocrats and commoners viewed each other with increasing suspicion. This had a great deal to do with another traditional noble privilege: creating and enforcing law.

"The Dungeon of His Prisoners": Elves and Medieval Justice

The gap between ordinary people and princes was at its widest when medieval kings and nobles exercised their second great duty: dispensing justice and punishing wrong-doers. Thranduil, the Elvenking, exercises that power when he has Thorin and the other dwarves arrested as trespassers in his forest realm. Thorin, of course, is a king in his own right, and from a medieval perspective, should have been treated with greater courtesy by the Elvenking. But his journeys into Mirkwood are carried out in secret and the dwarves seem suspicious by their very nature to the wary, war-weary elves.

Thorin's encounter with the king of the Wood-elves resembles Richard I of England's dreadful experience at the hands of Emperor Henry VI in 1192. Richard the Lionheart, renowned as a warrior, crusader, and troubadour, didn't always get along with his fellow rulers. He challenged Philip Augustus of France over their rival claims to his family's land, and Emperor Henry was outraged when the English king supported Sicilian and German rebellions against his imperial crown. While returning to England, Richard was shipwrecked and came ashore in imperial territory. The king and his fellow crusaders disguised themselves as humble travelers but revealed themselves through their lavish spending and bold behavior. Loyal imperial lords quickly unmasked the English party. King Richard was captured just fifty miles short of freedom, and left to cool his heels as the emperor's prisoner for more than a year.[13]

Traveling in disguise violated medieval ideas of proper behavior: Only evil-doers like burglars or troublemakers would behave in that way. Bilbo's party isn't exactly in disguise while they travel through Mirkwood, but Thorin is careful to keep his royal heritage under wraps. He fears, and maybe rightly so, the elves' reaction to his claim on the long-lost treasure now hoarded by Smaug. Even without that information, Thranduil and the Wood-elves aren't disposed to think well of the dwarves. Tolkien's dwarves and elves are old enemies in the history of Middle-earth. But past hostility and even suspicions of disguise are secondary problems for the Elvenking. His biggest problem is that the dwarves are breaking Mirkwood's laws. When Balin questions how the dwarves are treated, Thranduil's response sums up his kingly rights:

> "It is a crime to wander in my realm without leave. Do you forget that you were in my kingdom, using the road that my people made? Did you not three times pursue and trouble my people in the forest and rouse the spiders with your riot and clamour? After all the disturbance you have made I have a right to know what brings you here, and if you will not tell me now, I will keep you all in prison until you have learned sense and manners!"(The Hobbit, 159)

Once captive, a medieval prisoner could be held indefinitely. The Elvenking's vow to hold Thorin until he confesses his true reasons for traveling in Mirkwood is remarkably similar to Emperor Henry's detention of King Richard. Henry sought political advantage and money from his high-ranking captive. The Elvenking only suspects Thorin's objective but that is enough to keep the dwarves locked up indefinitely.

Demanding a ransom for noble and royal prisoners was a common practice in the Middle Ages. Soldiers who surrendered on the battlefield expected to have to ransom themselves with the help of their friends back home. So, too, did King Richard have to rely on his family and royal servants to start to raise the extortionate amount, 100,000 silver marks, needed to ransom him from the Emperor's grasp. Rich and poor subjects across England paid heavy taxes to finance the king's ransom, as high as 25 percent of the value of their movable goods, such as tools, housewares, and jewelry, to fill the emperor's coffers and free their king.[14] The huge ransom and heavy burden it imposed make it seem as if Emperor Henry was greedy and covetous. Was he? A hundred years later, the poet Dante Alighieri claimed that emperors and kings were the only people fit to pass judgment or make laws because they theoretically owned everything and could covet nothing. "But there is nothing the monarch *could* covet, for his jurisdiction is bounded only by the ocean. . . . From this it follows that of all men the monarch can be the purest embodiment of justice."[15] Emperor Henry didn't fit this description: His ransom demands were outrageous. Similarly, the Elvenking has a weakness for treasure, "especially for silver and white gems; and though his hoard was rich, he was ever eager for more" (*The Hobbit*, 155). Clearly the gulf between the ideals and reality of noble virtue is as wide in Middle-earth as it was in medieval history.

The problems that Thorin and the other dwarves faced as the Elvenking's captives are as serious as that of any historical hostage. A hostage for ransom was an asset to be nurtured. A regular prisoner was a liability. In a medieval prison, food and drink weren't well-supplied: A loaf of bread a day might be all that a prisoner would receive, far from enough to sustain a life.[16] Thorin and the dwarves receive food and drink in Thranduil's dungeon, ensuring they would not starve or suffer as did many of their medieval counterparts. On the other hand, while escape from some medieval prisons was an easy feat, the dwarves are held securely. Even if they could work their way out of his dungeons, there is no way to leave the confusing and well-guarded underground palace. Thranduil knows his power over the prisoners, ordering Thorin's companions to be unbound once they stand before him. "There is no escape from my magic doors for those who are once brought inside" (*The Hobbit*, 158). Gloating wasn't a trait only found in elven kings. While holding Richard captive, Emperor Henry boasted to King Philip Augustus of France of his clever capture of the English king and vowed that their fellow monarch would be punished for his "treason, treachery and mischief." [17] One could imagine Thranduil treating Thorin in much the same fashion if his mission to claim his throne and treasure were discovered.

While the Elvenking is content to let Thorin languish in his dungeon as an unknown but suspicious traveler, Emperor Henry brought his captive out of the dungeon and into the law courts. Richard was put on trial during Easter 1193, accused of killing a fellow crusader,

Awe-inspiring: Rulers such as Charles VII of France (1422-61) and Thranduil used their royal position to intimidate.

Conrad de Montferrat, and breaking agreements made with the emperor. Richard defended himself with great ability in the court. We have the proof of it from a chronicler for the French king—a hostile witness if there ever was one!—who wrote: "When Richard replied he spoke so eloquently and regally, in so lionhearted a manner, that it was as though he had forgotten where he was and the undignified circumstances in which he had been captured and imagined himself to be seated on the throne of his ancestors at Lincoln or Caen."[18] Thorin makes no defense beyond the very real risk of starvation facing his party in the hostile woods. Beyond that justification, the leader of the dwarves opts for a dignified silence and is taken to the Elvenking's dungeon, just as Richard was kept prisoner after his trial.

However, whereas the English king languished in Emperor Henry's control for many months, Thorin and his company are soon freed by Bilbo Baggins, who packs them into barrels and floats his fellows down the river toward Lake-town and freedom. Their escape is just as dramatic as the historical escape from captivity of Prince Edward, who was held hostage by English rebels for much of 1264 and into 1265, two generations after Richard's reign. In May of that year, the future Edward I of England rode out with some of his captors and soon the prince was galloping to freedom. Stories differ as to whether this was the result of his own cleverness (trying all the different horses as a pretended game until he identified the fastest for his escape) or good planning (some accounts claim the prince had the assistance of half a dozen knights and squires).[19] In either case, the dramatic escape helped turn the tide for a brave royal warrior. Edward's family soon defeated the rebels and so secured his throne. Similarly, Thorin's escape allows him to pursue his own crown.

"To Defend the Elvenking": Sieges, Stones and Chivalry

The Elvenking soon learns the truth of the dwarves' escape and of Thorin's royal ambition. His captain of the guard and butler seem to have been punished for their lapses in security—a bit unfair given that Bilbo had a ring that made him invisible. Rather than linger on the failures in his household security, the Elvenking is more interested in Thorin's plans to claim the treasure. Knowing the dangers that Smaug presented and their small numbers, Thranduil predicts that "they will all come to a bad end, and serve them right!" (*The Hobbit*, 184).

The end isn't as bad for Thorin and company as the Elvenking expects, but that is only because the people of Lake-town pay the greatest price. Their city is destroyed and many of their people die. It is Lake-town's brave archer, Bard, also the heir to the old kings of Dale, who shoots down Smaug and ends his destructive rampage. When Thorin rebuffs Bard's demand for a fair share of the treasure that his people had paid for with their lives and goods, war is in the offing. Bard's ally in this war is none other than the Elvenking. Together, their armies lay siege to Thorin's stronghold.

Sieges were risky and expensive undertakings in the Middle Ages, both for those taking refuge behind fortress or city walls and for the besiegers. Attackers had to batter down imposing defenses, tunnel mines beneath them to cause their collapse, or spend months waiting out their starving opponents. Medieval knights and rulers planned well for sieges. Attackers tried to cover all avenues of entrance or escape while they plotted ways to bring down the stronghold. Defenders ensured that they were protected by not only strong walls, but also supplied with food and water. Many sent out the call to allies to come and rescue them or "lift" the siege.

Many historical sieges failed, just as Bilbo suggests Thranduil's will both because of Thorin's strong position (it's hard to undermine a mountain) and the coming of Dain Ironfoot's dwarven army. Medieval sieges were harder to predict, as King Richard I found, to his dismay. After Emperor Henry VI released the king in 1194, Richard returned to find his French territories slipping from his grasp, thanks to the wily offers of the French king, Philip Augustus. Richard the Lionheart went to war against his former subjects, laying siege to one stronghold after another. While scouting the castle of Châlus-Chabrol in March 1199, Richard was shot by a crossbow bolt and died soon after, bringing an end to his campaign.[20] The prospective siege of Thorin's kingdom also ends suddenly, but less tragically, when Bilbo gives Bard and Thranduil the key to force Thorin into the open: the great royal symbol of the Arkenstone.

Medieval nobles and monarchs had their own great symbols of power and lost them at their peril. In 1296, the former crown prince Edward, now king of England in his own right, defeated the army of the Scots king John Balliol and seized the Stone of Destiny, also known as the Stone of Scone, which was the traditional coronation seat of Scotland's rulers.[21] Edward had the stone installed beneath the coronation seat of English rulers in Westminster Abbey, where it remained for 700 years. Thorin's Arkenstone is returned to him much more quickly than the Scots' stone to Scotland, restored in 1996, but still not fast enough: The King under the Mountain is buried with the Arkenstone after the devastating Battle of the Five Armies.

When the goblins and wolves threaten annihilation, the armies of humans, dwarves, and elves join together for one cause. It was Thranduil's elven warriors who draw first blood. The elven foot soldiers charge the goblins and the wolves with spears and swords while archers rain down arrows upon their foe. Thranduil, like many a medieval noble, directs his soldiers from high ground away from the battle. That isn't cowardice, but an effective military strategy that others respected. We see that in the way that both Gandalf and Bilbo seek out the Elvenking's company at the battle's climax, a deliberate choice on the hobbit's part, who felt that "if he was going to be in a last desperate stand, he preferred on the whole to defend the Elvenking" (*The Hobbit*, 258–59). Such dauntless chivalry recalls medieval precedent such as the loyal knights who accompanied blind King John of Bohemia into battle at Crécy in 1346. Chronicles admiringly recalled the group's brave attack, hampered by the fact that John's loyal followers protected their king at their own cost, lashing the royal mount to his guard's horses. The Bohemians' bravery so impressed their opponents that the English royal heir, the young Black Prince, adopted their king's crest of three white feathers and his motto, *Ich Dien* (I Serve), and the Prince of Wales uses these symbols to this very day.[22] Thranduil is less suicidal than King John, but still the noble leader with whom chivalric Bilbo wants to fight to the finish.

At the end, Bilbo's friends save the day, but only with a great loss of life. As well as Thorin; his nephews, Fili and Kili; and great numbers of Dain's followers; the allies bury many soldiers from Bard's and Thranduil's armies. The elf-host that returned to Mirkwood is "sadly lessened," but their king is accompanied by Gandalf, Beorn, and Bilbo until they all reach the forest borders. There Bilbo refuses all the royal offers of hospitality, still too fearful of the dreadful creatures that remain within the forest. Instead, he offers Thranduil a silver and pearl necklace out of Smaug's hoard as partial payment for the wine and bread that Bilbo confesses he stole from the king while his friends were captive. Thranduil accepts the gift gravely, dubbing his small companion "Bilbo the Magnificent" as well as "elf-friend and blessed." (*The Hobbit*, 266–67) Bilbo now shows that he shares many of the great qualities of medieval lords and great elf-lords: He is hospitable, fair, and brave.

"I Will Diminish, and Go Into the West": The End of the Elves and the Middle Ages

Bilbo's journey ends after a brief stopover at the Last (or First) Homely House in the West. But Elrond and the other remaining elves of Middle-earth face a stark choice Bilbo knows little of at this point: Travel over the seas and into the West, or, like the elves of medieval lore, dwindle into myth as the Age of Man begins. Galadriel, one of the mightiest of the elves, is relieved when she resists the temptation to accept the One Ring Frodo offers her. "I will diminish, and go into the West, and remain Galadriel" (*The Fellowship of the Ring*, 381).

In some ways, Galadriel's fate resembles that experienced by European aristocrats after the Middle Ages. Innovations in warfare, economics, and politics replaced noble rule in many places with some sort of representative government as early as the 17th century. Aristocrats could accommodate the rising merchant and manufacturing classes and their commercial ways of life through investments and even intermarriage, as some did in Great Britain and the Netherlands, or risk being destroyed by them, as others discovered in the French Revolution. Maintaining their grand lifestyle became impossible for great families in the modern world. By the late nineteenth and early twentieth century, many noble families in Britain had to sell or donate their estates to the government in order to pay rising taxes on inheritance of estates known as "death duties." This was a popular policy with ordinary Britons who couldn't dream of such luxuries and who felt the pinch of higher taxes on alcohol, tobacco, and their more modest income.[23]

There is another group whose decline brings to mind the fate of Tolkien's elves. These were the people of the oldest European state in the late Middle Ages: the Byzantines. The fall of Byzantium in 1453 is often cited as the end of the Middle Ages, just as the War of the Rings signals the end of the Third Age of Middle-earth. Understanding the end of the Byzantine Empire explains much about the fate of the elves in Tolkien's Middle-earth.

Why did Byzantium matter so much in medieval history, and how were its people like the elves? Byzantium is one of the names used for the Eastern Roman Empire after its great leader of the early fourth century, Constantine, moved his government from Rome, which had become an increasingly irrelevant settlement in the western fringes of his vast state, to Byzantium, a city on the straits of the Bosphorus, dividing Europe from Asia. Constantine poured his wealth and energy into the city that he renamed after himself: Constantinople. For centuries, it flourished as the center of a thriving empire, with successive emperors adding great new buildings such as *Hagia Sophia* (Holy Wisdom), the glorious church built on the orders of Emperor Justinian. To the people of Western Europe, the Byzantines seemed incredibly sophisticated and strange. The common language of their court had shifted from Roman Latin to Greek. Their fashions, their culture, and even their practices of Christianity were very different from those followed in Western Europe. Just as the elves are unearthly and remote to a hobbit, so too were the Byzantines to the European contemporaries.

It is no wonder that the medieval travelers who arrived in Constantinople formed strong impressions of the great city. Constantinople, modern-day Istanbul, differed from the cities of Europe as much as Rivendell contrasted with Hobbiton. The German historian and bishop, Liutprand of Cremona, arrived in the city in 949 and, rather like Bilbo admiring Rivendell, was enchanted by the wonders of the court. He described elaborate rituals of the royal household that appeared foreign to a westerner and marveled at the mechanical birds and beasts set up in the royal audience chambers to amaze the court. Returning in 968, Liutprand was far more critical of his hosts. He scorned their clothing as effeminate, their diet as disgusting, and their character as greedy and deceitful. The emperor was equally hostile: He said that Liutprand and his emperor, Otto, were "not Romans but Lombards," implying that the Europeans were barbarians.[24] Even Thorin didn't go so far in his hostility toward the Wood-elves or Thranduil to the dwarves!

The Empire was fading as the rival forces of the Islamic Caliphate, and later, the Ottoman Turks, came to dominate the region after the seventh century. So, too, were Tolkien's elves fading in the last days of the Third Age, when Bilbo and the dwarves journey to the Lonely Mountain. The elves are preparing to leave Middle-earth for the angelic realm of Valinor, far across the sea. Some Byzantines adopted a similar tactic: They fled their beloved "Queen of Cities" for safe haven in the Christian West, where a few discerning scholars welcomed their arrival as teachers of Greek and preservers of many ancient and valuable texts. But for many of the proudest Byzantines, that was a sad decline and, arguably, far more of a sacrifice than the elves face when they journey to the Havens or their immortal refuge of Valinor. The elves remain masters of their own destiny in the west, but the Byzantines in Europe would be subject to the kings and churchmen there. "Better a Turkish turban than a papal tiara" was the response of some Byzantine subjects to this proposition. Most refused to accept a European exile if it required them to relinquish their own Christian church for that of the Pope in Rome.[25] Exile in Tolkien's world is more appealing: Only a minority of Tolkien's elves stay in Middle-earth, including Elrond's children.

By the early fifteenth century, little was left of the great empire except for a small amount of territory immediately surrounding Constantinople itself. In spring 1453, Sultan Mehmed II laid siege to the walled city and within a few short weeks, Constantinople fell to his attacks. Renamed Istanbul, the city became the jewel in the crown of his vast Ottoman Empire, and today is the largest city in Turkey. Byzantine religion and culture continued as a distinct minority in Turkish Istanbul, but the Byzantines themselves faded as their population declined and their influence waned within the newly rededicated city. In this respect, they resemble those elves who choose, after the conclusion of the War of the Rings, to stay in Middle-earth and fade into mortality.

Bilbo lives in the last day of the elves of Middle-earth, experiencing all of their glory and grandeur. He enjoys the aristocratic hospitality of Elrond as well as the inadvertent hospitality of Thranduil. He witnesses the terror of royal justice and war as practiced by the elves, ancient masters of these noble arts. Bilbo realizes he is fortunate to experience all of this: The elves are rare visitors to the Shire in his lifetime and in the years to come, they will, like medieval elves and even medieval aristocrats, fade into obscurity.

Notes

1. All references to The Hobbit come from the reset 5th edition. J. R. R. Tolkien, *The Hobbit, or There and Back Again* (New York: HarperCollins, 2007). References to *The Fellowship of the Ring* come from the 1965 Houghton Mifflin edition.

2. Geoffrey Chaucer, *The Riverside Chaucer*, 3rd edition (Oxford: Oxford University Press, 2008), 116.

3. FJohn McKinnell, "The Context of *Volundarkviða*" in *The Poetic Edda: Essays on Old Norse Mythology* edited by Paul L. Acker (London: Routledge, 2002), 198–210.

4. For the broad context of elves in medieval legend and literature, see Alaric Hall, *Elves in Anglo-Saxon England: Matters of Belief, Health, Gender and Identity* (Woodbridge, UK: Boydell, 2007), 39–105.

5. Tolkien's Old English poem and a translation are available in T. A. Shippey, *The Road to Middle-earth: How Tolkien created a new mythology* (New York: Houghton Mifflin, 1983), 229–34.

6. Jack Zipes, *The Brothers Grimm: From Enchanted Forests to the Modern World*, 2nd edition (New York: Palgrave Macmillan, 2002), 67–68.

7. Angus Konstam, *British Forts in the Age of Arthur* (Oxford: Osprey, 2008), 9-25.

8. Felicity Heal, *Hospitality in Early Modern England* (Oxford: Oxford University Press, 1990), 68-69.

9. Kate Mertes, *The English Noble Household, 1250-1600* (Oxford: Blackwell, 1988), 18-25.

10. T. F. Tout, "Bowet, Henry (d. 1423)," rev. J. J. N. Palmer, *Oxford Dictionary of National Biography*, (Oxford: Oxford University Press, 2004), www.oxforddnb.com/view/article/3062.

11. Jean Coudert, "Pitance ou ripaille? Usages alimentaires et rituels d'hospitalité d'après les rapports de droits lorrains (1300-1635)", *Histoire et Societes Rurales* 29 (January, 2008), 13-21.

12. Lucinda M. Byatt, "The concept of hospitality in a cardinal's household in Renaissance Rome", *Renaissance Studies* 2:2 (1988), 314.

13. John Gillingham, 'Richard I (1157–1199)', *Oxford Dictionary of National Biography*, (Oxford: Oxford University Press, 2004), www.oxforddnb.com/view/article/23498.

14. Robert Bartlett, *England under the Norman and Angevin Kings, 1075-1225* (Oxford: Oxford University Press, 2000), 160-67.

15. Quoted in Spenser Pearce, "Dante: Order, Justice and the Society of Orders" *Orders and Hierarchies in Late Medieval and Renaissance Europe*, edited by Jeffrey Denton (Toronto: University of Toronto Press, 1999), 50.

16. Guy Geltner, "Medieval Prisons: Between Myth and Reality, Hell and Purgatory", *History Compass* 4:2 (2006), 263-64.

17. John Gillingham, *Richard I* (New Haven: Yale University Press, 2002), 222.

18. Gillingham, *Richard I*, 236-38.

19. Michael Prestwich, *Edward I* (Berkeley: University of California Press, 1988), 46-49.

20. Gillingham, "Richard I (1157–1199)".

21. Prestwich, 464-73.

22. Françoise Autrand, "The Battle of Crécy: A Hard Blow for the Monarchy of France", *The Battle of Crécy, 1346*, edited by Andrew Ayton and Philip Preston (Rochester: Boydell Brewer, 2007), 275-76.

23. David Cannadine, *The Decline and Fall of the British Aristocracy* (New Haven: Yale University Press, 1990), 46-48.

24. Liutprand of Cremona's views are contrasted in Averil Cameron's "The Byzantine Book of Ceremonies" in *Rituals of Royalty: Power and Ceremonial in Traditional Societies*, edited by David Cannadine and Simon Price (Cambridge: Cambridge University Press, 1992), 119-20. For Liutprand's writing as a reflection of Western culture, see Christopher Brooke, *Europe in the Central Middle Ages, 962-1154*, 3rd edition (New York: Longman, 2000), 16-17.

25. Judith Herrin, *Byzantium: The Surprising Life of a Medieval Empire* (Princeton: Princeton University Press, 2007), 299-309.

PART TWO

From Hobbit-holes to Riddle-Games in the Middle Ages and Middle-earth

"Riddles were all he could think of. Asking them, and sometimes guessing them, had been the only game he had ever played with other funny creatures sitting in their holes in the long, long ago, before he lost all his friends and was driven away, alone, and crept down, down, into the dark under the mountains."

—*The Hobbit*, 69

CHAPTER 5

Dreaming of Eggs and Bacon, Seedcakes and Scones

Kristen M. Burkholder

"So he sat himself down with his back to a tree, and not for the last time fell to thinking of his far-distant hobbit-hole with its beautiful pantries. He was deep in thoughts of bacon and eggs and toast and butter when he felt something touch him."

—*The Hobbit*, 134-35[1]

Food is one of the basic necessities of life, as we all know. Without food we starve and die. Indeed, the original meaning of the Old English *steorfan* was simply "to die," not necessarily of hunger, but in recent centuries it has come to mean primarily just that.

What characters eat or do not eat, and how they treat others with regard to food and eating, are important aspects of both characterization and plot in *The Hobbit*. Acquiring food is a frequent matter of concern for the dwarves and hobbit during their quest—their most difficult moments are marked by hunger—and food and eating are important throughout the story. The details of who, how, and what were informed by Tolkien's own experiences and the context in which he lived, as this chapter will demonstrate.

Concerning Hobbits and Comfort

A recipe from Hannah Glasse's 1747 *The Art of Cookery Made Plain and Easy:* "A *Rich* Seed Cake, *called the* Nun's Cake."

> TAKE four Pound of your finest Flour, and three Pound of double refin'd Sugar beaten and sifted, mix them together, and dry them by the Fire till you prepare your other Materials; take four Pound of Butter, beat it with your Hand till it is soft like Cream, then beat thirty-five Eggs, leave out sixteen Whites, and strain off your Eggs from the Treds, and beat them and the Butter together till all appears like Butter. Put in four or five Spoonfuls of Rose or Orange-flower Water, and beat again; then take your Flour and Sugar, with six Ounces of Carraway Seeds, and strew it in by Degrees, beating it up all the Time for two Hours together. You may put in as much Tincture of Cinnamon or Ambergrease as you please, butter your Hoop, and let it stand three Hours in a moderate Oven. You must observe always in beating of Butter to do it with a cool Hand, and beat it always one Way in a deep Earthen Dish.[2]

Hobbits love to eat, and eat well.

This is made plain in the opening paragraphs of *The Hobbit*, in which the comfort of a hobbit-hole is explicitly contrasted with "a dry, bare, sandy hole with nothing in it to sit down on or eat," and in which Bilbo's own home, Bag End, is described as having "lots" of pantries. (*The Hobbit*, 11) Bilbo first meets Gandalf shortly after eating breakfast, and at the end of their somewhat uncomfortable conversation, he invites the wizard for tea the next day. Thus the dwarves are introduced, appearing in ones and twos and fours and fives; all of them come to tea and expect a meal.

Bilbo Baggins and J.R.R. Tolkien would have both felt at home
in this traditional English kitchen

"Tea," as the name for a meal, in this instance seems to be closer
to the working-class evening meal than the afternoon tea with finger
foods that was generally considered suitable for ladies of the middle
and upper classes. Tolkien specifies the items that Bilbo provides at
this impromptu tea party: seedcake and tea, beer, ale, porter, and coffee, then buttered scones. When the final group of five dwarves plus
Gandalf arrives, they are quite demanding and request a variety of
foodstuffs, including raspberry jam, mince-pies, salad, cold chicken,
and similar substantial dishes. Bilbo reluctantly does the polite thing
of asking his unwanted guests to stay for supper, and indeed they stay
the night—although the supper seems to go by the wayside, never
again mentioned.

The next morning, the dwarves get their own breakfasts in Bilbo's
kitchen while their host continues to sleep. When Bilbo finally arises,
he has breakfast, clears up the mess in the kitchen, and then begins
eating a second breakfast before Gandalf comes back to chivvy him
into joining the dwarves on their quest. This second breakfast occasions no surprise; apparently, it is quite normal for a hobbit to eat
more than three meals a day. Bilbo's initial impression of adventuring

is positive, as it involves only riding through pleasant countryside, and the only aspect he doesn't care for is that meals with the dwarves don't come often enough.

Later in the story, Bilbo repeatedly wishes to be back in his hobbit-hole, or dreams of it. In many of these instances, he thinks of food and drink, such as bacon and eggs, or the kettle singing to make tea.[3] All of these items are traditional breakfast and supper foods; there is nothing extravagant, merely homely, hearty meals, akin to the common English meal.

That Bilbo's food preferences are typically English is what a reader might expect. Tolkien described himself as a hobbit, and gave to Bilbo and the race of hobbits as a whole many of his own distinctive likes and dislikes. He liked "good plain food" (as contrasted with French cooking), "unmechanized farmlands," "ornamental waistcoats," and so forth.[4] These characteristics understandably reflect both Tolkien's own life and idealized English custom.

The Food of the Shire

From Hannah Glasse's *The Art of Cookery Made Plain and Easy*: "*To dress* Cabbages, c."

> Cabbage, and all Sorts of young Sprouts must be boiled in a great deal of Water. When the Stalks are tender, or fall to the Bottom, they are enough; then take them off, before they lose their Colour. Always throw Salt into your Water before you put your Greens in. Young Sprouts you send to Table just as they are, but Cabbage is best chop'd and put into a Sauce-pan with a good Piece of Butter, stirring it for about five or six Minutes till the Butter is all melted, and then send it to Table.[5]

In his later novel, *The Lord of the Rings*, Tolkien makes clear that the Shire is a pre-industrial society that has not yet been sullied by factories, pollution, and modernization. There is a mill on the north bank of The Water, the river near Hobbiton, but it is operated by a waterwheel, a type of mill dating back to European antiquity. Under Bilbo's cousin Lotho Sackville-Baggins's direction, this old mill is destroyed. Its replacement is industrial in nature and produces pollutants and filth, fouling The Water.[6] Tolkien abhorred the destruction of the landscape in real life, although he lived nearly his entire adult life in town suburbs.[7]

Tolkien couldn't do anything about industrialization in England, but he could create a bucolic, peaceful countryside for Middle-earth in his writing. After the Battle of Bywater and the eviction of Saruman's adherents from the Shire, the new mill is torn down.[8] The Shire of *The Hobbit* clearly predates the nineteenth and twentieth centuries, the era of destruction that occurred after the industrialization of England.

The food in *The Hobbit* also suggests pre-industrial England. Hobbits as a race are largely self-sufficient, interacting little with men, elves, or dwarves.[9] Bilbo is a notable exception to this insular, isolationist attitude. Trade must occur between the hobbits and these other groups, considering tea, coffee, and some of the ingredients in Bilbo's pantry (like nutmeg and lemon for making mincemeat) could not grow in the temperate climate of the Shire.

Tolkien's avowed purpose in writing *The Hobbit, The Lord of the Rings,* and his other tales of Middle-earth was to provide "a mythology for England."[10] Placing the Shire in the northwest part of Middle-earth implies that it is merely England at an earlier time, and thus it would have a similar climate. Citrus might have been grown in southern Gondor, or it might have had to come through trade with Harad or other southerly countries of Middle-earth.

This may, of course, presume too much for *The Hobbit* in terms of seeking consistency for Middle-earth with the modern world. Although it was connected to the overall body of mythology that Tolkien created, this tale originated in stories he told to his children, and was published many years before *The Lord of the Rings,* fixing the narrative in ways that Tolkien sometimes regretted later.[11] He took the opportunity to make some changes to *The Hobbit* for the second edition in 1951, fourteen years after the original, most notably in chapter five, "Riddles in the Dark."[12] These changes brought *The Hobbit* into better alignment with the more complex narrative and characterization needs of *The Lord of the Rings*.

In his revisions to *The Hobbit*, Tolkien removed a first-edition reference to tomatoes, making pickles the replacement in the second edition, considering tomatoes derive from the Americas. Tobacco (consistently called "pipeweed" in *The Lord of the Rings*) remained, however, as did potatoes ("taters" in *The Lord of the Rings*).[13] Other mentioned foodstuffs of non-English origin were at least from the Old World, and thus, plausibly obtainable by trade; perhaps this is why Tolkien allowed them to remain in *The Hobbit* despite the opportunity for revision.

If we draw a parallel between the Shire and the "real world" of Tolkien's England, that would place Bilbo's life into the equivalent of the eighteenth or early nineteenth century. In English history, that would come after worldwide trading contacts had been established, enabling the importation of tropical products such as tea, coffee, sugar, and spices on a substantial scale, but before the large-scale industrialization that began during the nineteenth century.

Virtually every dish mentioned in chapter 1 of *The Hobbit*, "An Unexpected Party," can be found in the popular eighteenth-century cookbook by Hannah Glasse, *The Art of Cookery Made Plain and Easy*.[14] This work was first published in 1747, and was issued in revised and expanded editions for a century, long after the author's death. According to Glasse's own introduction, her intended audience was servants, but her cookbook was frequently used by minor gentlewomen and housewives.[15] Techniques and even specific dishes that appear in Glasse's book continued to be used and enjoyed into the twentieth century.[16] Although Glasse included a few foreign dishes, the bulk of her recipes were traditional English preparations, some even going back to the Middle Ages; for example, furmity, a preparation of wheat kernels simmered in milk. Tolkien, who once wrote that he "detest[ed] French cooking," was unlikely to have been personally familiar with Glasse's cookbook, but the type of cookery that she promoted was exactly the sort he favored.[17]

Another popular cookbook of the nineteenth century, and again one that was reissued in expanded editions for many decades—

indeed, cookbooks deriving from it are still available in the twenty-first century—was Isabella Beeton's *The Book of Household Management*, first published in 1861.[18] Aimed at the middle-class housewife, it incorporates a great deal of information on appropriate behavior and the supervision of servants, but a large proportion of the book consists of recipes. Like Glasse, Beeton leaned toward traditional preparations, though she also included recipes for such dishes as "Fillets of Turbot a l'Italienne" or "Ravigotte, a French Salad Sauce." Beeton organized her book to give seasonal availability of the various ingredients, costs, and sometimes bits of history along with the recipes. We can easily imagine Bilbo transported to nineteenth-century England, eagerly thumbing through *The Art of Cookery* or *The Book of Household Management* and preparing to try out a new recipe or two.

A Drink of Tea

From Isabella Beeton's *The Book of Household Management*: "TO MAKE TEA."

> 1814. There is very little art in making good tea; if the water is boiling, and there is no sparing of the fragrant leaf, the beverage will almost invariably be good. The old-fashioned plan of allowing a teaspoonful to each person, and one over, is still practised. Warm the teapot with boiling water; let it remain for two or three minutes for the vessel to become thoroughly hot, then pour it away. Put in the tea, pour in from 1/2 to 3/4 pint of boiling water, close the lid, and let it stand for the tea to draw from 5 to 10 minutes; then fill up the pot with water. The tea will be quite spoiled unless made with water that is actually 'boiling', as the leaves will not open, and the flavour not be extracted from them; the beverage will consequently be colourless and tasteless, — in fact, nothing but tepid water. Where there is a very large party to make tea for, it is a good plan to have two teapots instead of putting a large quantity of tea into one pot; the tea, besides, will go farther. When the infusion has been once completed, the addition of fresh tea

adds very little to the strength; so, when more is required, have the pot emptied of the old leaves, scalded, and fresh tea made in the usual manner.[19]

Although he also consumes wine on several occasions, Bilbo drinks tea the most. As a warm beverage, tea would have seemed far more comforting than wine to Bilbo when he was deep in the goblins' caves or shivering in Mirkwood—iced tea is a relatively recent innovation and even now is not particularly popular in England; certainly it was not in Tolkien's day, and thus would not have been a beverage Bilbo longed to have.

A native of China, the tea plant (*camellia sinensis*) first arrived in Europe as an item of trade in the early seventeenth century, and reached England by the middle of the century. Diarist Samuel Pepys mentioned drinking it for the first time on September 25, 1660.[20] Tea began as a luxury item, but the East India Company's large-scale importation of tea from the subcontinent eventually helped to bring the price down, especially after the Commutation Act of 1784.[21] By the mid-nineteenth century, tea was an everyday beverage for much of English society. Between the late eighteenth and late nineteenth century, tea consumption in workers' households increased more than sixfold.[22]

As noted earlier, the word "tea" came to be used not only for the beverage, but for the snack or meal that accompanied it: "afternoon tea" in the former case, "high tea" in the latter. Anna Maria Russell, the nineteenth-century Duchess of Bedford, is credited with the creation of afternoon tea as a meal to fill in the gap between the light meal of luncheon and the increasingly late dinner hour (often 8 p.m. or later for the fashionable).[23] High tea, on the other hand, seems to have developed after industrialization, when it became impossible for the working classes to leave their jobs to have a hot midday meal. Thus, late afternoon or early evening became the time to drink strong hot tea and eat hearty food, which might include cold meat, cheese, or pie, or hot dishes like Welsh rarebit, along with bread, butter, and preserves.[24]

Bilbo belongs to the leisured class; he owns a comfortable hobbit-hole and there is no evidence that he has to work for his living. With his afternoon tea he always has a cake, and perhaps more. His friend Balin the dwarf notices that Bilbo's waistcoat has grown more extensive by the time of his visit some years after their mutual adventures, undoubtedly the result of such delicious teatime indulgences.

A Lamb for the Slaughter

From Hannah Glasse's *The Art of Cookery Made Plain and Easy*: "MUTTON and LAMB."

> AS to roasting of Mutton; the Loin, the Saddle of Mutton (which is the two Loins) and the Chine (which is the two Necks) must be done as the Beef above: But all other Sorts of Mutton and Lamb must be roasted with a quick clear Fire, and without Paper; baste it when you lay it down and just before you take it up, and drudge it with a little Flour; but be sure not to use too much, for that takes away all the fine Taste of the Meat. Some chuse to skin a Loin of Mutton, and roast it Brown without Paper: But that you may do just as you please, but be sure always to take the Skin off a Breast of Mutton.[25]

Bilbo's stereotypically English food longings should be seen in the context of, and in contrast to, those of other characters in *The Hobbit*. The types of foods that Tolkien associates with particular individuals or species give clues to their character, their worthiness of respect, and even their existence. This type of connection would be developed further in *The Lord of the Rings*, but already appears here.

The trolls, for instance, see the dwarves and the hobbit as potential food, superior to the mutton they have been eating—or at any rate, a desirable change of pace. This is not technically cannibalism, considering trolls and dwarves are different species. Nevertheless, Tolkien assumes that his readers will agree that it is inappropriate for one sentient being to eat another. The trolls get their comeuppance when they take so long discussing the best method for cooking the dwarves that they delay going into their cave, and end up being turned to stone by the rising sun. Gandalf assists in this delay by throwing his voice to confuse the trolls into being unsure what cooking method they have agreed upon.

Other beings who turn out to be enemies try to eat the hobbit and the dwarves. The Great Goblin of the caverns orders the other goblins to "Bite them! Gnash them!" (*The Hobbit*, 62). After the company escapes from the mountains, the goblins work together with the Wargs to recapture the company, and Tolkien makes clear that the Wargs would eat anyone whom the goblins did not keep away from them. The goblins, too, would not hesitate to engage in quasi-cannibalism, as their doggerel indicates: "O what shall we do with the funny little things? / Roast 'em alive, or stew them in a pot; / fry them, boil them and eat them hot?" (*The Hobbit*, 94-95).

The creature Gollum makes raw fish the basis of his diet, but he also eats goblins when he can catch them from behind and strangle them. Tolkien makes clear that Gollum plans to do the same to Bilbo, and is only thwarted because Bilbo has found and makes use of Gollum's magic ring of invisibility. Gollum's description and the events of this chapter changes considerably between the first and second editions of *The Hobbit*,[26] but even in the first edition he intends to kill and eat the hobbit if he can. Readers familiar with *The Lord of the Rings* may find this section particularly disturbing, since in the later novel Gollum is revealed to have originally been a hobbit himself.

Lastly, the dragon Smaug cannot (of course) be a cannibal because there are no other dragons in the story, but he does eat the dwarves' ponies. Whether or not he would eat the dwarves and hobbit is more ambiguous. Smaug attacks the Lake-town, Esgaroth, in his rage at failing to locate and kill the dwarves, but he sets fire to the buildings rather than directly attacking the people who live there. Tolkien does say that Smaug plans to hunt the fleeing inhabitants later, but the purpose seems to be for the dragon's sport or entertainment, not necessarily for food. On the other hand, when describing Smaug's initial ravages, Thorin explicitly notes that the dragon has carried away maidens from Dale to eat, so it is probably safe to assume that he would eat the dwarves, Bilbo, and the inhabitants of Esgaroth if he has the time or appetite to do so.

Every enemy that the hobbit and dwarves encounter threatens not just to kill them, but also to eat them. Bilbo's initial apprehension about the entire adventure is not at all misplaced. His travels place him in a position where he might well be served up in the cook-pot of a goblin, far from his comfortable role as host where the story began.

Good Hosts and Good Food

From Mrs. Becton's *The Book of Household Management*: "PORK PIES (Warwickshire Recipe)."

835. INGREDIENTS.—For the crust, 5 lbs. of lard to 14 lbs. of flour, milk, and water. For filling the pies, to every 3 lbs. of meat allow 1 oz. of salt, 2-1/4 oz. of pepper, a small quantity of cayenne, 1 pint of water.

Mode.—Rub into the flour a portion of the lard; the remainder put with sufficient milk and water to mix the crust, and boil this gently for 1/4 hour. Pour it boiling on the flour, and knead and beat it till perfectly smooth. Now raise the crust in either a round or oval form, cut up the pork into pieces the size of a nut, season it in the above proportion, and press it compactly into the pie, in alternate layers of fat and lean, and pour in a small quantity of water; lay on the lid, cut the edges smoothly round, and pinch them together. Bake in a brick oven, which should be slow, as the meat is very solid. Very frequently, the inexperienced cook finds much difficulty in raising the crust. She should bear in mind that it must not be allowed to get cold, or it will fall immediately: to prevent this, the operation should be performed as near the fire as possible. As considerable dexterity and expertness are necessary to raise the crust with the hand only, a glass bottle or small jar may be placed in the middle of the paste, and the crust moulded on this; but be particular that it is kept warm the whole time.

Sufficient. — The proportions for 1 pie are 1 lb. of flour and 3 lbs. of meat.[27]

Feeding a guest is a traditional sign of a good host, in literature dating back at least to the time of Homer's *The Odyssey*. In contrast to the trolls, Wargs, and goblins, the eagles that rescue the company from their predicament — which Bilbo compares to being a piece of bacon in a pan — do not threaten to eat them, despite Bilbo's worry about "being torn up for supper like a rabbit" (*The Hobbit*, 97). Instead, the eagles do the opposite, bringing rabbits, hares, and a sheep to feed their unexpected guests, along with fuel for cooking.

The men of Esgaroth also treat the dwarves and hobbit well after their arrival there. Tolkien does not specify what food they are given, but they are fêted at banquets, and within a few days are completely recovered from their time in the elvish dungeons and their trip down the river nailed in barrels. The Lake-town men give them provisions and baggage animals for the last part of the journey to the Lonely Mountain, a generous gesture even if they expect compensation when the dwarves defeat the dragon and reclaim their treasure.

To turn back in the story somewhat, the next being the travelers encounter after their escape from the goblins is Beorn, who is a "skin-changer" — a man part of the time, but a bear the rest (*The Hobbit*, 103). He is also a vegetarian, as are the animals with which he lives. Tolkien's choice to present Beorn in this way has interesting implications.

Vegetarianism has a long history in Europe. As a philosophical and moral position, it dates back at least to the teachings of Pythagoras in the sixth century B.C.[28] Early and medieval Christians traditionally abstained from eating flesh foods on certain days of the week and seasons of the year, although which days and seasons changed somewhat over time, and eggs, dairy products, and fish might be permitted even on days of fasting. When the Protestant Reformation resulted in a split in the western Christian church, the Roman Catholic branch continued the fasting tradition. As a Catholic, his mother having converted to the faith after his father's early death, Tolkien would have been well acquainted with the principles of fasting whether or not he always strictly adhered to the practice.[29] Thus, Beorn's vegetarianism suggests a degree of sympathy with restraint of indulgence, or self-control generally, in the service of belief.

On the other hand, in early twentieth-century Britain, vegetarianism was widely considered to be a somewhat affected and odd mode of life. George Bernard Shaw was a vegetarian, but spoke lightly of his dietary habits. Aldous Huxley and George Orwell both disliked and made fun of vegetarianism, with Orwell going so far as to describe a vegetarian as "a person out of touch with common humanity."[30] Tolkien is unlikely to have agreed with such an extreme statement, but he would have been familiar with the attitude. Beorn, of course, is not strictly human, and perhaps Tolkien chose to make him vegetarian to also emphasize that difference.

Beorn is an excellent host. He provides the travelers with ample (vegetarian) food at his home, protects them during the night, and sends them off laden with both provisions and good advice. The dwarves and Bilbo do not follow this guidance, however, which results in the Wood-elves taking all of them prisoner except for the hobbit.

The Wood-elves are humane in their treatment of the imprisoned dwarves, feeding them regularly with coarse but decent food and drink. Bilbo, who escapes imprisonment, uses his magic ring of invisibility to skulk about the elves' caverns, pilfering whatever provisions he can. Being no hunter, he cannot obtain better food without revealing himself.

Bilbo eventually comes up with a plan to free the dwarves by sending them down-river packed in barrels, most of which had previously contained foodstuffs the elves purchased from the Lake-men. His scheme succeeds, although one of the dwarves, Fili, complains afterward that the smell of apples in his barrel as he drifted for many hours made him hungry for anything in the world—*except* apples. Bilbo travels outside of a barrel, since there was no one to pack him into it as he had done for the dwarves, and upon arrival steals a bottle of wine and a pie from the raft-elves. Tolkien does not specify what sort of pie, but most likely had in mind a meat pie. Of the 43 recipes that Hannah Glasse included in *The Art of Cookery*, 36 were for meat, fish, or other savory ingredients, and only seven for sweet fillings, a propor-

tion that might surprise modern readers who are more accustomed to
fruit and other sweet pies.

The dwarves' final hosts during their journey are the Lake-men,
who aid the dwarves after their escape from the elves. Unlike Beorn,
the Lake-men are not hosts out of pure generosity, but expect some
degree of repayment if and when the dwarves manage to kill the
dragon Smaug and regain the treasure of their ancestors. Here again,
Tolkien leaves the foods the dwarves are given undescribed, although
we can probably assume that they were largely items intended
for travel, since the Long Lake is some distance from the Lonely
Mountain that is the dwarves' destination.

Hard Times and Traveling Foods

From Isabella Beeton's *The Book of Household Management*:
"BISCUITS."

1712. Since the establishment of the large modern biscuit
manufactories, biscuits have been produced both cheap and
wholesome, in, comparatively speaking, endless variety. Their
actual component parts are, perhaps, known only to the various makers; but there are several kinds of biscuits which have
long been in use, that may here be advantageously described.

1713. Biscuits belong to the class of unfermented bread, and
are, perhaps, the most wholesome of that class. In cases where
fermented bread does not agree with the human stomach, they
may be recommended: in many instances they are considered
lighter, and less liable to create acidity and flatulence. The
name is derived from the French *bis cuit*, "twice-baked,"
because, originally, that was the mode of entirely depriving
them of all moisture, to insure their keeping; but, although that
process is no longer employed, the name is retained. The use of
this kind of bread on land is pretty general, and some varieties
are luxuries; but, at sea, biscuits are articles of the first necessity.

1714. SEA, or SHIP BISCUITS, are made of wheat-flour from which only the coarsest bran has been separated. The dough is made up as stiff as it can be worked, and is then formed into shapes, and baked in an oven; after which, the biscuits are exposed in lofts over the oven until perfectly dry, to prevent them from becoming mouldy when stored.

1715. CAPTAINS' BISCUITS are made in a similar manner, only of fine flour.[31]

At several points during *The Hobbit*, Bilbo, the dwarves, and Gandalf go hungry. Tolkien may well have been remembering his own childhood—after his father's death, his family (himself, mother, and younger brother) experienced a severely limited income[32]—but more likely he recalled the situation during World War I. During the Great War, as it was called at the time, official measures were taken both to increase food production and to restrain consumption in Britain. "Government bread" had other grains or potato flour that partially replaced white wheat flour, wartime cookbooks promoted the use of lentils and beans in lieu of meat, and eventually food rationing was put into effect.[33] Tolkien served in France for part of the war, but was wounded and invalided back home, so he would have experienced the results of food shortages in both places.[34]

Soldiers carried "iron rations" of hardtack and preserved meat that were provided for emergencies only, such as during battle when other food was unavailable. Daily rations for British soldiers in the trenches included a pound or more of meat, often bacon or stew; a pound and a quarter of bread; and jam, most commonly plum or apple. Some units, at the discretion of their commanding officer, might also receive a rum ration.[35] Food rations were usually adequate in terms of calories, but often unappetizing. They might also be unfamiliar and disliked for that reason; rabbit, brawn, and sardines were at times provided as the meat ration, and one soldier recalled his disgust at being served tripe and onions for breakfast.[36]

Tolkien may well have had the hardtack of his iron rations in mind when he described the cram given to the dwarves by the men of Esgaroth as "being in fact very uninteresting except as a chewing exercise" (*The Hobbit*, 207). Hardtack kept better than fresh bread and was therefore commonly substituted for it in soldiers' rations, but it was both tasteless and difficult to eat for men with false teeth. One solution was to soak it in water to make a kind of porridge, which was then sweetened with jam.[37]

By the time of writing *The Lord of the Rings*, Tolkien had imagined a better sort of traveling food: *lembas*, made by the elves of Lothlórien. This bread tastes better than *cram* or even Beorn's honey-cakes, stays fresh for months if kept in the leaf wrappings the elves use, and sustains not only life, but also the will of the eater. Tolkien acknowledged that the concept of *lembas* owed something to the teachings of the Catholic Church regarding the Eucharist.[38]

Although Tolkien explicitly denied that his tales of Middle-earth were allegorical,[39] it is difficult to imagine that his own experiences of war and hardship did not influence his writing, including his descriptions of both food and hunger. Many British had difficulties coping with the aftermath of the Great War, despite various private and public efforts to ease the transition from war to peace.[40] That Tolkien preferred not to acknowledge a close link between his personal history and his writing should not surprise us.

Food and Friendship

From Isabella Beeton's *The Book of Household Management*: "FRIED RASHERS OF BACON AND POACHED EGGS."

802. INGREDIENTS.—Bacon; eggs.

Mode.—Cut the bacon into thin slices, trim away the rusty parts, and cut off the rind. Put it into a cold frying-pan, that is to say, do not place the pan on the fire before the bacon is in it. Turn it 2 or 3 times, and dish it on a very hot dish. Poach the eggs and slip them on to the bacon, without breaking the yolks, and serve quickly.

Time. — 3 or 4 minutes. Average cost, 10d. to 1s. per lb. for the primest parts.

Sufficient. — Allow 6 eggs for 3 persons.

Seasonable at any time.[41]

Repeatedly throughout *The Hobbit,* Bilbo dreams or imagines that he is home at Bag End, with his kettle singing, and eating comforting foods such as bacon and eggs, and toast and butter. These are idealized meals, plain, hearty, and delicious, and in the end Bilbo does achieve his dream. At the end of the book, after his return to the Shire, he notes that "the sound of the kettle on his hearth was ever after more musical than it had been even in the quiet days before the Unexpected Party" (*The Hobbit,* 254).

His contentment — and satisfaction in the comforts of the kitchen-hearth — is well deserved after his travails. Even the dwarves acknowledge that perhaps Bilbo's preference for a content and well-fed life is desirable. On his deathbed, Thorin Oakenshield, who claimed the title of King under the Mountain and whose possessiveness over the gold that Smaug had hoarded led to the Battle of the Five Armies, told Bilbo, "If more of us valued food and cheer and song above hoarded gold, it would be a merrier world" (*The Hobbit,* 243).

Bilbo and Balin — perhaps his closest friend among the dwarves — part after their adventures by sharing the wish to eat together once more. The two statements are very different in style, but virtually identical in meaning. Balin says, "If ever you visit us again, when our halls are made fair once more, then the feast shall indeed be splendid!" Bilbo's reply is far less flowery: "If ever you are passing my way, don't wait to knock! Tea is at four; but any of you are welcome at any time!" (*The Hobbit,* 246). Eating together as a mark of friendship has roots stretching back to time immemorial, both in history and in literature; the hospitality offered to the disguised Odysseus on his return home is but one example. The exchange between the hobbit and the dwarf connects *The Hobbit* to this long tradition.

Bilbo's journey to the Lonely Mountain comes to life through his experience of food and drink. His sorrow at leaving the comforts of his very own hobbit-hole, in the cozy community of the Shire, is all the more understandable as he bewails all that he leaves behind. While some of his stops along the way are marked by good food, as in Beorn's hall or with the provisions he takes from the Wood-elves, Bilbo and the dwarves experience more than their share of threats and deprivation. The food that fills Bilbo's dreams is very much the food that Tolkien himself admired above all: traditional English fare that drew from both medieval traditions and modern trade. In the end, the best people, including Bilbo himself, were marked in part by the food they served and their generous attitudes to their guests who arrived for second breakfast, tea, or supper.

Notes

1. J. R. R. Tolkien, *The Hobbit: Or There and Back Again*, rev. ed. (Boston: Houghton Mifflin, 1988). All parenthetical citations are to this edition of *The Hobbit*.

2. Hannah Glasse, *The Art of Cookery Made Plain and Easy* (London: Prospect Books, 1983, facsimile of 1747 first edition, with modern glossary and notes and index), 139.

3. Bilbo expresses explicit food-longings in chs. 2, 3, 5, 7, and 8. In ch. 16 he dreams of eggs and bacon.

4. Letter to Deborah Webster, 25 October 1958, in J. R. R. Tolkien, *The Letters of J. R. R. Tolkien*, ed. Humphrey Carpenter (Boston: Houghton Mifflin, 1981), 288–89. Hereafter cited as *Letters*.

5. Glasse, *The Art of Cookery*, 10.

6. J. R. R. Tolkien, *The Return of the King*, 2nd ed. (Boston: Houghton Mifflin, 1993), 292–93.

7. Humphrey Carpenter, *Tolkien: A Biography* (Boston: Houghton Mifflin, 1977), 124–25.

8. Tolkien, *The Return of the King*, 302.

9. Bree and the other villages in the Bree-land were another exception; there, both men and hobbits lived in mixed communities [J. R. R. Tolkien, *The Fellowship of the Ring*, 2nd ed. (Boston: Houghton Mifflin, 1993), 161–62].

10. Carpenter, *Tolkien*, 89.

11. Carpenter, *Tolkien*, 176–79.

12. J. R. R. Tolkien, *The Annotated Hobbit*, ed. Douglas A. Anderson, rev. ed. (Boston: Houghton Mifflin, 2002), 128–31, note 25. Hereafter cited as *Annotated Hobbit*.

13. *Annotated Hobbit*, 41, note 26.

14. The most notable exception is scones. Baking powder, the usual leavening for modern scones, was not invented until the nineteenth century. Glasse does have recipes for various other types of small cakes and biscuits, for which the leavening (if any) is usually yeast or beaten egg whites [Glasse, *The Art of Cookery*, ch. XV].

15. Glasse, *The Art of Cookery*, i; Stephen Mennell, *All Manners of Food: Eating and Taste in England and France from the Middle Ages to the Present*, 2nd ed. (University of Illinois Press: Urbana, 1996), 116.

16. For instance, Glasse's recipe for a "Beef-Stake-Pye" calls for thin slices of raw beef, seasoned, placed in a pie dish, which is then half-filled with water before the crust is put on top [Glasse, *The Art of Cookery*, 71]. Nearly two centuries later, another cookbook instructed its readers to slice steak thinly, dip into seasoned flour and roll up, place in a pie dish, and half-fill the dish with stock before covering with pastry [Mary Duke Gordon and Eleanour Sinclair Rohde, Cookery (London: Longmans, Green and Co., 1922), 76–77].

17. Letter to Deborah Webster, 25 October 1958, in *Letters*, 289.

18. The "Mrs Beeton" name has even been licensed to food manufacturers in the United Kingdom for a whole range of products, from trifle sponge slices to chutney [Kathryn Hughes, *The Short Life & Long Times of Mrs Beeton* (London: Harper Perennial, 2006), 490, 422–23].

19. Isabella Beeton, *The Book of Household Management* (1861; Project Gutenberg, 2003), entry 1814, www.gutenberg.org/cache/epub/10136/pg10136.html.

20. Samuel Pepys, *The Diary of Samuel Pepys*, ed. Henry B. Wheatley, vol. 1 (Random House: New York, 1946), 168–69; see also www.pepysdiary.com/diary/1660/09/25/.

21. Helen Saberi, *Tea: A Global History* (London: Reaktion Books, 2010), 106.

22. Gregory Clark, Michael Huberman and Peter H. Lindert, "A British Food Puzzle, 1770-1850," *The Economic History Review*, New Series, vol. 48, no. 2 (May 1995): 223, doi:10.2307/2598401.

23. United Kingdom Tea Council, "A Social History of the Nation's Favourite Drink," www.tea.co.uk/a-social-history#afternoontea.

24. Saberi, *Tea*, 106.

25. Glasse, *The Art of Cookery*, 4.

26. *Annotated Hobbit*, 128-31, note 25.

27. Beeton, *The Book of Household Management*, entry 835, www.gutenberg.org/cache/epub/10136/pg10136.html.

28. Colin Spencer, *The Heretic's Feast: A History of Vegetarianism* (Hanover, NH: University Press of New England, 1995), ch. 2.

29. Perry C. Bramlett, *I Am in Fact a Hobbit: An Introduction to the Life and Work of J. R. R. Tolkien* (Macon, GA: Mercer University Press, 2003), 4.

30. Quoted in Spencer, *The Heretic's Feast*, 299.

31. Beeton, *The Book of Household Management*, entries 1712–1715, www.gutenberg.org/cache/epub/10136/pg10136.html.

32. Carpenter, *Tolkien*, 17, 24.

33. Ian F. W. Beckett, *Home Front 1914–1918: How Britain Survived the Great War* (Kew: The National Archives, 2006), 112–22.

34. Carpenter, *Tolkien*, 80–85.

35. Neil M. Heyman, *Daily Life During World War I* (Westport, CT: Greenwood Press, 2002), 36.

36. Rachel Duffett, "A War Unimagined: Food and the Rank and File Soldier of the First World War," in *British Popular Culture and the First World War*, ed. Jessica Meyer, *History of Warfare* vol. 48 (Leiden: Brill, 2008), 51–52.

37. Duffet, "A War Unimagined," 54–55.

38. Letter to Deborah Webster, 25 October 1958, in *Letters*, 288.

39. E.g. in letters to Herbert Schiro, 17 November 1957, and to Walter Allen of the *New Statesman*, April 1959, in *Letters*, 262, 297–98.

40. Juliet Nicolson, *The Great Silence: Britain from the Shadow of the First World War to the Dawn of the Jazz Age* (New York: Grove Press, 2009).

41. Beeton, *The Book of Household Management*, entry 802, www.gutenberg.org/cache/epub/10136/pg10136.html.

CHAPTER 6

Battle of Wits, Battle of Words:

Medieval Riddles and
The Hobbit

Christina Fawcett

The thing all things devours
Birds, beasts, trees, flowers
Gnaws iron, bites steel
Grinds hard stones to meal
Slays king, ruins town
And beats high mountain down![1]

From the Riddle of the Sphinx in *Oedipus Rex*[2] to a challenge facing Harry Potter in *The Philosopher's Stone* and *The Goblet of Fire*,[3] riddles transcend time, appearing across Western culture. Challenges of intelligence and demonstrations of cleverness are used as plot devices throughout literature to build character or create conflict. Wordplay and wit echo throughout literary history as modern authors draw upon either classical or medieval traditions; in popular

literature, there is no text where the antiquity and significance of riddles are made more prominent than in J. R. R. Tolkien's *The Hobbit*.

Tolkien, as a medievalist, regularly reflected and echoed medieval
characters, names, and narratives in his texts. His use of historic materials gives his tales weight and a sense of grounding, connecting his
modern fantasies to Anglo-Saxon, early Germanic, and Norse narratives. His use of riddles as a central plot element and his use of clever
wordplay as a means of sidestepping violence in *The Hobbit* tie the
text to the riddle traditions of the Anglo-Saxons, specifically the collection of 95 found in the *Exeter Book*.

In the course of his adventure, Bilbo Baggins is faced with numerous challenges and trials, some of which he manages to overcome
with quick wits and quicker words. When facing Gollum in the tunnels below the Misty Mountains, Bilbo is able to use riddles as a
form of combat, as each participant must stump the other in order to
achieve victory. He sings songs and teases giant spiders in three languages in order to free his friends from sticky captivity in Mirkwood.
Later, in Smaug's den, Bilbo uses enigmatic language, providing a
string of epithets to give Smaug puzzles rather than answers. Tolkien's
narrative draws not only on the larger riddle tradition seen throughout
Western history, but more specifically on a set of Anglo-Saxon riddles
that demonstrate the contrasting verbal antagonism and domesticity
seen in Bilbo's quick words.

The History of Riddles

The Riddles of the *Exeter Book* are of tremendous antiquity. The
book is dated to 975 A.D., but scholars have agreed that the riddles
themselves have much older sources.[4] As scholar A. J. Wyatt notes,
"[t]he literary origin, as distinguished from the prevalence of popular riddles, of all these collections is to be found in the *Aenigmata* of
one Symphosius," an elegant collection of Latin riddles, composed
in the fourth century.[5] Latin riddles were well known in educated
Anglo-Saxon circles, and provided inspiration for many of the riddles
of the *Exeter Book*;[6] other scholars and writers also composed or copied riddles, including Aldhelm: Bishop of Sherborne and Abbot of

Malmesbury. Aldhelm was a scholar whose Latin texts were important both for spiritual and pedagogical reasons; his works were standard curriculum in monastic schools from the time of their writing in the seventh century until the Norman Conquest in 1066. His writings were some of the first to introduce elements of the *Aenigmata* and other Latin riddles to an Anglo-Saxon audience.

The *Exeter Book*, appearing around 200 years later, not only echoes poetry from earlier Northumbrian manuscripts, but also incorporates segments that are a clear translation of Aldhelm's Latin text. Other collections of riddles exist that were written either around the same time or before the *Exeter Book*, demonstrating the wide appeal of riddle texts throughout educated Anglo-Saxon circles.[8] The small collection of 95 riddles found in the *Exeter Book* drew upon the larger tradition, recording a selection of what would have been vernacular riddles of the time.

The riddles found in the *Exeter Book* vary, as they are drawn from different sources and authors into a single text. Many named writers of the time engaged in riddling, as enigmas have been found written by medieval scholars such as the Venerable Bede or Alcuin, a deacon of York, among others.[9] These monastic and religious figures preserved and created riddles. As long as humanity has had language and metaphor, we have had riddles; these games and challenges have passed through generations and, through written language, passed from one era to another. So, from early Greek traditions to Latin texts to Anglo-Saxon poetry, riddles have passed through Western culture. It is this tradition that Tolkien draws upon in *The Hobbit*, as his narrator describes "the riddle game [. . .] of immense antiquity" (*The Hobbit*, 104). Tolkien's riddles echo the form and content common to Anglo-Saxon riddles, like those found in the *Exeter Book*. While the riddles of *The Hobbit* play on the enigmatic and figurative language found in all riddles, their personal connection, emotional investment, and focus on common or familiar objects tie the riddles found in *The Hobbit* to the largest existing collection of Anglo-Saxon riddles.

The riddles in the *Exeter Book* are striking in their focus on the domestic details of day-to-day life, which also makes them important for our understanding of the history of the Anglo-Saxons in a broader sense. While some of the Exeter riddles focus on animals or fabulous beasts, most of them focus on domestic items. The riddles are thus revealing of Anglo-Saxon culture, but often difficult to solve. We no longer have the same domestic tools or terms as Anglo-Saxons did. Michael Alexander points out that there is an appeal to this sense of the familiar, even if it's a domestic life from another time: "[t]here is often charm as well as an anthropological interest in the domestic riddles, and in the natural ones an inwardness that we have lost."[10] We learn about the people of Anglo-Saxon England through these riddles, seeing what they paid attention to, how they played, and how they put their ideas into words. The language of the riddles, while difficult for a modern reader, was clear and accessible to the contemporary audience. We get a glimpse of their culture and home life in many of these riddles, as the simple concepts tie us back to the past. The answer to most riddles tended to be something drawn from common knowledge of the period, whether a domestic or militaristic object, well-known animal, or Biblical reference. For example, Riddle Five asks the reader to guess what object is speaking:

> I am alone wounded by iron weapons,
> Damaged by blade, a weary soldier,
> Tired of the sword-edge. Often I see war
> Fiercely fought. I do not hope for solace
> That to me should come comfort in the battle,
> Before I should perish with the men,
> Or be struck with that made by the hammer,
> The hard edged war-gear, the handiwork of the smith,
> Bites at the burg; I ought to pray for
> The hostile meeting of weapons. Never any healer
> Among the people might I find
> That with herbs can heal my wounds,
> But I with sword-wounds increase in worth
> Through death-blows day and night.[11]

The answer to this riddle is a shield. The riddle is focused around an object that is familiar in the hand of the warrior and prominent in the broader culture. The voice of the shield is brave and inspires some pathos: It is tired of battle, facing the rush of the attack, and holds no hope. It cannot be healed, and must suffer through sword slashes and death wounds. The language appeals to the audience, engaging their sympathies for an everyday object. Through personification, the object speaks directly to us, and we must hear its experiences not as an object, but as an articulate, sentient being. As Alexander explains, "[s]omething speaks to us from twelve hundred years ago, directly, however mysteriously, and, in the first person, asks us to guess its name."[12] The language these objects use in the riddles is clear and brief, appealing to a wide audience. While the game is intended to be challenging, the game is in the wordplay and metaphor, and the language is not deliberately obscure. However, while accessible, the riddles are not easy: We must work to discover the answer for ourselves.

"Answers were to be guessed not given"

The 95 riddles in the *Exeter Book* are interspersed with other poetic pieces. Each riddle has no answer provided in the text, but instead asks a direct question, followed by another separate voice posing a new question. There is no cheat sheet, no answer key; the reader will either succeed at the challenge or not. Modern scholars are still often stumped by the ambiguous language of the riddles, as evident through Jonathan Wilcox's descriptions of the complications surrounding Riddle 19, whose answer is unclear to us nowadays:

> Riddle 19, like riddle 86, is difficult to solve and, since there is no titled Latin analogue to make it easier, the solution is still contested. An additional level of difficulty is created by the presence of the clusters of runic letters. Commentators agree that the runes spell out words in reverse but there is little agreement on the solution to the riddle.[13]

While solutions may be proposed and argued, there are many riddles for which no consensus has been reached. We have options, but no definitive answers. Unlike riddles that are used as literary devices, where the discovery of the solution is part of the plot, the riddles of the *Exeter Book* provide us with no such resolution. So, like the flustered Gollum sitting under the Misty Mountains, we are forced to ponder possible solutions, being denied any actual answer.

Saga hwaet ic hatte: Say what I am called

The language of the riddles is also notable not only in its simplicity, but its sense of the personal. The objects themselves are asking the questions. A personified thing is challenging us, over a thousand years later, to play its game. The language of these domestic objects is, naturally, just as familiar. The riddles do not possess the heroic or poetic language found in other sections of the *Exeter Book*, but reflect their supposed speakers. As Edith Whitehurst Williams points out, "[t]he essence of riddling is personification, and in many instances, the simple artifacts of daily living speak with the voice of the contemporary Anglo-Saxon."[14] The objects take on the voice and class of the person most associated with it: The shield uses language of a warrior and household items reflect their user. This language would have spoken directly to the original audience, adding another layer to the wordplay.

The simplicity of these medieval brainteasers is part of their appeal. "The riddles are also attractive to readers with any curiosity: unlike most Old English poetry, they are frequently neither heroic nor improving. Dr. Johnson[15] would have found many of them low and mean—but they are also innocent and disarming."[16] We hear the voice not of the court or monastery, but of the home: the tone and timbre of the common man.

The language of the riddles speaks directly to their audience, asking for an answer. Yet, instead of being simply friendly or playful, there is a challenge presented. Like the original audience, we are asked to fulfill a task. The tone of the riddles, their direct engagement, and their assertive language also meant that they could serve the social function of providing a safe space for aggression and competition. Marie Nelson points to the innate challenge in the riddle as significant within Anglo-Saxon society:

Difficult as it is to determine with certainty what some of them are about, the Old English riddles of the Exeter Book seem, without much doubt, to have served at least three important social purposes: the riddle game provided a structure for the competitive exercise of verbal skills; and within that structure some riddles permitted performers to play aggressive roles sanctioned by the culture of which the game itself was a part, while others presented well thought out responses to destructive forces of the natural world."[17]

When discussing Riddle 71, Nelson points to the innate aggression and challenge visible in the phrasing. Rather than simply being a voice speaking to us from over a thousand years ago, as Alexander characterizes it, the tone of the Riddles is antagonistic. We are being challenged to outsmart the text:

These words carry a challenge that can be paraphrased "Prove you are smart enough to guess the answer and say the right word." At the same time, Wiga, the word that precedes this challenge, may suggest a metaphoric role to be played by the would-be riddle-solver, who is presumably to accept the challenge with a certain verbal aggressiveness.[18]

The term Wiga means "warrior"; as such, the use of such a term as part of the address of a riddle establishes clearly what role the reader is taking on. So, the riddle as a construct is a safe space for aggression. Rather than having a literal battle, there can be challenge and either victory or defeat without drawing a sword.

The riddle as a concept has been a challenge throughout history: a way of testing one's intellect, proving one's worth, and showing one's bravery in battle. Tolkien, then, has a powerful and ancient weapon featured as central to the plot of his children's tale; and he puts the weapon in the hands of a "little fellow in a wide world" (The Hobbit, 365).

Riddles in the Dark

Bilbo, an unassuming and domestic person, is the primary wielder of riddles and enigmatic language in Tolkien's children's story. Wholly out of his element, Bilbo is thrown into a perilous journey by the good intentions of Gandalf. Bilbo's purpose in the company is to act as a burglar: a role he cannot fulfill successfully without the aid of a magic ring. As the reader discovers quite early on, his skills truly lie in his ability to talk his way into and out of situations. He wraps himself in words, inadvertently promising himself to the dwarven expedition:

> I don't pretend to understand what you are talking about, or your reference to burglars, but think I am right in believing [...] that you think I am no good. I will show you. [...] Tell me what you want done, and I will try it, if I have to walk from here to the East of East and fight the wild Were-worms in the Last Desert. (*The Hobbit*, 32)

Without knowing the details of the excursion, Bilbo speaks in hyperbole, assuring the dwarves of his credentials and tenacity. He trips over his sense of dignity and his words fail him. He is caught up in a journey that he did not intend to join. Yet, despite his ill-founded assurances, when faced with real danger, he draws upon words and riddles to get himself out of it.

There are two main versions of "Riddles in the Dark," a quintessential chapter in *The Hobbit*. In chapter 5 of the text, Bilbo is faced with Gollum, who is "as dark as darkness" (*The Hobbit*, 94). When challenged, Bilbo agrees to the riddle game, which was "sacred and of immense antiquity" (*The Hobbit*, 104). Gollum starts the game simply enough, asking Bilbo "*What has roots as nobody sees / Is taller than trees / Up, up it goes / And yet never grows?*" (*The Hobbit*, 97). When Bilbo answers "Mountain, I suppose" (*The Hobbit*, 97) with ease, the terms of the game are established. In Tolkien's original text, released in 1937, the contest between Bilbo and Gollum ends with Gollum trying to fulfill his promise of a gift: his precious ring. While Bilbo draws Sting and fears Gollum's retaliation, he need not have been frightened. For one thing the Gollum had learned long long ago was never to cheat at the riddle-game. Also there was the sword. He simply sat and blubbered.

"What about the present?" said Bilbo, not that he cared very much; still he felt he had won it, and in very difficult circumstances too.

"Must we give it the precious; yes we must—we must fetch it precious, and give it to the thing the present we promised."[19]

While Bilbo still wins the game with his questionable riddle, "[w]hat have I got in my pocket," Gollum intends to provide Bilbo with the ring, the precious. The competition in this early version has an element of urgency, as Gollum sets the terms: "It must have a competition with us precious. If precious asks, and it doesn't answer, we eats it my precious. If it asks us and we doesn't answer, we gives it a present: Gollum."[20]

There are two slightly different later editions, both of which involve a much more purposeful bargain. In neither does Gollum offer a gift for victory, but instead offers escape and freedom: "We does what it wants, eh? We shows it the way out, yes!" (The Hobbit, 97). In the 1966 text, he still threatens a possible violent outcome to the game with the line "If precious asks, and it doesn't answer, we eats it my precious,"[21] which was removed in the 1978 edition. This change almost entirely eliminates the threat of a brutal end offered to Bilbo.

The later editions also have a different end to the riddling game, as Gollum is not trying to fulfill a promise, but attempting instead to double-cross Bilbo after he is tricked:

Gollum did mean to come back. He was angry now and hungry. And he was a miserable wicked creature, and already he had a plan. [...] "It won't see us, will it, my precious? No. It won't see us, and its nassty little sword will be useless, yes quite." (The Hobbit, 105; 106)

He is not going to relinquish the ring, but use it to throttle Bilbo. Tolkien shifted the tone and events of the text to fit into his later mythology of *The Lord of the Rings*. By removing Gollum's willingness to part with the Ring, its power and importance are highlighted. In the original text, the metal band is worthy of being a prize in a game, whereas the later text shows that the game literally carries the weight of life and death.

The changes in the later editions, however, from Gollum's open threat to the mortal danger being unspoken, allow us to feel greater sympathy. The reader can feel pathos for this lost little creature beneath the Misty Mountains, despite the threat he embodies. The reader's response to Gollum changes, but the desperation of the situation is preserved. Even though Bilbo must win to survive in any version of the text, his longer-term survival and escape from the caverns are also bound up in his successful completion of the game. This is no trite game with simple prizes: This is Bilbo fighting for his life.

Riddles: Resonance and Revelation

In the chapter "Riddles in the Dark," Gollum seeks to discover more about his visitor through a riddling competition. Despite his intent, it is the readers who find out a great deal through the game, discovering hints of Gollum's past life through his chosen riddles and recollections. Through the game, there is mention of Gollum playing such challenges of wits with his friends aboveground when he lived in the sun and in a hole on a riverbank. First, Gollum recollects "the only game he had ever played with other funny creatures sitting in their holes in the long, long ago" (*The Hobbit*, 96). Later, as Bilbo tries to stump him with a riddle about flowers, Gollum recalls living "with his grandmother in a hole in a bank by a river" (*The Hobbit*, 98). This passing mention by the narrator should catch the reader's eye, as this points to Gollum potentially being akin to hobbits. As Gandalf points out in *The Fellowship of the Ring*, Smeagol, Gollum's earlier name before he fled under the Misty Mountains, came from a happier life:

... there lived by the banks of the Great River on the edge
of Wilderland a clever-handed and quiet-footed little people.
I guess they were of hobbit-kind; akin to the fathers of the
fathers of the Stoors, for they loved the River and often swam
in it, or made little boats of reeds. There was among them a
family of high repute [... t]he most curious-minded of that
family was called Smeagol. He was interested in roots and
beginnings; he dived into deep pools; he burrowed under
trees and growing plants; he tunneled into green mounds.
(*The Fellowship of the Ring*, 51)[22]

Gollum, through his chosen riddles and discovery of answers, shows
himself not as a monster, but as a fallen creature who has lost his past.
The riddling game with a distant relative of his own kind brings up
memories of his loss. "[The riddles] reminded him of days when he
had been less lonely and sneaky and nasty, and that put him out of
temper" (*The Hobbit*, 98). So, while being an antagonistic battle of
wits, we as readers actually develop sympathy for the poor lost creature, bound to the caves of the Misty Mountains.

Bilbo, we discover, is familiar with the game. Hobbits know wordplay, as evidenced by Bilbo's ability to draw on familiar riddles from
the outset. He knows the rules and strategies of the game just as well
as Gollum. He trusts his very life to them, engaging in the game until
its conclusion. Though afraid of the stakes of the game, Bilbo even
gives in to nervous habits, such as putting his hand in his pocket
mid-battle; this is not exactly a defensive stance. In fact, it's more like
a defenseless one. So, Bilbo is willing to trust the creature and the
game, at least at first. It is only when he has defeated Gollum that
Bilbo brandishes his sword. When Gollum answers incorrectly, he is
"very much relieved; and he jumped at once to his feet, put his back
to the nearest wall, and held out his little sword" (*The Hobbit*, 104).

As the riddles of ancient and medieval manuscripts are so
frequently associated with the domestic space, it is appropriate that
the vision of domesticity in an adventure tale should be the individual familiar with the play of riddles and words. Gollum, as he plays
with Bilbo, finds the "ordinary above ground everyday sort of riddles

[. . .] tiring" (*The Hobbit,* 98). This familiarity points quite specifically to Tolkien's characterization of the riddles as domestic and common. Rather than letting the reader come to this conclusion, he has the narrator state the idea outright, reminding us how riddles play upon the conventions of shared vocabulary and knowledge of the everyday.

The topics of the riddles Gollum and Bilbo use are also interesting. Instead of drawing directly from the language of texts like the *Exeter Book,* Tolkien creates his riddles in a different form. He carries on the poetic tradition, constructing the riddles as poems: set off from the text in italics, indented as verse. But he does not use the "say what I am called" form found so frequently in medieval riddles. Instead, the text provides us with the riddlers so there is no need to provide a personified voice to give the riddle weight, because the narrative has given us two characters with clear motivations and voices. The riddles themselves still address the mundane details of daily life, but are not necessarily as domestic. Answers like teeth, dark, eggs, time, and fish are not all matters of the hearth and home, but certainly point to what is familiar for the characters. Each draws on riddles he knows, and the most readily at hand are those that discuss common objects or ideas, as darkness or fish are for Gollum and eggs or sun on flowers are for Bilbo. Each speaks from his space of comfort, using the familiar as his weapon of choice.

Wits: A Wee Warrior's Weapon

We see most clearly in "Riddles in the Dark" the use of the riddle as a weapon, a means of battle. Though Bilbo is carrying a sword, he does not instinctively strike Gollum, even after the proposed battle of the riddles. In the 1966 edition of *The Hobbit* and those before it, Gollum states his intentions clearly: "If precious asks, and it doesn't answer, we eats it, my preciousss."[23] In later editions this direct threat is omitted, yet Bilbo seems certain of the danger he is in; after the proposal of the riddle game, he is "nearly bursting his brain to think of riddles that could save him from being eaten" (*The Hobbit,* 97). While the 1978 edition does not include the direct statement of threat, there is no question that Bilbo is potentially in mortal danger; yet, he does not draw his sword. He takes up the challenge and agrees to the terms of the battle, leaving his sword at his side and instead parrying with his wits.

In Mirkwood, when faced with the clutter of giant spiders, Bilbo cannot rely on his blade to win the day. While he does fight off the first spider he sees, cutting himself free and stabbing it in the eyes, he recognizes that he cannot fight them by himself: "Bilbo saw that the moment had come when he must do something. He could not get up at the brutes and he had nothing to shoot with" (*The Hobbit*, 195). Instead, he decides to infuriate them. He sings and throws rocks, taunting and teasing with ancient words rather than ancient steel:

> The idea came to him to lead the furious spiders further and further away from the dwarves, if he could; to make them curious, excited and angry all at once. [...] then dancing among the trees he began to sing a song to infuriate them and bring them all after him, and also to let the dwarves hear his voice. (*The Hobbit*, 196–97)

The language he chooses is not aggressive, but mocking. He antagonizes them with taunts about his ability to escape, to evade their webs and nippers. Interestingly, Tolkien, in this moment, has layers of wordplay in Bilbo's song. While the narrative voice undercuts Bilbo's musical attempts, saying that it is "[n]ot very good perhaps" (*The Hobbit*, 197), Bilbo is drawing upon two different ancient languages in his mockery of the spiders. *Attercop* is the Old English, or Anglo-Saxon, word for "spider," while *cob* is the Old German term.[24] Thus, Bilbo is mocking the spiders in a few different languages, playing with the rhyme and meter of the ancient words. So, even in a moment of levity and frivolous verse, Tolkien links this wordplay back to ancient languages, making Bilbo's teasing song a demonstration of knowledge.

When faced with the incredible moment of meeting a dragon, Bilbo once again relies on his words to keep him safe. When discussing with the dwarves how to deal with Smaug, Bilbo points out that "I was not engaged to kill dragons, that is warrior's work" (*The Hobbit*, 267). And when caught in a moment of panic with the great Smaug,

Bilbo does not draw a blade, but turns to witticisms and wordplay. He does not provide Smaug with his name, but instead grants himself a series of epithets; this is noted by the narrator as a wise choice. One does not refuse a dragon or reveal too much, so speaking in riddles is the safest way to face such an opponent. As A. J. Wyatt describes the riddles of the *Exeter Book*, "The riddles, it will be seen, are not riddles in the modern sense of the word, but enigmas, descriptions of an object which are intended to be at once accurate and misleading: the more misleadingly accurate and accurately misleading, the better."[25]

This puzzling construction is akin to Bilbo's banter with Smaug. He is not necessarily asking the question "say what I am called," but he is a literal enigma. His words are not structured verse, but they take on an almost poetic quality in their rhythm: "I am the clue-finder, the web-cutter, the stinging fly" (*The Hobbit*, 270). And as Bilbo is invisible, and an unfamiliar smell, Smaug must rely on Bilbo's words to puzzle through who the impossible invader might be.

As readers, we are provided with a sense of superiority: We know of what Bilbo speaks. The narrator even points to this; while Smaug does not fully understand, "[the narrative voice] expects you do, since you know all about Bilbo's adventures to which he was referring" (*The Hobbit*, 270–71). We are in the know, and thus are part of the riddling. Through the text, we have moved from being a spectator of Bilbo and Gollum's clever words to an insider. We are now party to his tale, and find no challenge in his enigmatic language. While Smaug may be briefly befuddled by Bilbo's banter, we are not.

Bilbo's seemingly playful approach contrasts our usual idea of heroics. When considering how to deal with such a beast, and contemplating his one patch of weakness, the dwarves reflect upon:

> dragon-slayings historical, dubious, and mythical, and the various sorts of stabs and jabs and undercuts, and the different arts, devices and stratagems by which they had been accomplished. The general opinion was that catching a dragon napping was not as easy as it sounded, and the attempt to stick one or prod one asleep was more likely to end in disaster than a bold frontal attack. (*The Hobbit*, 277)

Despite their grand assertions, Bilbo is the only one brave enough to go down the tunnel and potentially face the dragon, either asleep or awake. The idea of bravery and honor is central to the dwarves, yet Bilbo's methods are far more effective. It is his banter that reveals Smaug's weakness, and his sharing of the information that leads to Bard's defeat of Smaug. Bilbo's weapons are words, and he wields them to help bring down a dragon.

Wisdom and Words

In *The Hobbit*, riddling and witty speech play important roles. When facing the unknown, Bilbo uses riddles and proverbial wisdom, two medieval language traditions, to get out of tight scrapes. Words and witticisms are Bilbo's strongest weapon, as he turns to these when strength or Sting would fail. Medieval manuscripts like the collection of the *Exeter Book* draw together riddle games and wisdom poetry: Texts that challenge us or teach us are given space side by side. Bilbo echoes this pairing, as Tolkien, in his construction of Bilbo, draws upon both the riddling skill and the proverbial wisdom. As Tom Shippey discusses in "A Fund of Wise Sayings: Proverbiality in Tolkien"[26], Bilbo is a font of proverbial phrases, both those he repeats and those he creates. He coins his own form of wisdom, "[n]ever laugh at live dragons" (*The Hobbit*, 275), just as he comes up with his own riddle of sorts when asking "[w]hat have I got in my pocket?" (*The Hobbit*, 103).

Bilbo, as a character, has strong ties to medieval poetry and riddles; when Bilbo engages with other characters that participate in riddles and quips, he is the central figure of sophisticated and ancient language in the book. His challenges revolve around words and wits: While there is conflict and battle, Bilbo's contributions are not in physical strength. He is instead "the friend of bears and the guest of eagles. [He is] Ring-winner and Luckwearer" (*The Hobbit*, 270). He is a warrior of words.

Notes

1. Unless otherwise noted, all parenthetical citations are from *The Hobbit* by J. R. R. Tolkien (London: Collins Modern Classics, 1998).

2. "What is it that has one name that is four-footed, two footed, and three footed?" Apollodorus, quoted in *Classical Mythology*, Seventh Edition, ed. Mark Morford and Robert Lenardon (Oxford: OUP, 2003), 283.

3. Harry, too, faces a sphinx, who provides him with the following riddle in the middle of the maze-challenge:

"First think of the person who lives in disguise,
Who deals in secrets and tells naught but lies.
Next, tell me what's always the last thing to mend,
The middle of middle and end of the end?
And finally give me the sound often heard
During the search for a hard-to-find word.
Now string them together, and answer me this,
Which creature would you be unwilling to kiss?"

J. K. Rowling, *Harry Potter and the Goblet of Fire*. (Vancouver: Raincoast Books, 2000), 546.

4. Wyatt, *Old English Riddles*. (Boston & London: D. C. Heath, 1912), xx. *The Exeter Book*, ed. George Krapp and Elliott Dobbie (London: Routledge & Kegan Paul Ltd. 1936), lxvii. Michael Alexander, *Old English Riddles from the Exeter Book* (London: Anvil Press Poetry. 1980), 8.

5. Wyatt, xx.

6. Wyatt, xx.

7. Anita Redinger, "Formulaic Style in the Old English Riddles" *Studia Neophilologica* 76 (2004), 31.

8. Wyatt, xviii.

9. Wyatt, xviii.

10. Alexander, 8.

11. Ic eom anhaga iserne wund,
bille gebennad, beadoweorca sæd,
ecgum werig. Oft ic wig seo,
frecne feohtan. Frofre ne wene,
þæt me geoc cyme guðgewinnes,
ær ic mid ældum eal forwurðe,
ac mec hnossiað homera lafe,
heardecg heoroscearp, hondweorc smiþa,
bitað in burgum; ic abidan sceal
laþran gemotes. Næfre læcecynn
on folcstede findan meahte,
þara þe mid wyrtum wunde gehælde,
ac me ecga dolg eacen weorðað
þurh deaðslege dagum ond nihtum. (Krapp & Dobbie 183–84)
Translation is my own, derived from *An Anglo-Saxon Dictionary* from Joseph Bosworth, ed. T. Northcote Toller (London: OUP, 1898).

12. Alexander, 7.

13. Jonathan Wilcox, "Mock-Riddles in Old English: Exeter Riddles 86 and 19" *Studies in Philology* 93.2 (1996), 185.

14. Edith Whitehurst Williams, "Annals of the Poor: Folk Life in Old English Riddles" *Medieval Perspectives* 3 (2), 68.

15. Dr. Samuel Johnson is a famous English lexicographer and creator of *The Dictionary of the English Language*, the standard English Dictionary from its publication in 1755 until the publication of the Oxford English Dictionary in 1928.

16. Alexander, 7.

17. Marie Nelson, "Four Social Functions of the Exeter Book Riddles" *Neophilologus* 75 (1991), 445.

18. Nelson, 446.

19. John D. Rateliff, *The History of the Hobbit: Part One Mr. Baggins* (London: HarperCollins Publishers, 2008), 160.

20. Rateliff, 156.

21. Tolkien, *The Hobbit* (London: George Allen & Unwin, 1966).

22. Tolkien, *The Fellowship of the Ring* (London: HarperCollins Modern Classics, 2001).

23. Tolkien, *The Hobbit* (London: George Allen & Unwin, 1966).

24. Rateliff, 322.

25. Wyatt xxviii

26. Tom Shippey, "A Fund of Wise Sayings: Proverbiality in Tolkien" *Tolkien 2005 Conference Proceedings* edited by Sarah Wells (UK: The Tolkien Society, 2008).

CHAPTER 7

Bilbo's Ring:

Magical Objects in Middle-earth and Medieval Europe

Laura Mitchell

"His head was in a whirl of hope and wonder. It seemed the ring he had was a magic ring: it made you invisible!"

—*The Hobbit*, 81[1]

When Bilbo discovers Gollum's magic ring in the bowels of the Misty Mountains, it is a turning point for the hobbit and for the story of Middle-earth. What was J. R. R. Tolkien's inspiration for this small but vital object? We can never know the sources of Tolkien's Ring for certain; he alternately claimed his academic work had no influence, or that it did, but that it was indirect. In one letter to his publishers he wrote, "in any case—except for the runes (Anglo-Saxon) and the dwarf-names (Icelandic) . . . I am afraid my professional knowledge is not directly used."[2] However, he also wrote to the editor of the *Observer* newspaper in 1938 that, "*Beowulf* is among my most valued sources; though it was not consciously present to the mind in the process of writing."[3] Nevertheless, whichever of these stories is closest to the truth, we can see glimpses of medieval magic from history and fiction in *The Hobbit*. By examining these together, we can get a sense of the types of sources influencing Tolkien's work and gain a better understanding of the Ring and its place in Middle-earth.

First, we'll take a look at the various genres of magic and the principles on which magic worked in both medieval Europe and Middle-earth—including an overview of the powers that Bilbo's Ring possesses. With the proper background in place, we can then explore some of the possible sources for the Ring, beginning with magical objects from ancient myth, medieval magic, and medieval romance, and even less obvious influences such as medieval spells of invisibility. We'll also look at aspects of Bilbo's Ring that can be found in medieval legend and in the charms and rituals of medieval magic.

The Magic of Medieval Europe

In medieval Europe, as in Middle-earth, there were many different kinds of magic. Medieval magic was divided into folk and learned magic.[4] Folk magic consisted of charms, amulets, and natural magic. Learned magic was made up of the complex ritual magic of necromancy, image magic, and other magical rituals. Learned magic was more difficult and theoretical than folk magic and it was written in Latin, which meant that it was performed only by educated Europeans, such as monks and clerics. Folk magic, on the other hand, was found at all levels of society, from the lowliest peasant to members of the nobility. In the next few pages, we will look at each of these branches of medieval magic and explain their different categories in order to set the stage for the magic of Middle-earth.

One of the most common types of folk magic was charms. Charms were spoken or written formulas that were transmitted through oral and written traditions. Their guiding principle was the use of holy words and phrases and Biblical stories to impart the desired effect, whatever that may be.[5] Charms were used for a wide variety of purposes, including in medicine, against thieves, for love, and for protection. Amulets were similar to charms in that they also often relied on special letters, words, or phrases in order to work. Amulets could be pieces of parchment, brooches, rings, or almost any object that could be carried or worn against the body.[6] The physical aspect was required for amulets to work, which was not necessarily true of charms, most of which could simply be read or recited to produce the desired effect. Amulets were inscribed with images, such as crosses, or words and phrases taken from charms; consequently, amulets were inexorably linked with charms. An excellent example of this link is a ring that survives from fifteenth-century Coventry, England. The Coventry ring, made to protect the wearer from danger and illness, is inscribed on the outside with a figure of Christ and a description of the five wounds of Christ on the cross (which was a common late medieval devotional text), and the inner band is inscribed with the words of a charm against epilepsy.[7] Like charms, amulets could be used for many different purposes, but most of the surviving examples were for protection, like the Coventry ring.[8]

Natural magic was based on the belief that all natural objects, like metals, stones, animals, and plants, possessed special properties, which people could tap into and use for various endeavors, from love magic to medicine. These properties could often be controlled by using sympathetic associations thought to exist between certain objects. Sympathetic associations could be based on appearance, such as using a liver-shaped plant to treat diseases of the liver, or they could be based on other associations, which are not immediately obvious to us in our modern world, but for which a medieval audience hardly needed explanation. Carrying betony (a flowering herb), for example, was widely believed to ward off demons as long as it was picked before dawn in the month of August.

In learned magic, the two predominant kinds of works were image magic and necromancy. Image magic was heavily influenced by the work of neo-Platonists, and especially by the ninth-century Arab writer, al-Kindi.[9] The theory behind this magic is highly philosophical and full of complexities, but essentially, it was thought to work through the manipulation of rays that came to Earth from the celestial forms; that is, the stars and planets. The magician used a form or image that was connected to the celestial form, using sympathetic associations in accordance with the proper astrological knowledge and special prayers and rituals. Once the power of the rays was drawn down to the image, the desired goal could be achieved. The magician might then wear the image as an amulet in order to complete the ritual. As with folk magic, the goals of image magic were wide-ranging and covered topics from making someone love you to destroying one's enemies. The magician was confined only by the properties in the stars and planets that could be drawn down.

By the later Middle Ages, necromancy had evolved considerably. It originally and literally meant divination—foretelling the future—by conjuring the spirits of the dead, who would offer predictions to the magician. But by the late medieval period, the focus of this branch of magic was on conjuring demonic spirits to do the magician's will.[10] Necromancy was openly demonic and made no pretensions of using natural or heavenly forces as other magical texts did. Necromancy used long, complex rituals, explicit invocations of demons, and often appropriated and adapted orthodox Christian rituals, such as saying Mass or reciting Psalms. Necromantic rituals usually began with intense preparations in which the practitioner wore specific clothing, fasted, and recited certain prayers for days, and even weeks, before the actual ritual began. These operations were very long and usually involved making rings, drawing intricate patterns, or performing animal sacrifices in order to conjure demons and other spirits who were compelled to do the magician's bidding.

Once these spirits were conjured, they could be compelled to do anything—whether that was to foretell the future, transport the practitioner around the world on a demonic horse, or create majestic illusions. In one fifteenth-century operation, the magician conjured up fifteen spirits to create an illusory castle, complete with armed guards and a moat.[11] The instructions for this illusion end with the author's boastful story of how he once used this illusion to trick an unnamed emperor and his entire retinue of nobles. The power of necromancy appears even in Bilbo's time as Sauron, disguised as the Necromancer of Dol Guldur, plots to recover his lost Ring.[12]

What bound all of these distinct types of magic together was the underlying power that was brought out by the words used in the rituals and charms, and which was an innate part of plants, stones, and other objects used in the various magic rituals and experiments. In all these different operations, there was a belief that the powers drawn down or embedded in objects ultimately came from God. The words used in charms and in magic rituals were thought to possess holy powers, either because of what the words referenced (such as liturgical verses and Biblical stories) or because of the language that was used. As the language of the Church, Latin was automatically instilled with a level of holiness that was not found in vernacular languages like English or French. This holiness was meant to increase the power and efficacy of the incantation. Latin was also the language of the educated elite, and as a result, it possessed a higher level of authority. Reciting these words or writing them on objects passed on that holiness and authority to the object or to the intended subject of the operation. A similar effect can be seen in the words of power written on the Ring in the Black Speech of Mordor. The Ring's words of power had been inscribed in a language that was spoken only by the servants of Mordor (such as the orcs and the Nazgûl) and is thus associated with evil.

The Magic of Middle-earth

Medieval magic can be categorized in a wide range of approaches and philosophies, and aspects of all of these categories are found in Tolkien's conception of magic in Middle-earth. Tolkien has woven together different elements from each kind of magic—both folk and learned—to form his own unique vision. These different kinds of magic used in the Middle-earth of *The Hobbit* provide a framework in which to place Bilbo's Ring.

The magic of Middle-earth is not as clearly delineated as medieval magic. There is good and evil magic, and there is a distinction between the kinds of magic performed by the various races that populate Middle-earth. For example, as one of the Maiar, near immortals sent by the Valar to protect Middle-earth, Gandalf possesses powers

that other races of Middle-earth do not have. He is especially adept
at controlling fire and light, which is seen when he kills the goblins
that are attempting to kidnap him with a flash of light, and when he
throws pinecones ablaze with magic flames at the attacking wolves
outside the Misty Mountains.

Much of the magic in Middle-earth is focused on enhancing or

The people of the Middle Ages
feared necromancers just as much
as the people of Middle-earth.

weakening the inherent properties of objects in much the same way
as medieval natural magic. Elves and dwarves are especially skilled at
crafting magical objects using these principles, such as the dwarfish
blade that Bilbo names Sting, which can detect goblins. We also see
the use of charms in Middle-earth when the dwarves bury the troll's
treasure and speak "a great many spells" over it. (*The Hobbit*, 42)
Above all, however, the greatest distinction in Middle-earth magic is
who is doing it, rather than what kind it is. Unlike medieval Europe,
where various kinds of magic were repeatedly condemned throughout
the period, magic is viewed as a normal part of Middle-earth—the
distinction made here is whether the magic is done for good or evil.
The Necromancer, for example, is called so not because he summons
spirits, but because he is a force of evil.

Although there is not a one-to-one relationship between the magic of Middle-earth and medieval Europe, there are some similarities between these two worlds. For example, as noted above, the manipulation of the inherent properties of objects is found in both Middle-earth and in the natural magic of medieval Europe. In addition, the spells of protection that the dwarves speak over their buried treasure are paralleled by the many protective charms against thieves that survive in medieval manuscripts.[13] Tolkien's title for Sauron, the Necromancer, reflects the negative connotations associated with necromancy in the Middle Ages and the numerous condemnations to which it was subject. These parallels continue to appear when we turn to the topic of magic rings and invisibility.

Rings, Invisibility, and Hobbits

This discussion of magic in medieval Europe and in Middle-earth is all well and good, but how does Bilbo's Ring fit into this? Now that we have a clear understanding of how magic was conceived of and operated in both worlds, we can look more closely at the Ring itself and its medieval counterparts.

Let's begin by looking at what *The Hobbit* tells us about the Ring—its powers and limitations. The abilities of the Ring are first revealed when Gollum is searching for it after he has lost the riddle competition; "he [Gollum] wanted it because it was a ring of power, and if you slipped that ring on your finger, you were invisible; only in the full sunlight could you be seen, and then only by your shadow, and that would be shaky and faint" (*The Hobbit*, 77). The Ring can make its wearer invisible, but with certain caveats. It has not yet become the powerful Ring in *The Lord of the Rings* that controlled the other rings of power, or that gave Frodo the ability to see what is invisible, such as when he can see the features of the Ringwraiths on Weathertop in *The Fellowship of the Ring*.[14] Neither can the Ring conceal physical traces left behind or sounds, such as when Bilbo's thievery by the river is found out by the wet footprints he leaves behind and by his sneezing.

Invisibility, of course, can come in handy in many different situations. Bilbo uses the Ring for protection when he hides from the spiders in Mirkwood and during the Battle of the Five Armies. Not that invisibility offers complete protection: Bilbo is still hit by an errant stone during the battle and left unconscious in the cold for hours because no one can find him with his Ring on. As Bilbo says upon awakening on the empty battlefield, "this invisibility has its drawbacks after all" (*The Hobbit*, 264). Bilbo also uses the Ring to sneak about and spy on people and creatures, as he does while the dwarves are held captive by the elves of Mirkwood and when the dwarves are trying to decide how to defeat Smaug the dragon. He even uses the Ring to play a joke on the dwarves after he has first found it, sneaking up on them after they have escaped the goblins. Despite the Ring's limitations in the sunlight and Bilbo's problems with wet feet and errant rocks, the hobbit and the dwarves are very keen on the Ring and what it can do to help them. "For they [the dwarves] saw that he [Bilbo] had some wits, as well as luck and a magic ring—and all three are very useful possessions" (*The Hobbit*, 155).

What kinds of sources influenced Tolkien when he was creating this ring of invisibility? Rings appear in all forms of medieval magic and for very different purposes. In medieval ritual, magic rings were used either as a component in the operation or as the instrument through which the experiments were performed. In necromancy, rings were consecrated and used as conduits to summon demons, such as in one fifteenth-century procedure that used demonic powers to seduce women. When the spirits are initially called forth, they are invoked by the virtues and powers of various holy beings, but they are also invoked by a ring that the magician brings with him.[15] Rings were important in image magic as the receptacles of power, as described in a book of image magic in a fifteenth-century manuscript in the Cambridge University Library.[16] In this work, titled *The Book of Angels, Rings, Characters and Images of the Planets,* rings are filled with the power of the planets and are then used to perform different functions. For example, the ring of the sun is made of gold and inscribed with the names of the angels associated with the sun; it will help someone to summon a magical horse that will carry them wherever in the world they wish to go.[17]

Rings for protection often appear in natural magic, especially rings that had been set with precious gems (like the toadstone, which was thought to be from the head of a toad but was really the fossil of a fish) or holy relics (such as a fragment of a saint's bone).[18] In these cases, the gems and relics were believed to possess special qualities that gave the rings power, whether that was because of the inherent powers of the stones, or because of the holy powers associated with the relics. Some rings were powerful because of the words written on them, as demonstrated by a common cure for epilepsy that used a ring inscribed with powerful religious phrases, in a similar manner as the Coventry ring mentioned earlier.[19] Cramp rings were rings that had been blessed and touched by monarchs on Good Friday to cure epilepsy, cramp, and palsy. The king's touch was believed to cure scrofula (tuberculosis of the lymph glands, also known as the king's evil) and this healing power could be passed on to the rings that he touched.[20]

In addition to the Coventry ring, there are a number of rings with magical inscriptions that survive from the Anglo-Saxon period in England (c. 400–1066). Some of the more important rings from this period are the Bramham Moor Ring (ninth century), the Kingmoor Ring (also called the Greymoor Hill Ring, ninth or tenth century), and the Linstock Castle Ring (ninth century?).[21] Each is inscribed with runes for protection. The Bramham Moor and Kingmoor Rings are both inscribed with *"ærkriulft | kriuriþon | glæstæpon | tol."* The phrase is nonsense, but *ærkriu* resembles the phrase *ærcrio* or *ær crio* that appears in an Anglo-Saxon charm to staunch blood.[22] The Linstock Castle Ring is inscribed with runes that spell out *"ery . ri . uf . dol . yri . uri . þol . wles . te . pote . nol."*[23] Like the Bramham Moor and Kingmoor rings, this is a nonsense phrase. The exact purpose of these rings is not known, but they were probably worn for protection or to cure illnesses, like the later surviving rings. Likewise, we do not know how much these rings influenced Tolkien's work, but we can see similarities between the use of inscriptions in the Anglo-Saxon rings and the protective effect of the magical inscription on the ring of Tolkien's creation. Because Tolkien was at one time a professor of

Anglo-Saxon literature at Oxford, it is quite possible that these rings had a role in his creation of the ring in *The Hobbit*.

There is one magical ring in medieval myth that we can definitively cross off the list of potential sources for Tolkien. This was the Ring of the Nibelung, otherwise known as *Andvaranaut* (Andvari's gift), which was a ring in Norse mythology that was stolen by the god Loki and ultimately caused the death of the hero Sigurd.[24] At the suggestion that this ring and the ring in *The Hobbit* and *The Lord of the Rings* were in any way similar, Tolkien wrote, "both rings were round, and there the resemblance ceases."[25] While TTolkien was never entirely clear about the sources for his ring, he was always quick to point out inaccuracies and errors in interpretation.

Rings were rarely used in medieval magic for invisibility. What we do find in the manuscript sources instead are magical gems, enchanted cloaks (like Harry Potter's—J. K. Rowling seems to be familiar with these older beliefs), beans, and even the hairs of a dead man. Opals were thought to be so brilliant that whoever wore one would be hidden by the gem's radiance.[26] A fifteenth-century German necromantic manuscript (known as the Munich handbook) in the Bavarian state library has two sets of instructions for invisibility. In the first operation, a number of demons are conjured and when they appear, the magician asks for a cloak "so that when I wear it no one can see or sense my presence."[27] This is only a temporary cloak, however, as it must be burned within three days or else the magician will die. The second operation instructs the reader on how to grow a bean plant that, with the right rituals (including the sacrifice of a black cat), will make invisible whoever holds a bean from that plant in their mouth.[28]

A similar set of instructions is presented in a natural magic experiment described in an Ashmole manuscript from the Bodleian Library in Oxford. In this version, the bean plant is planted over the buried body of a dead dog. Once the bean plant has sprouted, the magician has only to place one of the beans in his mouth and he will become invisible.[29] Another passage from this manuscript states that invisibility can be obtained by carrying a stone taken from a certain nest.[30] The Ashmole manuscript also contains instructions for invisibility in which the practitioner takes four hairs of a dead man, mixes them with the blood of a bat, and then places them on top of his own head.[31] Presumably, he becomes visible again once this mixture has been washed off.

To find rings of invisibility, however, we must turn to ancient legend and medieval myth. One of the first and most well-known ancient stories of a ring of invisibility is that of the ring of Gyges. In Book 2 of Plato's *Republic*, Plato's brother Glaucon tells Socrates the story of a shepherd of Lydia.[32] This shepherd found a ring that would make him invisible when the settings were turned toward the palm of his hand. When he discovered this, he immediately used the ring to seduce the king's wife and get her help to overthrow the king, kill him, and take over the kingdom. This story was used to argue that no man can be truly just, but will be corrupted if given the opportunity. It has been argued that this story was the source for Bilbo's ring, but this seems unlikely given the moral tone of this tale.[33] Unlike the characterization of the Ring in *The Lord of the Rings*, Bilbo's Ring in *The Hobbit* has no corrupting influence. In *The Hobbit*, the Ring is simply a magic ring that Bilbo uses to do good and help others (and to occasionally hide from unwanted guests).

The twelfth-century romance *Yvain*, which was composed by the French writer Chrétien de Troyes, also contains a magic ring that works in the same way as the ring of Gyges.[34] This story, especially its thirteenth-century Welsh redaction as *Owein*, or *Chwedyl Iarlles y Ffynnawn (The Lady of the Fountain)*, may be the most direct influence on Tolkien's conception of the Ring.[35] The hero of the story, Yvain, is given a ring by the maiden Lunette (or Luned, as she is called in the Welsh version) that will make him invisible when its stone is turned inward. However, Yvain must also remain completely still or else he will be seen. Yvain at first uses the ring to evade a mob in the castle of Escolade the Red, whom he has mortally wounded.[36] He then remains hidden in the castle, and watches the Lady Laudine, Escolade's widow. He falls in love with her and eventually Lunette persuades Laudine to marry Yvain.[37] While this does not exactly parallel Bilbo's Ring, the similarities are remarkable.

The Ring in *The Hobbit* shares many similarities with medieval magic rings in both history and literature. Its ability to make its wearer invisible is seen in ancient legend and the work of Chrétien de Troyes. Like the rings used in necromancy, image magic, and charms, Bilbo's Ring is inscribed with magical words of power (although this is unknown during the events of *The Hobbit* and is not revealed until the beginning of *The Fellowship of the Ring*). Rings and the power of invisibility make frequent appearances in all manner of medieval magic. Although we can never know the exact sources that influenced Tolkien's conception of the Ring in *The Hobbit*, these examples give us possible ideas as well as provide us with the medieval context in which to view Bilbo's ring.

Notes

1. All quotations from *The Hobbit* are taken from the paperback 70th anniversary edition published in Canada by HarperCollins in 1996.

2. Humphrey Carpenter, ed., *The Letters of J.R.R. Tolkien*, with the assistance of Christopher Tolkien (Boston and New York: Houghton Mifflin Company, 2000), 21.

3. *Letters*, 31.

4. On this division see Owen Davies, *Cunning-Folk: Popular Magic in English History* (London: Hambledon and London, 2003), X.

5. Lea Olsan, "Charms in Medieval Memory," in *Charms and Charming in Europe*, ed., Jonathan Roper (Great Britain: Palgrave Macmillan, 2004), 60.

6. Don C. Skemer, *Binding Words: Textual Amulets in the Middle Ages* (University Park, PA.: Pennsylvania State University Press, 2006), 1.

7. Edina Bozoky, "Private Reliquaries and Other Prophylactic Jewels: New Compositions and Devotional Practices in the Fourteenth and Fifteenth Centuries," in *The Unorthodox Imagination in Late Medieval Britain*, ed. Sophie Page (Manchester and New York: Manchester University Press, 2010), 123-24.

8. Other examples of protective amulets include two textual amulets from thirteenth-century England, which offered protection against demons, elves, apparitions, and all evil in general for their owners, Adam and Osanna. An English amulet from the fourteenth century, owned by a woman named Lucy, offered protection against toothache, fever, and gout, as well as protection from evil and enemies. See Skemer, *Binding Words*, 185-88.

9. See Pinella Travaglia, *Magic, Causality and Intentionality: The Doctrine of the Ray in al-Kindi* (SISMEL: Edizioni del Galluzzo, 1999) for an overview of al-Kindi's life and works, especially chapter 1, "al-Kindi in his historical context."

10. This partly came about because medieval writers assumed that the appearance of the dead in ancient stories of necromancy were really demonic spirits in disguise. Richard Kieckhefer, *Magic in the Middle Ages* (1989; repr., Cambridge: Cambridge University Press, 2000), 152.

11. The complete description of this experiment can be found in Richard Kieckhefer, *Forbidden Rites: A Necromancer's Manual of the Fifteenth Century* (University Park, PA.: Pennsylvania State University Press, 1997), 50-54.

12. For mention of Sauron as the Necromancer of Dol Guldur at this time, see Appendix B of *The Return of the King*.

13. There are countless examples in the medieval manuscript record. For example, Oxford, Bodleian Library, Ashmole MS 1435, a fifteenth-century English notebook, contains several charms to find thieves as well as charms to protect against them. San Marino California, Huntington Library HM 58, a fifteenth-century medical notebook, has a Latin conjuration against thieves. London, British Library, Additional MS 34111, another fifteenth-century medical notebook, contains three operations to find thieves. Published examples can be found in Curt F. Bühler, "Middle English Verses against Thieves," *Speculum* 33:3 (1958): 371-372; Curt F. Bühler, "Middle English Verses against Thieves," *Speculum* 34:4 (1959): 637-638; and Tony Hunt, *Popular Medicine in Thirteenth-Century England: Introduction and Texts* (Cambridge: D.S. Brewer, 1990).

14. *Letters*, 152.

15. Kieckhefer, *Forbidden Rites*, 128.

16. Cambridge, Cambridge University Library MS Dd.Xi.45. An edition and translation of this work is in Juris G. Lidaka, *"The Book of Angels, Rings, Characters and Images of the Planets: Attribute to Osbern Bokenham,"* in *Conjuring Spirits: Texts and Traditions of Medieval Ritual Magic*, ed. Claire Fanger (University Park, PA.: Pennsylvania State University Press, 1998), 32-75, which includes the instructions for making the ring of the sun discussed here.

17. Lidaka, *"The Book of Angels,"* 47.

18. Kieckhefer, *Magic in the Middle Ages*, 102-03.

19. Suzanne Eastman Sheldon, "Middle English and Latin Charms, Amulets, and Talismans from Vernacular Manuscripts" (PhD diss., Tulane University, 1978), 216.

20. "Cramp rings," in *Oxford Dictionary of English Folklore*, ed. Jacqueline Simpson and Steve Roud (Oxford: Oxford University Press, 2000), 82-83.

21. R.I. Page, *An Introduction to English Runes* (London: Methuen & Co.: 1973), 30.

22. Page, *English Runes*, 30, 114; "finger-ring," The British Museum, accessed May 8, 2011, http://www.britishmuseum.org/research/search_the_collection_database/search_object_details.aspx?objectid=88694&partid=1.

23. Page, *English Runes*, 114.

24. Snorri Sturluson, *The Prose Edda: Tales From Norse Mythology*, trans. Jean I. Young (Berkeley: University of California Press, 1966), 111. This story is famously one of the central parts of Richard Wagner's opera *Der Ring des Nibelungen (The Ring of the Nibelung)*.

25. In a letter to his publishers, Allen & Unwin, in February, 1961. *Letters*, 306.

26. Kieckhefer, *Forbidden Rites*, 59.

27. Kieckhefer, *Forbidden Rites*, 60.

28. The instructions are as follows: The practitioner kills a black cat that was born in March. He cuts out its eyes and places heliotrope seeds in its eyes and mouth; then he buries the cat while reciting certain conjurations. Once the plant has sprouted, the magician takes each sprouted bean and puts them in his mouth one by one while gazing into a mirror until he turns invisible. Kieckhefer, *Forbidden Rites*, 60-61; 240.

29. Page 25: *"Si vis esse inuisibile: accipe vnum canem mortuum et sepilles eum et plantes super eum fabus et vnam in ore tuo et sine dubio eris inuisibile."* [If you wish to be invisible: take a dead dog and bury it and plant a bean plant over it and place one in your mouth and without a doubt you will be invisible.]

30. Page 12: *"vt sis inuisibile: vade ad nidum et inuenies lapidem, quem porta tecum."* [So that you should become invisible: go to a nest and you will find a stone, which you should carry with you.]

31. Page 25: "Take four hers of A dedman and þe blod of a rermowse [a bat] and lay þem togeder and lay þem on þi hed and no mon schall se þe."

32. Plato, *Republic*, book 2, 359d-360c.

33. See John D. Rateliff's discussion of this in *The History of the Hobbit, Part One: Mr. Baggins* (Great Britain: HarperCollins Publishers, 2007), 176-77.

34. Chrétien de Troyes, *Yvain* or *the Knight with the Lion*, trans. Ruth Harwood Cline (Athens: University of Georgia Press, 1975), ll. 953-1058.

35. This connection is also analyzed in *The History of The Hobbit*, 177-79.

36. ll. 965-1058.

37. ll. 1302-2024.

CHAPTER 8

"Roads Go Ever Ever On": Rambling and Roughing It in *The Hobbit*

Bram Mathew

"They had not been riding very long, when up came Gandalf very splendid on a white horse. He had brought a lot of pocket-handkerchiefs, and Bilbo's pipe and tobacco. So after that the party went along very merrily, and they told stories or sang songs as they rode forward all day, except of course when they stopped for meals. These didn't come quite as often as Bilbo would have liked them, but he still began to feel that adventures were not so bad after all."

—*The Hobbit*, 371[1]

Bilbo Baggins' idyllic home life is the foundation upon which Tolkien builds the story of *The Hobbit*. The homey setting of Bilbo's dwelling at Bag End that the book presents at the beginning contrasts with the rough and rambling remainder of Tolkien's account. *The Hobbit* tells of a lengthy journey relying mostly on one mode of transportation: peregrination, or traveling by foot, with all the hardships that might entail.

Traveling on foot wasn't just an artifact of an earlier era before trains, planes, and automobiles. In Tolkien's time, "rambling" in the countryside was a popular pastime. The question of why Tolkien evoked the joys and trials of rambling in *The Hobbit* involves the history of his own time as much as the reality of a world without trains and automobiles. There are many parallels between Bilbo's long trek in *The Hobbit* and the experiences of adventuresome men and women in Victorian and Edwardian Britain. During these periods, the countryside played a critical role in shaping how people lived and travelled.[2] Even midway through the twentieth century, when Tolkien was writing his stories of Middle-earth, the ideal of spending time enjoying the countryside was important to many Britons.[3]

The scouting movement in Britain can also be connected to *The Hobbit*. Bilbo embodies key values the scouts emphasized, such as integrity and decency. The scouts of the Edwardian era also walked the breadth and width of Britain in their pursuit of a healthy life, and they embodied the same sense of brotherhood and active living that Thorin's party represents. This idealized notion of a rural way of life wasn't just a creation of Tolkien, but was popular in ordinary experience as well as major literary works of the nineteenth and early twentieth centuries. In both Middle-earth and Tolkien's Britain, rambling in the countryside was a model life (but only as long as the comforts of home weren't forever lost).

The Home of a Hobbit

"It was a hobbit-hole, and that means comfort."

—*The Hobbit*,[3]

The Hobbit begins with a detailed description of Bilbo Baggins' home, and this passage shows how important home life was for hobbits. Bilbo's hobbit-hole was one of "comfort" as opposed to a simple hole in the ground. The entrance of the home boasts a "perfectly round door," "painted green" with a "shiny yellow brass knob" (*The Hobbit*, 3). While round doors weren't common, the elements of color and decoration on this hobbit's door are typical for Victorian architecture.[4] The emphasis is on homey warmth, which Tolkien continues by describing the various features of Bilbo's abode, such as its "very comfortable tunnel with no smoke" and "the deep-set round windows looking over his garden, and meadows beyond, sloping down to the river" (*The Hobbit*, 3). This picturesque description of the hobbit's surroundings was similar to the ideal of the English country life in the nineteenth century and found in the work of notable English novelists of that era, such as Dickens, Gaskell, and Eliot.[5]

Overall, the features of the hobbit's home evoke a warm, comfortable, and companionable environment that, except for the round door and low ceilings, would have fit in with many of the domestic ideals of Tolkien's youth. Bilbo's hole reflects the nostalgia for a past that was both homey and grand, which was a powerful cultural force in Victorian and Edwardian Britain. Bilbo enjoyed a home life that would be the envy of many English gentlemen and ladies who valued nature, leisure, and artistic contemplation.[6] But nature was much more manageable from the window of a hobbit-hole than it would prove to be in the wilds of Middle-earth: Tolkien dwelled upon Bilbo's comfy lifestyle only to use it to point to his later homesickness and discomfort.[7] So, too, did the English explorers and young men who were part of the new scouting movement occasionally long for home when their adventures took an uncomfortable or soggy turn. Nevertheless, Britons took great enjoyment in the countryside and nature, hiking, trekking, and camping their way across the nation for much of the later nineteenth and early twentieth centuries. Tolkien drew upon these very British pastimes and traditions in crafting the stories of Bilbo's adventures trekking across Middle-earth.

The Tradition of a Traveling Life

"'You will have to manage without pocket-handkerchiefs, and a good many other things before you get to the journey's end.'"

— Dwalin, *The Hobbit*, 36

Once he joins the dwarves on their journey, Bilbo soon learns that his enjoyment of the comforts of home has come to an end. He realizes that he has embarked on an adventure of sorts, one sparked by the interference of the wizard, Gandalf. Bilbo describes adventures as "nasty, disturbing, uncomfortable things!" (*The Hobbit*, 7). Despite Bilbo's initial opposition to such quests, he is drawn to them just as many Britons were in the modern age.

The sharp contrast to growing industrial towns and cities attracted the people of the Victorian and Edwardian eras out into the countryside. Steadily increasing industrialization in Britain during the nineteenth century meant that the living conditions of urban centers became increasingly congested and dirty.[8] Those who lived in the busy and heavily polluted cities suffered from different aliments associated with overcrowding and a lack of public health measures: typhus, smallpox, tuberculosis, and cholera, to name a few. The countryside offered a way of escaping from the industrialized parts of Britain. Although the initial portions of the story emphasize the dreary aspects of traveling in Middle-earth, like the Victorian and Edwardian tourists whose values influenced Tolkien, Bilbo eventually learns to appreciate his life on the road even if the hardships are overwhelming at times.

Rambling is probably as old as civilization, but it was not until the late eighteenth and nineteenth century that it began to be an important social phenomenon.[9] People didn't just wander without a purpose, they followed well-established paths crisscrossing the British countryside. Literary walking, touring sites made famous in novels and stories, became a popular activity before Tolkien's birth.[10] Tolkien himself reminisced happily about the walking tour of the Swiss Alps he'd made with school friends in 1911: "We went on foot carrying great packs practically all the way from Interlaken, mainly by mountain paths, to Lauterbrunnen, and so to Mürren. . . . We slept rough — the

men-folk—often in hayloft or cowbyre, since we were walking by map
. . . ."[11] Walking was often seen as a healthy and even manly activity in Victorian and Edwardian Britain. Not just well-to-do men and
boys at their leisure enjoyed these rambles, but ordinary laborers and
their families, too.[12] While trekking wasn't always a restful holiday, the
adventurous appeal was undeniable, just as Bilbo discovers while lis-
tening to one of the dwarves' songs: "Then something Tookish woke
up inside him, and he wishes to go and see the great mountains, and
hear the pine trees and waterfalls, and explore the caves, and wear a
sword instead of a walking-stick" (*The Hobbit*, 19). Despite his home-
body instincts, Bilbo fosters an interest in exploring the wider world;
by the end of the book, he has shown that he has a lot common with
other ramblers of the English countryside in the nineteenth century.

Victorian thoughts and feelings about the joys of rural life and
exploration probably contributed to Tolkien's emphasis on this setting
in *The Hobbit* as well as his own experience.[13] He had a lot of company in this, in both his and his parents' generation. The Victorian
journalist, Richard Blatchford, echoed these feelings in his socialist
newspaper, *The Clarion*, when he stated that, "I never wander in the
stuffy sordid London streets nor in the squalid gruesome Northern
slums, but I think of the dancing sea waves, of the flower starred
meadows, and the silky skies of [rural] England."[14] Blatchford praised
the English countryside in contrast to the urban life, "And by the
same token the sweet air and the sunny landscapes and still green
woods bring up before my eyes with painful vividness the breath-
less courts and gloomy lanes, the fever beds and vice traps of horrible Liverpool, and horrible Manchester, and horrible Glasgow."[15]
Tolkien and his brother moved to grimy, industrial Birmingham after
their mother's death in 1904. There the countryside was but a distant
smudge past an endless sea of rooftops and smoking chimneys, and
Tolkien deeply resented its loss.[16]

The love of the countryside led to the creation of popular tools
and guides for the rambling life. We see this, for example, in the use
of walking sticks in *The Hobbit*. More than tools, an interest in hiking
or rambling was a key part of the English culture from which Tolkien
drew. Walking sticks could be used not only to aid in rambling, but

also as a potential weapon; the two dwarves Bifur and Bofur use their walking sticks in this fashion. Considering the rough terrain that was being covered in Middle-earth by the adventurers, we shouldn't be surprised by the numerous mentions of walking sticks in the story, which illustrates their importance to the adventurers.[17]

Bilbo's own hobbit-hole suggests he was as fond of rambling as any Victorian squire might have been. Like them, he decorates with maps that bring back memories of his country jaunts: "He loved maps, and in his hall hung a large one of the Country Round with all his favourite walks marked on it in red ink" (*The Hobbit*, 25). Bilbo might have thought his adventuring days were over now that he had reached a comfortable middle age. The mission that Thorin Oakenshield describes sounds daunting even as it conjures up memories of when Bilbo was once "a fine adventurous lad in those days, always wandering about" (*The Hobbit*, 29). But Bilbo would now rather read about adventures or reminisce about his youthful rambles than take on such a challenge.

Victorian and Edwardian book sales show us that Bilbo was hardly unusual in wanting to read about country explorations. Rambling was so popular by the early twentieth century that it spawned a new literary genre called countryside writing.[18] For example, the Victorian travel writer, George Borrow, made frequent reference to his love of the countryside and "long peregrination" in his influential autobiography, *Lavengro*.[19] The celebration and recreation of the English landscape was sustained in literature well into the twentieth century.[20] This British love of exploration and rambling in the picturesque countryside was balanced by wariness toward strangers, as seen in Lord Dufferin's *Letters from High Latitudes*, first published in 1856. Dufferin's initial description of the Icelanders suggests that the consummate Victorian nobleman found these foreigners unimpressive.[21]

This hesitation is similar to Bilbo Baggins' first experiences with the dwarves he would later accompany. Dufferin's *Letters* also included fond reference to the "smells, hills and sunshine" of the Iceland countryside he explored, even as he frequently complained about the peculiar ways of the people and occasionally of the dull and sullen wet weather.[22] *Letters* has additional similarities to Tolkien's work: Dufferin described the daunting "lava mountains" he spotted from horseback (or from ponyback, as Icelandic mounts were better sized for dwarves and hobbits than for a tall man).[23] Tellingly, Lord Dufferin concluded his description of his adventure in Iceland with a comment that he experienced a "most happy time" in that land.[24] Bilbo Baggins would also acquire a taste for adventure, but it took a while to develop.

Bilbo, the Reluctant Rambler

"'I wish I was at home in my nice hole by the fire, with the kettle just beginning to sing!'"
    —Bilbo Baggins, *The Hobbit*, 38

Once the group of adventurers sets off on their journey, Bilbo's complaints begin almost immediately. The stark contrast between Bilbo's life on the road and the comforts of his hobbit home are striking. "It was after tea-time; it was pouring with rain, and had been all day; his hood was dripping into his eyes, his cloak was full of water; the pony was tired and stumbled on stones; the others were too grumpy to talk" (*The Hobbit*, 39).

The custom of teatime was cherished by Victorian Englishmen and women as well as by Bilbo Baggins, and its lack is a keenly felt discomfort for the hobbit for the remainder of his journey. Teatime is a quintessentially British activity, although tea isn't grown in Britain. The tea that filled the pots and cups of Victorian Britons was cultivated in China or India, the farthest ports reached by the ships of the British Empire. G. G. Sigmond, a Victorian doctor, promoted tea's healthful effects. The Englishman was, in his view, "deeply indebted to the tea plant" that "imparts all the charms to society which spring from the enjoyment of conversation."[25] On the road, with Bag End but a distant memory, Bilbo has neither tea nor conversation to give him comfort.

Bilbo's experience of camping in *The Hobbit* begins on a dreary note. During their first night of setting camp, "they all sat glum and wet and muttering, while Oin and Gloin went on trying to light the fire, and quarrelling about it" (*The Hobbit*, 39). Although the rain is certainly not Thorin's or Gandalf's fault, it makes their outing seem all the more miserable, especially in contrast to the idyllic trips of imagination. "Bilbo was sadly reflecting that adventures are not all pony-rides in May-sunshine" (*The Hobbit*, 39). In this perfect vision of adventures and camping, Bilbo demonstrates that he isn't far off from his Victorian counterparts.

There were many campsites in Victorian Britain and a great amount of pleasure and enjoyment was attached to camping.[26] Camping grounds flourished well into the early twentieth century and such places were used frequently by nature enthusiasts.[27] These Victorian camping grounds were far finer than the dreary, damp and, dark site that Bilbo faced at the end of his first long day among the

This comfortable Victorian camp is probably what Bilbo expected
when he agreed to go on his adventure

dwarven company. There isn't even a tent for him to sleep in, as Lord Dufferin's party enjoyed in Victorian Iceland.[28] The literary and popular British image of camping was one thing, but Bilbo's experience of it is quite another.

Some heroes were better at roughing it than others. Tolkien's close friend and fellow Oxford English professor, C. S. Lewis, drew on the appeal of the outdoor life in *Out of the Silent Planet*, which appeared in print in 1938, one year after *The Hobbit* was published. In the opening pages of the *Silent Planet*, its central character, Elwin Ransom, "has a map and took shelter under a large chestnut tree."[29] But unlike in Tolkien's world, where Bilbo notes many minute details of his travels, Dr. Elwin Ransom "wasted no time on the landscape."[30] He may not have been as fond of the countryside as Bilbo, but Ransom was a "good walker."[31] He eventually came to appreciate the "solemn landscape" and "mountain air" he encountered in his explorations.[32]

Not every experience of the outdoors went so smoothly. The hardships connected to this rambling lifestyle become positively harrowing by the time Bilbo and the dwarves reach Mirkwood. There, the band of travelers develop an intense hostility toward the dark forests surrounding them: "It was not long before they began to hate the forest as heartily as they had hated the tunnels of the goblins, and it seemed to offer less hope of any ending" (*The Hobbit*, 164). The group encounters a variety of dangers while traveling through these woods, the worst of which is contact with the Wood-elves of Mirkwood. The dwarves and hobbit become entranced after a few sightings of the elves as they revel and celebrate. But when the elves vanish after the travelers come too close, the dwarves are captured by the giant spiders of Mirkwood and Bilbo is left by himself in the forest. Soon after the capture of the dwarves, "the cries of the others got steadily further and fainter, and though after a while it seemed to him they changed to yells and cries for help in the far distance, all noise at last died right away, and he was left alone in complete silence and darkness" (*The Hobbit*, 180).

Indeed, Bilbo Baggins is now alone in Mirkwood, and it "was one of his most miserable moments" (*The Hobbit*, 180). To escape this helpless moment, Bilbo goes "deep in thoughts of bacon and eggs and toast and butter when he felt something touching him" (*The Hobbit*, 180). It appears that Bilbo still longs for his comfy home in times of desperation, but the battle with the spiders changes him profoundly. After slaying his first spider, Bilbo "felt like a different person, and much fiercer and bolder in spite of an empty stomach" (*The Hobbit*, 181). Bilbo changes with each challenge he faces and conquers, becoming more "Tookish" in his own description. (Bilbo's mother was a member of the Took clan — wealthy, adventurous hobbits who only lacked respectability.) Yet, Bilbo still loves food and contentment, reminding the reader of the hobbit's home-loving roots. Bilbo saves the dwarves from the giant spiders, but shortly after this, the group (minus Bilbo) is taken captive by the Wood-elves, leading to new troubles on the road.

Bilbo's Tookishness becomes an asset as he faces danger time and again. The hobbit's role as a thief (and hero) grows after his rescue of his dwarven friends from the Wood-elves of Mirkwood. Infiltrating the Elvenking's gate, Bilbo constructs a plan to smuggle the dwarves out of the forest via an underground river system.

Getting out of Mirkwood doesn't end Bilbo's troubles: The band of travelers endures further hardships until they land upon the "doorstep" of the Lonely Mountain. "They spent a cold and lonely night and their spirits fell" (*The Hobbit*, 234). "There was no laughter or song or sound of harps, and the pride and hopes which had stirred in their hearts at the singing of old songs by the lake died away to a plodding gloom" (*The Hobbit*, 235). At least the adventurers are close to their goal of destroying Smaug the Magnificent, but this is a prospect that makes even the bravest hobbit quiver in fear. However, Bilbo becomes a better and braver, more Tookish hobbit as a result of his adventures, a transformation predicted by Gandalf early in the story.

Bilbo the Boy Scout

"...and while the dwarves were still singing songs he (Bilbo) dropped asleep..."

—*The Hobbit*, 152

Not all of Bilbo's experiences as a rambler are as challenging as facing down Wood-elves or dragons. Singing songs around a campfire seems like something right out of a Scouting manual. Indeed, some parts of Bilbo's experience on the road with Thorin and company read like moments from a Boy Scout's life. A number of parallels emerge over the course of the story between the early British Scouting movement and *The Hobbit*. Scouting originated in Britain around 1907; the movement's first leader was Robert Baden-Powell.[33] It built upon an earlier tradition of camping expeditions for boys combined with organized group activities and extensive outdoor training in the nineteenth century.[34]

Companionship in the countryside was a key part of the Scouting ethos, along with other older traditions. Baden-Powell infused into his ideology of the Scouting movement aspects of the legend of King Arthur and the Knights of the Round Table.[35] This is apparent in the manual he wrote: "in Baden-Powell's best-selling *Scouting for Boys*. . . . Chapter VII is devoted to 'The Chivalry of the Knights.'"[36] The model of the Knights of the Round Table is also reminiscent of the gathering of the hobbit, dwarves, and Gandalf for their own quest, especially since, like the Round Table, their group includes a king, his loyal followers, and a wizard.

When the dwarves sing of their goal, they are singing of adventures and quests that any early twentieth-century British Boy Scout would have admired. "Far over the misty mountains cold, To dungeons deep and caverns old, We must away ere break of day, To seek the pale enchanted gold" (*The Hobbit*, 18). The song suggests that the dwarves excel at rambling and that they are eager to obtain the treasures found at the end of this journey. Companionship grows between the group of adventurers, not only in song but also through their journey together. The dwarves' songs reveal the levels of camaraderie that develop rapidly between the travelers: In fact, the first song offered by the dwarves makes light of Bilbo's attention to neatness and order in his hobbit home, with mock threats to his cups and plates. The second song by the dwarves, about their quest, awakens feelings of joy and warmth in Bilbo's heart. Tolkien uses music and the ideal of adventuring to foster companionship between the hobbit and his dwarven friends.

As well as the practical experience outdoors, Baden-Powell's Scouts were supposed to build the "inner man" in character and qualities. One key aspect of the Scouting movement in early twentieth-century England was its emphasis on "goodness."[37] Bilbo demonstrates such goodness, particularly as it involves caring for others, when he rescues his comrades from the giant spiders of Mirkwood. Bilbo's goodness is expressed, for example, when he exclaims "What a mess we are in now! We! I only wish it were we: it is horrible being all alone" (*The Hobbit*, 180). The hobbit could have deserted the dwarves, but instead makes it a priority to save them. By doing so, Bilbo's dedication to the group becomes clear, and his role as a hero emerges.

Another character trait of Bilbo's that was also celebrated by the early British Scouting movement was that of "cheerfulness."[38] One example of the hobbit's cheerfulness occurs when Bilbo attempts to initiate conversation in the second chapter of the book. Shortly after the journey starts it begins to rain, and the hobbit observes, "To think it will soon be June!" (*The Hobbit*, 38). None of the dwarves has a response to this comment as they steadfastly trudge along in the rain and mud. But it is this cheerfulness that makes Bilbo so appealing.

Another example of Bilbo's merriness is displayed when the hobbit rescues the dwarves from the giant spiders. While invisible due to his ring of power, Bilbo hurls stones at the spiders. He then sings a song to infuriate the creatures, taunting "Old fat spider spinning in a tree! Old fat spider can't see me!"(*The Hobbit*, 185). Bilbo sings another song while attacking the spiders:

> Lazy Lob and crazy Cob,
> Are weaving webs to find me,
> I am far more sweet than other meat,
> But still they cannot find me!
> Here am I, naughty little fly;
> You are fat and lazy.
> You cannot trap me, though you try,
> In your cobwebs crazy. (*The Hobbit*, 186)

His dwarven companions are still somewhat dizzy, but Bilbo is in complete control of the situation, and rather cheerful about it.

Bilbo repeatedly exhibits other qualities of an ideal Boy Scout, such as morality and righteousness, even if his job in Thorin's company is supposed to be that of a burglar. This morality, along with being "honourable, truthful and reliable," was as important an aspect of early Scouting as it was for Bilbo and company.[39] As well as individual character traits, Scouting emphasized bonds among the boys of the group. Bilbo's inclusion among the adventurers displays a similar sense of "brotherhood" to that promoted in the scouts.[40]

As much as it seemed an organization of peaceful recreation, Scouting in Edwardian Britain prepared young men for life as soldiers of the British Empire. Bilbo's time with Thorin and company is also quite martial, beginning with his fortunate discovery of arms and armor from the trolls' lair: Orcrist, Glamdring, and the knife in a leather sheath that "was as good as a short sword for the hobbit" (*The Hobbit*, 41). Like a Scout with a pocketknife and camp tools, Bilbo must learn to use his new weapon, but his companions are already skilled warriors. Their abilities are critical in the first battle against the goblins of the Misty Mountains.

While Scouts wouldn't have expected to face goblins in their excursions, they might have had sympathy for Bilbo's challenge: the giant spiders of Mirkwood. Baden-Powell's Scouts learned to recognize and deal with all sorts of wild and domestic animals in their training. The forest and the woodland were also part of their study. Bilbo bravely faces fears of the forest and its creatures as he attempts to save his dwarven companions from the spiders. When the hobbit's friends are captured by the spiders, Bilbo is able to avoid them with the invisibility connected to his ring of power. After surprising the spiders, the hobbit frees the dwarves and a large-scale battle ensues. Tolkien notes that "Some of the dwarves had knives, and some had sticks, and all of them could get at stones; and Bilbo had his elvish dagger" (*The Hobbit*, 189). As the battle wears on, some of the dwarves are still weary from the spider poison. Bilbo puts on his ring again and "darted backwards and forwards slashing at spider-threads, hacking at their legs, and stabbing at their fat bodies if they came too near" (*The Hobbit*, 191). After this impressive display of fighting from the hobbit, the spiders grow tired and fearful of Bilbo's sword and they leave the group alone. Bilbo has saved his friends. One of the main goals of the Scouting movement was to produce confident, respectable, and commendable young men ready for military service. Bilbo's adventures have done precisely that.

Homecoming: Bilbo's Experiences Leave a Mark

"'You are not the hobbit that you were.'"
>—Gandalf, *The Hobbit*, 347

The Hobbit relies heavily on rambling to complete its plot: In order for Bilbo and his fellows to travel from Bag End to the Lonely Mountain, the most efficient and effective—and really, only viable— way to cross these distances is on foot. And once the destination is reached, the dragon slain, and their enemies defeated, the only place to go is home again.

After all of the hardships of his trip, home is a welcome sight for Bilbo, who truly comes full circle in his travels. The hobbit is satisfied with his comfortable surroundings before embarking on his journey, and the return home brings him much joy. Adventures are memorable, but they are draining. This is evidenced by the song that Bilbo sings in response to catching a vision of his hill upon returning to the Shire:

> Roads go ever ever on,
> Over rock and under tree,
> By caves where never sun has shone,
> By streams that never find the sea;
> Over snow by winter sown,
> And through the merry flowers of June,
> Over grass and over stone,
> And under mountains in the moon.
>
> Roads go ever ever on,
> Under cloud and under star,
> Yet feet that wandering have gone

Turn at last to home afar.
Eyes that fire and sword have seen
And horrors in the halls of stone
Look at last on meadows green
And trees and hills they long have known. (*Hobbit*, 346–47)

Bilbo's song describes the life of the rambler in all of its glory and grief: He has climbed mountains and worked through dangerous forests, ventured deep into caves, and seen horrors as well as wonders on his way. No ordinary rambler could have done so much, but any one of them could appreciate his happiness upon seeing the green meadows of home once more. "He [Bilbo] was quite content; and the sound of the kettle on his hearth was ever after more musical than it had been even in the quiet days before the Unexpected Party" (*The Hobbit*, 348). In both his love of home and his proud memories of his adventures, Bilbo perfectly embodies the ideals of Victorian and Edwardian British ramblers, Scouts, and countryside explorers.

Notes

1. All book quotes are taken from the British edition by J. R. R. Tolkien as follows: *The Hobbit* (London: HarperCollins, 1995).

2. Jeremy Burchardt attempts to define what the countryside consisted of since 1800, in his introduction of *Paradise Lost: Rural Idyll and Social Change in England Since 1800*, (London; New York, I. B. Tauris, 2002). This book explains the significance of the English countryside in the nineteenth and twentieth centuries.

3. The Countryside Code, the Countryside Commission and the Countryside Agency were formed in 1951, thus illustrating the countryside's prolonged significance in Britain. See Peter Merriman, "Respect the Life of the Countryside: The Country Code, government and the conduct of visitors to the countryside in post-war England and Wales", *Transactions of the Institute of British Geographers*, New Series, 30, no. 3 (Sept. 2005), 336–50.

4. G.E. Mingay refers to the application of different colors to Victorian countryside houses. See Mingay, *The Victorian Countryside* 2, (London: Routledge & Kegan Paul, 1981), 400.

5. Burchardt, *Paradise Lost*, 8.

6. Burchardt, *Paradise Lost*, 2.

7. Mingay, *The Victorian Countryside*, 401. Mingay makes note that by the 1870s, the suggestion of comfort and coziness could be found in Victorian architecture.

8. Burchardt, *Paradise Lost*, 17.

9. Burchardt, *Paradise Lost*, 121.

10. Ibid., 121.

11. Quoted in Humphrey Carpenter, *Tolkien: A Biography* (New York: Ballantine Book, 1977), 56.

12. John Langton, "Proletarianization in the Industrial Revolution: Regionalism and Kinship in the Labor Markets of the British Coal Industry from the Seventeenth to the Nineteenth Centuries", *Transactions of the Institute of British Geographers*, New Series 25, no. 1 (2000), 31–49.

13. Ibid., 2.

14. David Prynn, "The Clarion Clubs, Rambling and the Holiday Associations in Britain Since the 1890s", *Journal of Contemporary History*, 11 (1976), 66 in *The Scout-A Journal for Socialist Workers* (June 1895), I, no. 3.

15. Ibid., 66.

16. Carpenter, 35–36.

17. See pages 17, 19 and 36 of *The Hobbit* for just a few of the many references to walking sticks.

18. Catherine Brace, "Publishing and Publishers: Towards an Historical Geography of Countryside Writing, c. 1930–1950", *Area* 33, no. 3 (2001), 287–96.

19. George Borrow, *Lavengro* (New York: Dutton, 1965), 479.

20. Brace, "Publishing and Publishers," 288.

21. Dufferin and Ava, Frederick Temple Blackwood, Marquis of, *Letters from High Latitudes* (London: Dent, 1910), 6.

22. Ibid., 8–25.

23. Ibid., 86.

24. Ibid., 241.

25. Julie E. Fromer, *A Necessary Luxury: Tea in Victorian England* (Athens: Ohio University Press, 2008), 29-30.

26. Beatrice M. Swainson, "Rural Settlement in North West Devon, England," *Economic Geography* 11, no. 1 (1935), 80.

27. Ibid., 84.

28. Dufferin, *Letters from High Latitudes*, 151.

29. C. S. Lewis, *Out of the Silent Planet*, (New York: J.M. Dent and Sons, 1996), 7.

30. Ibid., 7.

31. Ibid., 7.

32. Ibid., 99

33. John S. Wilson, *Scouting Round the World* (London: Blandford Press, 1959), 13.

34. Ibid., 13.

35. Ibid., 13. See also Michael John Foster, *The Complete History of the British Boy Scouts: The History of an Early "Breakaway" Movement*, (Aylesbury, Brotherhood of British Scouts, 1989), 2nd ed., revised, 1.

36. Mark Girouard, *The Return to Camelot: Chivalry and the English Gentleman* (New Haven: Yale University Press, 1981), 254.

37. D.C. Spry, "One Scouting World," *International Journal* 3 (1948), 156–59.

38. Foster, 54.

39. Wilson, *Scouting Round the World*, 14, 54.

40. Spry, "One Scouting World," 156.

41. Sam Pryke, "The Popularity of Nationalism in the Early British Boy Scout Movement," *Social History* 23, no. 3 (Oct. 1998), 309–24.

PART THREE

Wizards and Bears and Monsters, Oh My!:

Magic and Mystery in Middle-Earth

"Then Gandalf lit up his wand. Of course it was Gandalf; but just then they were too busy to ask how he got there. He took out his sword again, and again it flashed in the dark by itself. It burned with a rage that made it gleam if goblins were about; now it was bright as blue flame for delight in the killing of the great lord of the cave."

—*The Hobbit*, 62

Merlin, Odin, and Mountain Spirits:

The Story of Gandalf's Origins

Leila K. Norako

"If you had heard only a quarter of what I have heard about him, and I have only heard very little of all there is to hear, you would be prepared for any sort of remarkable tale."

—*The Hobbit*, 31

A s a shaper of events, a counselor to ring-bearers and kings alike, and a powerful wizard who aids the peoples of Middle-earth against the forces of evil, Gandalf proves himself a figure of immense powers throughout *The Hobbit* and *The Lord of the Rings*. To create him, Tolkien drew on an array of figures from the mythologies and literatures of medieval Europe—Odin and Merlin most especially. But even as Gandalf resembles these figures, he differs from them in important ways and stands, as a result, as a unique extension of the storytelling traditions from which Tolkien drew. Gandalf exists, in other words, as a perfect example of Tolkien's creative process as he drew from a variety of literary traditions to create the world of Middle-earth.

More than a Mountain Spirit: Gandalf's Beginnings

Tolkien claimed that Gandalf's appearance was inspired by a painting by Josef Madlener called *Der Berggeist*, "The Mountain Spirit."[1] Tolkien owned a postcard of the painting, and on its paper cover he wrote "the origin of Gandalf" at an unknown date. The image certainly resembles the Gandalf we encounter in *The Hobbit* and *The Lord of the Rings*: It features an old, grey-bearded man wearing a cape and a wide-brimmed hat. Madlener did not paint *Der Berggeist* until the mid-1920s, however, and reproductions of it were not available in postcard form until 1930.[2] By that date, Tolkien was already well underway in his work on *The Hobbit* and on the Gandalf character, which makes the possibility of *Der Berggeist*'s direct influence on Gandalf's development somewhat unlikely. The fact that we cannot date Tolkien's inscription on the postcard makes it even harder to determine when he came across the image, and as a result, exactly how it might have exerted influence. As we'll discuss later in this chapter, the features that Gandalf shares with *Der Berggeist* could just as easily have come from various representations of Odin or Merlin. Nevertheless, Tolkien's inscription suggests that he acknowledged an affinity between the mountain spirit and Gandalf.

The origins of Gandalf's name are far easier to trace than the influence of this particular painting. "Gandalfr" appears in the catalog of dwarven names (*Dvergatal*, or "dwarf tally") in *Völuspá*, the first poem in the Old Norse *The Poetic Edda*. The name also appears in *Gylfaginning*, a tale included in *The Prose Edda*.[3] In early drafts of *The Hobbit*, the character we know as Gandalf was originally referred to as Bladorthin, with "Gandalf" serving instead as a name for the character eventually known as Thorin Oakenshield.[4] For reasons unknown, Tolkien eventually changed the wizard's name to "Gandalf." The name, however, retains a certain aptness. "Gandalfr" comes from the Old Norse *gandr* (a wand or staff) and *álfr* (elf). While not an elf, Gandalf is an otherworldly figure, since we learn (from Tolkien's later writings) that he is a Maia—an immortal spirit that has existed since the beginning of time—and one of the Istari, the five wizards sent to help the peoples of Middle-earth in their struggles against Sauron.[5] His staff, moreover, becomes particularly important: It serves as his primary source of defense and as a conduit for his magical powers.[6]

While Gandalf's physical appearance remains largely the same across Tolkien's stories, his abilities and his role as a powerful advisor and shaper of events become more pronounced as the events of Middle-earth unfold. There are, according to Michael Stanton, three Gandalfs who emerge throughout *The Hobbit* and *The Lord of the Rings*. "The first and least impressive," he argues, "is the Gandalf in *The Hobbit*; the second more powerful one is in *The Fellowship of the Ring*, and the third and most majestic Gandalf appears in the last two parts of *The Lord of the Rings* after his return."[7] In this configuration, the Gandalf we encounter in *The Hobbit* serves as but an organizer of the adventure and as a counselor to the dwarves; because he is absent for most of the narrative and on the surface, he does not have as much influence over the course of events that take place in *The Hobbit* as he does in *The Lord of the Rings*.

Nevertheless, suggestions of his greater powers do exist. *The Hobbit* gradually reveals him as a figure well known and influential throughout Middle-earth. Creatures and peoples everywhere either respect or fear him (depending on whether they are good or evil). He communes with Beorn and the Eagles, rescues the company from trolls and goblins, and is instrumental in the outcome of the Battle of the Five Armies. His abrupt departure earlier in the story from the company of dwarves is even explained: He leaves in order to attend "a great council of the white wizards, masters of lore and good magic; and . . . [to drive] the Necromancer from his dark hold in the south of Mirkwood"[8] (*The Hobbit*, 357). He might appear elusive and even downright grumpy in *The Hobbit*—far more so than in *The Lord of the Rings*—but he remains a figure with immense powers at his disposal.

These abilities are more fully formed in Tolkien's work after *The Hobbit*. In a 1954 work entitled "An Essay on the Istari," Tolkien describes Gandalf as one of the Istari sent by the Valar to aid the peoples of Middle-earth against the forces of evil. Gandalf and his fellows are "forbidden to reveal themselves in forms of majesty, or to seek to rule the wills of Men or Elves by open displays of power."[9] They are, instead, to serve and advise the inhabitants of Middle-earth. Tolkien explains, however, that the only Istari who remains faithful to their goals and to their vows is Gandalf:

> [He] was named among the Elves Mithrandir, the Grey Pilgrim, for he dwelt in no place, and gathered to himself neither wealth nor followers, but ever went to and fro in the Westlands from Gondor to Angmar, and from Lindon to Lórien, befriending all folk in times of need. Warm and eager was his spirit . . . for he was the Enemy of Sauron . . . . [H]is joy, and his swift wrath, were veiled in garments grey as ash, so that only those that knew him well glimpsed the flame that was within. Merry he could be, and kindly to the young and simple, and yet quick at times to sharp speech and the rebuking of folly; but he was not proud, and sought neither power nor praise, and thus far and wide he was beloved among all those that were not themselves proud. . . . [H]e would at times work wonders among them, loving especially the beauty of fire; and yet such marvels he wrought mostly for mirth and delight, and desired not that any should hold him in awe or take his counsels out of fear.[10]

Much later in his life, Tolkien even describes Gandalf as an angelic being:

> We must assume that they [the Istari] were all Maiar, that is persons of the 'angelic' order, though not necessarily of the same rank. The Maiar were 'spirits,' but capable of self-incarnation, and could take 'humane' (especially Elvish) forms.[11]

These post-production writings reveal, in no uncertain terms, the continued activity of the author's creative process, particularly in terms of how he sought to resolve and explain aspects of the character (his name, his shifting attitudes, the different ways the peoples of Middle-earth perceive him) that might otherwise be difficult to understand. The "little old man," encountered in the first edition of *The Hobbit*, is, to be sure, a far cry from the magisterial wizard of *The Return of the King*, let alone from the angelic being described by Tolkien in his later writings. And in fact, Tolkien eventually abandoned the description of Gandalf as "a little old man" for that very reason, truncating the phrase to "old man" in later editions of *The Hobbit*. The original phrase appears only in the 1937 edition, and while it endured well into drafts of *The Lord of the Rings*, Tolkien seems to have gotten rid of it because of how it began to conflict with other developing aspects of the character.[12] While minor, this editorial change reveals that Tolkien ultimately desired for Gandalf to be read as a consistent figure across *The Hobbit* and *The Lord of the Rings*.

Gandalf and Odin: Wanderers and Wonder-workers

Out of the sources of inspiration from which Tolkien drew, Gandalf bears the closest resemblance to Odin, the chief god of the Norse pantheon. Tolkien himself readily acknowledged the connection, referring to Gandalf at one point in his letters as "the Odinic wanderer."[13] Like the Norse god, Gandalf appears in different forms and guises depending on the problem at hand. The hobbits, for instance, view Gandalf as a meddlesome—but largely benevolent—"wandering wizard," known primarily for his fireworks, his captivating tales, and his tendency to inspire wayward hobbits to go off on "mad adventures" (*The Hobbit*, 34–35). Even in *The Hobbit*, however, many others understand him as a being endowed with far greater powers. He commands the respect of the great eagles and of Beorn, and he works with other wizards to rid Mirkwood of a powerful necromancer (later revealed as Sauron). Because of his ability to shift roles—from affable entertainer, to counselor, to strategist, to warrior—Gandalf is known in *The Hobbit* and in *The Lord of the Rings* by different names: Mithrandir (The Grey Pilgrim), Tharkun, Olorin, Greyhame, Stormcrow, The White Rider, and Incanus, among others. Many of these epithets, as Marjorie Burns has discussed, derive from those given to Odin throughout Norse mythology, such as Lore-Master, Broad-Hat, Truth-Getter, Long-Hood, Long-Beard, Greybeard, Bearer of the (Magic) Wand, One Who Rides Forth, Wayweary, Wayfarer, and Wanderer.[14] According to Burns:

These attributes are applied to Odin when he travels—as he frequently does—through his own middle-earth, the middle-earth of Norse mythology, disguised as a grey-bearded old man, carrying a staff and wearing either a hood or a cloak (nearly always blue) and a wide-brimmed, floppy hat.[15]

Gandalf frequently uses this particular disguise in *The Hobbit* and *The Lord of the Rings*. Consider his first appearance in *The Hobbit* as seen through the eyes of Bilbo Baggins: "[a]ll that the unsuspecting Bilbo saw that morning was an old man with a staff. He had a tall pointed blue hat, a long grey cloak, a silver scarf over which his long white beard hung down below his waist, and immense black boots" (*The Hobbit*, 32). In *The Lord of the Rings*, Frodo composes an elegy for Gandalf (after his "death" in Khazad-dûm) and describes the wizard in similar terms—as "an old man in a battered hat" who wanders far and wide "at will," who knows the "secret tongues" of the races of Middle-earth, and who uses a "thorny staff for support" (*The Lord of the Rings*, 350–51). In *The Two Towers*, Gandalf appears to members of the broken fellowship in a similar guise: "They could not see his face: he was hooded, and above the hood he wore a wide-brimmed hat, so that all his features were overshadowed, except for the end of his nose and his grey beard" (*The Lord of the Rings*, 482).

Bilbo's initial meeting with Gandalf draws on other aspects of the Norse god. The wizard's mixed reputation among the hobbits—who find him both suspicious and fascinating—mirrors Odin's tendency to either work wonders or disrupt the lives of those he encounters in his journeys. In the *Lay of Grimnir*, for instance, Odin's wife Frigg sends a warning to Geirrod—Odin's would-be host—"lest he be bewitched by a warlock [Odin] who was then come into the land."[16] Geirrod eventually loses his life because he fails to identify the god. Much like Odin, the inhabitants of Tolkien's Middle-earth often have a difficult time recognizing Gandalf. Bilbo has to ask for his name (*The Hobbit*, 6), and in *The Lord of the Rings*, Gandalf surprises members of the broken Fellowship and the corrupted court of Theoden in his new form as the White Wizard (*The Lord of the Rings*, 502–03).

As these previous examples make clear, Gandalf shares Odin's affinity for wandering. Odin journeys in disguise in the aforementioned *Lay of Grimnir*, and Heimskringla states that "[His followers] put all their trust in him. Often he was away so long as to be gone for many years . . . ,"[17] In the *Lay of Vafhruthnir*, Odin speaks of his journeys, saying, "far have I fared and much afield have I been."[18] In like fashion, Gandalf's travels take him far and wide, and he often disappears at curious and seemingly inopportune times. He parts from the dwarves' company in *The Hobbit*, for instance, just as they are about to embark on the most treacherous part of their journey; he leaves them to their own devices for much of the story and only reappears in time for the Battle of the Five Armies. This pattern repeats itself in *The Lord of the Rings*: Gandalf leaves Frodo for a number of years in order to uncover the origins of Bilbo's ring, only returning years later once he has amassed all the knowledge available to him and has reason to believe it dangerous. Later, in *The Fellowship of the Ring*, Gandalf is presumed dead after falling into a chasm while fighting the Balrog; he also departs before the Battle of Helm's Deep just as it seems the army needs him most. But while both Odin and Gandalf share an affinity for travel and disappearance, their motivations are quite different. The Norse god's absences are often either unexplained or self-serving, whereas Gandalf's absences—initially mysterious as they might be—are always for the betterment of Middle-earth and its inhabitants. Unlike Odin, then, Gandalf always takes care to return and help those who need him.

In addition to extensive traveling, Gandalf shares Odin's linguistic prowess. According to *Heimskringla*:

> [Odin] spoke so well and so smoothly that all who heard him believed all he said was true. All he spoke was in rimes, as is now the case in what is called skaldship . . . He was also able with mere words to extinguish fires, to calm the sea, and to turn the winds any way he pleased . . . Odin knew all about hidden treasures, and he knew such magic spells as would open for him the earth and mountains and rocks and burial mounds; and with mere words he bound those who dwelled in them, and went and took what he wanted.[19]

Similarly, many of Gandalf's powers derive from his gifts of language and speech. In *The Hobbit*, for instance, he tricks a group of hungry trolls who are about to eat Bilbo and his fellow dwarves by mimicking their voices, creating an argument that keeps them from noticing the rising sun (the trolls of Tolkien's world, like those of Icelandic folklore, turn to stone in the sunlight). Just as the sun begins to crest over the hill, Gandalf, still mimicking a troll's voice, shouts, "Dawn take you all, and be stone to you!" and they all promptly turn to stone (*The Hobbit*, 80). In another example, he carves a runic symbol for "burglar"—which he knows will be deciphered only by the dwarves—on Bilbo's door in order to ensnare the hobbit in the dwarves' adventure (*The Hobbit*, 36, 49).

Finally, Gandalf and Odin share a deep-seated connection to various animals in Scandinavian myth and legend.[20] Eagles feature prominently in Scandinavian mythology and are, like Odin, ambiguous in nature, "representing both the power and threat of war and the power of transference between spiritual states or worlds."[21] Odin himself shape-shifts into an eagle in *Skáldskaparmál* in order to acquire the gift of poetry, and it is this aspect of the eagle—its ability to act as an agent of rescue—that resonates in the relationship with eagles that Gandalf possesses in Tolkien's world.[22]

Gandalf, unlike Odin, never shape-shifts into an eagle, but he does call on eagles for assistance. In both *The Hobbit* and in *The Lord of the Rings*, Gandalf relies on the giant birds of prey for rescue. Moreover, the description of the eagles in *The Hobbit* resonates strongly with their ambiguous representation in Scandinavian mythology. As the narrator tells us: Eagles are not kindly birds. Some are cowardly and cruel. But the ancient race of the northern mountains were the greatest of all birds; they were proud and strong and noble-hearted" (*The Hobbit*, 150). Threatening though they might be, these very birds, led by the Lord of the Eagles, rescue Gandalf, the dwarves, and Bilbo from a horde of goblins and wolves. The Eagles take the group to their eyrie, and Bilbo learns of Gandalf's relationship to the giant creatures:

> . . . he found all the others sitting with their backs to the mountain wall. The Lord of the Eagles was also there and was speaking to Gandalf. It seemed that Bilbo is not going to be eaten after all. The Wizard and the Eagle Lord appeared to know one another slightly, and even to be on friendly terms. As a matter of fact Gandalf, who had often been in the mountains, had once rendered a service to the eagles and healed their Lord from an arrow wound . . . He was discussing plans with the great eagle for carrying the dwarves and himself and Bilbo far away and setting them down well on their journey across the plains below." (*Hobbit*, 157-58)

In this respect, Gandalf's special affinity with these creatures and his consistent ability to broker agreements with them aligns him with Odin.

Gandalf also has an indirect relationship with wolves, animals that—like the eagle—are beasts of battle in Scandinavian mythology and that are linked directly to Odin himself. The Norse god has a varied relationship with wolves: He dies at Ragnarok in the jaws of the giant wolf Fenrir, but he also has two wolf companions, Geri and Freki. By contrast, Tolkien appears to have transferred only Odin's hostility toward wolves over to Gandalf. In *The Hobbit*, Gandalf reveals that he knows their "dreadful language," and his encounters with wolves are always antagonistic. He fights them in *The Hobbit* and battles a large wolf—sent by Sauron—in *The Lord of the Rings*, an encounter that bears an oblique resemblance to Odin's fateful encounter with Fenrir.[23]

Additionally, Gandalf's relationship with the horse Shadowfax bears undeniable similarities to Odin's relationship with his own horse, Sleipnir.[24] Both animals share supernatural origin stories: Sleipnir is the eight-legged offspring of Loki, and Shadowfax's sire "knew the speech of Men" (*The Lord of the Rings*, 425). Both of these horses, moreover, are remarkable in their abilities to remain calm around the dead; like Sleipnir, who rides into the underworld on more than one occasion in Norse mythology, Shadowfax is the only horse in Middle-earth unafraid of the Nazgul, the undead servants of Sauron.[25]

Finally, Gandalf's friendship with Beorn also reminds us of Odin. Beorn is a shape-shifter who can transform himself from man to bear. He is hospitable in human form, but warns his guests in *The Hobbit* not to venture out of doors at night (that is, while he is in his bear form), lest they be harmed. As Stefan Donecker discusses in chapter 10 of this book, Beorn resembles in many respects the berserkers of Norse mythology. These men were a key component of Odin's warrior host because of their ability to become animalistic in their rage prior to battle.

Even with all of these similarities, Gandalf is hardly a mere copy of Odin. He is not a god but an immortal agent sent on a mission, an envoy who answers to a deity. His enduring benevolence and devotion to the peoples of Middle-earth also distance him from the Norse god. Whereas Odin is often fickle and inconstant, Gandalf is reliable and trustworthy, lacking the mythical deity's self-centered behaviors. While he occasionally disrupts the lives of those he encounters (Bilbo and Frodo most notably), Gandalf does so with a broader, and largely benevolent, purpose in mind. Moreover, while he might run on his own schedule, he always arrives in time to save those who would otherwise be lost without him. The most important difference between

Odin and Gandalf, however, lies in the themes of self-sacrifice that run through both of their stories. Whereas Odin sacrifices himself on the World Tree (as described in *Hávamál*) in order to increase his own knowledge and power, Gandalf sacrifices himself for others—a character trait made most visible at the Bridge of Khazad-dûm in *The Fellowship of the Ring*. Like Odin, he is a consummate knowledge seeker, but his sacrificial death at the hands of the Balrog to save the Fellowship is much more like a Christian sacrifice of self (followed by a "resurrection" in *The Two Towers*) than Odin's sacrifice on the World Tree for the sake of greater knowledge.

Tolkien's later writings on Gandalf also reveal that the wizard's faithfulness to his role as an Istari prohibits him from intimidating others and from revealing himself in majesty, as Odin is so frequently wont to do. In the *Lay of Grimir*, for instance, Odin eventually reveals himself and kills his ungracious host because of the host's unwitting insolence. Gandalf, by contrast, only intimidates those who warrant it, and even then he only reveals as much of his powers as is absolutely necessary. Early in *The Lord of the Rings*, for instance, he scares Bilbo into giving up the Ring, and later on he shocks the court of Theoden and bellows at Wormtongue, but only in an attempt to rescue Theoden from Saruman's grasp. Odin, moreover, has many wives and mistresses, while Gandalf remains decidedly chaste in Tolkien's fiction. These differences from Odin demonstrate that Tolkien was not interested in simply reinventing a single character from folklore and mythology, but instead was invested in creating something entirely new through a process of selective borrowing.

Wizard, Counselor, Prophet: The Many Faces of Merlin and Gandalf

Tolkien may not have drawn as heavily from representations of Merlin as he did from Norse mythology when creating Gandalf, but certain aspects of Gandalf's character do parallel the Arthurian counselor, prophet, and military strategist.[26] His status as a wizard, for instance, links him most obviously to Merlin, but not to the Merlin one might think. As Stephen Knight has so deftly observed, Merlin's role as a wizard is a decidedly modern invention:

> Merlin is an icon: a few lines will create him, sketching the pointed hat and the long beard, plus a magic wand and someone to teach. So T. H. White described him in *The Once and Future King,* Disney visualized the image in *The Sword in the Stone,* and Lerner and Loewe set it to music in *Camelot.* But that image is an illusion of modernity: medieval Merlin was not old and bearded, was wise rather than a wizard, guided countries rather that learners. The modern icon delineates an image not anciently mythic, but one we find both credible and consoling among contemporary anxieties.[27]

This Merlin—crafted by Victorian authors and later writers like White—is one upon which Tolkien seems to have drawn most readily. Gandalf, after all, is frequently referred to as a wizard throughout Tolkien's fiction; he wears the iconic pointed hat (though, as mentioned previously, this aspect of his attire also evokes Odin), works magic, and frequently adopts the role of counselor and teacher.

Gandalf, however, rejects opportunities to become all-powerful (refusing Frodo's offer of the Ring, for instance), and avoids the unnecessary use of magical powers; in these respects, he notably departs from the Merlin tradition.[28] Both Charles Williams and C. S. Lewis—colleagues of Tolkien—created Merlins who use their magical powers to intervene in human struggles; by contrast, Tolkien emphasizes Gandalf's role as an advisor, one who only uses magic when absolutely necessary. In this way, Tolkien "de-emphasizes the role of the wizard figure as a powerful magician who uses his powers to change human destinies."[29] Moreover, in his writings on the Istari, Tolkien states that the word "wizard" is ultimately an inadequate descriptor for Gandalf, and that the word—as it appears in his fiction—is a loose translation of the word *istari.* As with Tolkien's adaptations of Odinic narratives, this move "signals [his] attempt to create something new and original" out of the Merlin tradition, rather than simply replicate it.

Nevertheless, there are attributes that Gandalf certainly shares with the iconic wizard from the Arthurian tradition, the role of military strategist being but one of them. Merlin is frequently cast in stories as a military strategist in medieval literature. In Geoffrey of Monmouth's *History of the Kings of Britain*, for instance, he serves as a counselor and as a prophet to both Arthur and to the kings before him, advising them on a number of military matters.[30] In like fashion, the Gandalf encountered in both *The Hobbit* and *The Lord of the Rings* takes on very similar roles as an orchestrator and strategist. At the outset of *The Hobbit*, he deftly forces Bilbo's participation in the dwarves' quest, and at the story's conclusion he serves as a pivotal orchestrator (on the side of the dwarves, elves, and men) in the Battle of the Five Armies. He inhabits this role most fully, however, in *The Lord of the Rings* during the Battle of the Pelinnor Fields, where he advises and counsels from behind the walls of Minas Tirith, rides out into battle with the men, and actively defends the walls of the city from the Nazgul and the armies of Mordor

Gandalf most resembles Merlin, however, in his role as a counselor and teacher to various figures in both *The Hobbit* and in *The Lord of the Rings*.[31] Merlin consistently serves as an advisor and even as a prophet to the kings of Britain in Arthurian literature. In the *Historia*, the *Prose Merlin*, Malory's *Le Morte d'Arthur*, and other medieval works, he serves as a counselor and advisor not only to Uther but also to Arthur himself, advising and, in some cases, admonishing the young king in order to form him into a worthy ruler. This tradition is extended and developed further by writers such as T. H. White who, in *The Once and Future King*, describes in great detail the education young Arthur receives from Merlin

While it is uncertain which tales inspired Tolkien most directly, Gandalf strongly reflects this particular aspect of Merlin's character. In *The Hobbit* and *The Lord of the Rings*, Tolkien presents him as a dispenser of wisdom and guidance, a role later explained in Tolkien's description of the Istari. As such, Gandalf's primary goal is to advise and counsel the peoples of Middle-earth in their fight against the forces of evil led by Sauron. The dwarves in *The Hobbit*, for example, look to him for leadership and counsel, and they lament his departure because "the most dangerous part of all the journey" was about to begin (*The Hobbit*, 190). In *The Lord of the Rings*, Gandalf's role as a counselor extends to kings and leaders (Aragorn, Theoden, Denethor, Elrond, and Saruman, to name the most notable), though he also actively advises the lesser folk, the hobbits in particular.

But whereas Merlin often counsels kings in order to help them obtain and maintain power regardless of the ethics involved, Gandalf only bestows advice and counsel that will help the peoples of Middle-earth as a whole.[32] In a variety of Arthurian narratives, for instance, Merlin is not above arranging the adulterous liaison of Uther and Igraine (King Arthur's parents), and in certain portions of the Merlin tradition, the wizard finds himself attracted to and ultimately undone by an enchantress named Vivian (or some variation thereof). Gandalf, however, actively resists succumbing to or being swayed by the worldly desires for those he encounters; consider, for instance, how he unswervingly resists the temptations and threats of characters such as Denethor and Saruman.

As with the figure of Odin, Merlin undoubtedly influenced Tolkien's depiction of Gandalf, but Tolkien did not simply create another version of the iconic wizard. Rather, he took aspects that he felt would best suit the character of Gandalf and dispensed with those that would not. A study of both antecedents reveals a sometimes puzzling degree of overlap. It is very easy to wonder whether Gandalf's pointy hat was inspired by Merlin or Odin, or more pressingly, which antecedent inspired the depiction of Gandalf as a competent warrior strategist and as a repository of wisdom. Both Odin and Merlin—in their various iterations—adopt these roles. These overlaps are significant, because they make it impossible to neatly determine which figures are responsible for certain of Gandalf's traits and characteristics. This dynamic, and the somewhat unanswerable questions it produces, ultimately allows a reader's focus to return to the character himself, one who remains both rooted in literary traditions and distinct from them.

The Trickster Gandalf

While Odin and Merlin are the literary and mythological figures who had the most influence on Tolkien's development of Gandalf, many scholars have made compelling arguments about other possible sources of inspiration. Leslie Ellen Jones, for instance, has argued that Gandalf is a trickster figure inspired by a combination of accounts of Odin, Myrddinn (the Welsh antecedent of Merlin), and the Norse god Loki. To be sure, Gandalf seems to share some of the aspects of the archetypal trickster figure. Tricksters tend to be "ambiguous and anomalous, deceivers and trick-players, shape-shifters, situation-inverters, messengers and imitators of the gods, and sacred and lewd bricoleurs."[33] In Jones's formulation, Gandalf, as a "situation-inverter," disrupts Bilbo's life quite dramatically in *The Hobbit*; as a Maiar, he acts in some respects as a "messenger . . . of the gods"; and, in his creation of the company of dwarves in *The Hobbit* and his assistance in creating the Fellowship in *The Lord of the Rings*, he acts as a "sacred bricoleur."[34] And yet, the trickster tends to be a truly ambiguous figure with a substantially dark and subversive side. The Norse god Loki, in his cruel machinations that result in the tragic death of Baldur, is one example. There is, however, nothing subversive in the figure of Gandalf, and so he falls short of Loki and many classic trickster figures in this sense.

It has also been suggested that the Rübezahl—the legendary mountain spirit that inspired Madlener's painting *Der Berggeist*—may have influenced Tolkien's portrayal of the wizard. As Douglas A. Anderson describes:

> In tales the Rübezahl appears in various forms—as a guide, a messenger, or a farmer. He delights in leading travelers astray. There is a considerable Rübezahl tradition, and while much of this has not appeared in English, some tales . . . have been translated, including one entitled "Rübezahl" in *The Brown Fairy Book* (1904), edited by Andrew Lang. In illustrations, the Rübezahl often appears as a bearded man with a staff . . . and

thus may be the origin of some of Gandalf's behavior as well as his outward appearance.[35]

The Rübezahl, like Odin and Merlin, is known for his sudden appearances and disappearances, and Gandalf's similar entrances and exits might have been inspired by the Rübezahl as much as they were by Odin's wanderings. Gandalf repeatedly disappears at critical moments; he deserts the party just before they encounter the trolls, right in the midst of their capture by the goblins, and again on the borders of Mirkwood, but he always reappears when needed, actions that mirror those of the Rübezahl in German folklore.[36] This potential influence of the mountain spirit may, in fact, have been what Tolkien was alluding to in the message he wrote on the postcard of Madlener's painting; by saying that *Der Berggeist* was the origin of Gandalf, Tolkien could easily have been pointing to the broader Rübezahl tradition as source of inspiration rather than to Madlener's specific rendering of the figure.

"I Am Gandalf, and Gandalf Means Me!"

Although Tolkien borrowed the traits of many legendary characters to create Gandalf, in the end the wizard is identical to none of them, and this process of selective borrowing can, in fact, be seen throughout Tolkien's fiction. He drew on a variety of folkloric, mythological, and literary traditions, many of them medieval or rooted in medievalism, in his development of the peoples and cultures of Middle-earth. The elves, for instance, are inspired by descriptions of fairies and the Fairy Otherworld in medieval folklore and literature, and the Rohirrim were inspired by the culture represented in Anglo-Saxon literature. Like Gandalf, these imaginary peoples differ dramatically from their influences, making it impossible to see them as simple repetitions of medieval or mythological tropes. Studying the creation of Gandalf, then, provides us with a microcosmic example of Tolkien's creative process and allows us to appreciate both the nuances of Gandalf as a character and the careful work of the author who created him.

Notes

1. Humphrey Carpenter, *Tolkien: A Biography* (Boston: Houghton Mifflin, 1977), 51; Michael N. Stanton, "Gandalf," in *J.R.R. Tolkien Encyclopedia: Scholarship and Critical Assessment*, edited by Michael D. C. Drout (New York: Routledge, 2007), 230–32. Douglas A. Anderson, in *The Annotated Hobbit*, clarifies the matter of the painting and its possible influence in n. 14 (New York: Houghton Mifflin, 2002).

2. J. R. R. Tolkien, *The Annotated Hobbit* (revised and expanded edition), Introduction and annotations by Douglas A. Anderson (New York: Houghton Mifflin, 2002), 37 n. 14. All quotations from *The Hobbit* come from this edition. All quotations from *The Lord of the Rings* come from J. R. R. Tolkien, The Lord of the Rings (Boston: Houghton Mifflin, 2002?, c1994).

3. John D. Rateliff, *The History of the Hobbit, Part One: Mr. Baggins* (Boston: Houghton Mifflin, 2007), 15.

4. Ibid., 15. As Ratliff observes, this original configuration made a great deal of sense: The other dwarf names are also largely taken from the Dvergatal and Bladorthin was a Sindarin elvish name of Tolkien's own creation, which would have linguistically separated the character from his dwarfish compatriots in *The Hobbit*.

5. In Tolkien's world, the Maiar are "an order of semidivine spirits created to assist the Valar [that is, angelic beings born out of the thoughts of Eru, the one God] in protecting and preserving the ongoing creation and refinement of the world"; the Istari are "a special sub order of the Maiar" (Jonathan Evans, "Maiar," in the *J.R.R. Tolkien Encyclopedia: Scholarship and Critical Assessment* [New York: Routledge, 2007], 401–02).

6. Leslie Ellen Jones, *Myth and Middle-earth: Exploring the Medieval Legends Behind J.R.R. Tolkien's The Hobbit and The Lord of the Rings* (Cold Spring Harbor: Cold Spring Press, 2002), 69.

7. Stanton, "Gandalf," 231.

8. As Anderson explains in his note on the subject, Tolkien seems not to have "fully developed the idea of how many wizards there were, and what their colors might be" (357, n. 2). He will go on to name three of the five wizards in *The Lord of the Rings*, however, and in his ancillary writings explains their roles even further.

9. J. R. R. Tolkien, *Unfinished Tales of Númenor and Middle-earth*, edited by Christopher Tolkien (Boston: Houghton Mifflin, 2001), 390.

10. Ibid., 390–91.

11. Ibid., 394.

12. Anderson, *The Annotated Hobbit* 36, n. 13.

13. J. R. R. Tolkien, *The Letters of J.R.R. Tolkien* (Boston: Houghton Mifflin, 1981), 119.

14. As catalogued by Marjorie Burns, *Perilous Realms*, 96.

15. Ibid., 96–97.

16. Hollander, ed., *The Poetic Edda*, 54.

17. Snorri Sturluson, *Heimskringla: History of the Kings of Norway*, translated by Lee M. Hollander (Austin: University of Texas Press, 1964), 7.

18. Hollander, ed., *The Poetic Edda*, 42.

19. Sturluson, 10.

20. Burns, *Perilous Realms*, 100–06.

21. Ibid., 100.

22. Snorri Sturluson, *The Prose Edda*, translated and edited by Anthony Faulkes (London: Everyman, J. M. Dent, 1987), 58–59.

23. Burns, 103-04.

24. In *The Prose Edda*, we are told Sleipnir was the progeny of Svaðilfari, a giant's stallion, and Loki, disguised as a mare, (35–36).

25. Burns, *Perilous Realms*, 105.

26. Frank P. Riga, "Gandalf and Merlin: J.R.R. Tolkien's Adoption and Transformation of a Literary Tradition," *Mythlore* 27 (Fall/Winter 2008): 21–44; Leslie Ellen Jones, *Myth and Middle-earth*, 69–79.

27. Stephen Knight, *Merlin: Knowledge and Power through the Ages* (Ithaca: Cornell University Press, 2009), xi.

28 As Riga, Stephen Knight, and many others have observed, Merlin's origins (in some of the earliest versions of his story) contribute to his ambiguousness. In Geoffrey of Monmouth, for instance, he is revealed to be the child of a mortal woman and an incubus demon (*The History of the Kings of Britain*, translated by Lewis Thorpe [New York: Penguin, 1966] 166–169).

29. Riga, "Gandalf and Merlin," 31.

30. Geoffrey of Monmouth, *The History of the Kings of Britain*, 206–07.

31. Riga, "Gandalf and Merlin," 39–41.

32. Ibid., 36–39.

33. Jones, *Myth and Middle-earth*, 76. Jones relies here on William J. Hynes's 1993 essay "Mapping the Characteristics of Mythic Tricksters: A Heuristic Guide," in *Mythical Trickster Figures* (Tuscaloosa: University of Alabama Press, 1993), 33–45. And as Jones explains, the term *bricoleur*, as used by Claude Levi-Strauss, describes figures known for their ingenuity and ability to creatively resolve situations (*The Savage Mind*, 16–18).

34. Ibid., 76–77.

35. Anderson, *The Annotated Hobbit*, 189, no. 13.

36. Ibid., 190, n. 13.

CHAPTER 10

Berserkers, Were-Bears, and Ursine Parents:

Beorn the Skin-Changer and His Ancestors

Stefan Donecker

"I should say there were little bears, large bears, ordinary bears, and gigantic big bears, all dancing outside from dark to nearly dawn. They came from almost every direction, except from the west over the river, from the Mountains."

—*The Hobbit,* 121[1]

"**I**f you must know more, his name is Beorn. He is very strong, and he is a skin-changer." With these simple words Gandalf introduces one of the most impressive characters of *The Hobbit*—and

171

immediately prompts a rather inappropriate association from Bilbo: "'What! A furrier, a man that calls rabbits conies, when he doesn't turn their skins into squirrels?' asked Bilbo. 'Good gracious heavens, no, no, NO, NO!' said Gandalf. 'Don't be a fool Mr Baggins if you can help it; and in the name of all wonder don't mention the word furrier again as long as you are within a hundred miles of his house, nor rug, cape, tippet, muff, nor any other such unfortunate word! He is a skin-changer. He changes his skin: sometimes he is a huge black bear, sometimes he is a great strong black-haired man with huge arms and a great beard. I cannot tell you much more, though that ought to be enough'" (*The Hobbit*, 110)[1].

Soon thereafter, Bilbo and the dwarves encounter the redoubtable Beorn in person, who, after some initial reluctance, hosts them in his great wooden house, provides them with ponies and provisions, and advises them on the dangers that lie ahead on their quest. But the skin-changer proves to be far more than a random encounter on the journey to the Lonely Mountain; at the climactic Battle of the Five Armies, he returns in bear shape and decides the battle almost single-handedly: Beorn breaks through the goblins' ranks, slays their king Bolg, and scatters their army, thus saving the day for the dwarves, elves, and the Lake-men.

Interestingly enough, even Gandalf is uncertain about the origins of mighty Beorn: "Some say that he is a bear descended from the great and ancient bears of the mountains that lived there before the giants came. Others say that he is a man descended from the first men who lived before Smaug or the other dragons came into this part of the world, and before the goblins came into the hills out of the North. I cannot say, though I fancy the last is the true tale" (*The Hobbit*, 110).[2] It might seem presumptuous to try competing with Gandalf and tackle a question that not even the great wizard could answer with certainty—but the lore of the man-bear is too tempting to resist. In this chapter, we'll examine the ancestry of Beorn[3] and discuss the prototypes from history, literature, and folklore that Tolkien could draw upon in creating his "skin-changer".[4] In particular, we'll focus on three traditions, all linked to the idea of a human capable of transforming into a bear: the berserkers of Viking-age Scandinavia, the depictions of bears in medieval bestiaries, and the "were-bears" of early modern demonology.

"As Strong as Bears": Old Norse Berserkers

Among the historical inspirations for the character of Beorn, the berserkers of medieval Scandinavia are easily the most famous and recognizable. The frothing, bloodthirsty berserker is one of the most iconic representations of "the Viking age" in the popular imagination, and has become a stock character in modern fantasy fiction. The historical record reveals a rather more complex phenomenon—depending on the source, a berserker could be a reputable champion in the king's retinue, an antisocial thug, or a victim of a debilitating disease.

In medieval Scandinavian literature, the term *berserker* describes a warrior capable of entering an altered state of consciousness, the famous "berserker rage" or *berserkergang*. In this furious condition, he was impervious to pain and could not be harmed by most weapons. The thirteenth-century Icelandic historian and poet Snorri Sturluson provided an often-quoted description of these fearsome fighters: "[Odin's] men went to battle without coats of mail and acted like mad dogs or wolves. They bit their shields and were as strong as bears or bulls. They killed people, and neither fire nor iron affected them. This is called berserker rage."[5] It worth noting that Snorri relegates the berserkers to a mythical sphere: In his description, they are no mundane warriors participating in any historical or contemporary conflict, but champions of Odin, the enigmatic chief god of the Old Norse, a deity associated with ecstasy and sorcery (and, incidentally, one of the main inspirations for Tolkien's Gandalf).[6]

The word *berserker* literally translates as a man clad in a coat of bearskin. The oldest known usage of the term dates from the ninth century, in a poem praising the military prowess of King Harald I of Norway: "The berserkers bellowed as the battle opened, / the wolf-coats shrieked loud and shook their weapons."[7] The stanza seems to describe two groups of ecstatic warriors, the berserkers and the "wolf-coats" (Old Norse: *ulfheðnar*), distinguished by their garb made from the pelt of bears or wolves. It is quite likely that both terms are the invention of the poem's author, Thorbjörn Hornklofi. Thorbjörn was a skald, a Viking court poet, and skaldic poetry is known for creative metaphors and the invention of new words. Deciphering the deliberately complicated language was an intellectual challenge their audiences seemed to enjoy. The term *berserker* most probably originates in neither the reality of Viking warfare nor archaic mythology, but in the creativity of an individual poet.[8]

Thorbjörn's usage of the word remained an isolated occurrence for 250 years. In the twelfth century, however, the berserker motif resurfaced in Iceland.[9] Presumably, Icelanders rediscovered Thorbjörn's poem and found his image of bellowing lunatics in bearskins quite inspiring. Berserkers soon gained an enormous popularity and became a typical feature of Icelandic saga literature.

In some sagas, the berserkers are depicted as loyal retainers of Scandinavian kings, elite warriors who serve as royal bodyguards and as shock troops in battle. But in the majority of cases, they appear in a less respectable role: as violent sociopaths who abuse their combat prowess to terrorize the population and exact tribute and loot. As such, they differ significantly from Beorn as they battle, rather than assist, the sagas' heroes.

A typical example of such a thuggish berserker is Ljot the Pale from the thirteenth-century *Egils Saga*. An honorable matron asks the hero, Egil, for help against a berserker who troubles her family: "'I will tell you, Egil, how things stand here with us. There is a man named Ljot the Pale. He is a Berserk and a duellist; he is hated. He came here and asked my daughter to wife; but we answered at once, refusing the match. Whereupon he challenged my son Fridgeir to wager of battle.' [. . .] Fridgeir was not a tall man; he was slenderly built, comely in face, not strong. He had not been used to combats." Egil realizes that the young men would not stand a chance and agrees to face the berserker himself: "Ljot was a man of vast size and strong. And as he came forward on the field to the ground of combat, a fit of Berserk fury seized him; he began to bellow hideously, and bit his shield." Undaunted, Egil dispatches his opponent, and the saga provides a rather unkind obituary for the berserker: "Ljot's death was little mourned, for he had been a turbulent bully. [. . .] He had slain many worthy landowners, whom he had first challenged to wager of battle for their lands and heritages."[10]

Most berserkers in the medieval sagas lead similar lives, as itinerant duelists who extort wealth from the farmers. Occasionally, there are also tragic characters among them: *Vatnsdœla Saga,* a thirteenth-century family chronicle, for example, features a berserker who experiences his condition as a debilitating illness: "Thorir said himself to be the worst [among his brothers], 'because the berserker rage comes on me at times when I would least wish it, and I wish, brother, that you could do something about it.'"[11] But such reluctant berserkers are rare, compared to the numerous villainous thugs that oppose the saga heroes.

Researchers have argued that the berserker motif is rooted in notions of shape-changing.[12] By donning a bear pelt, the berserker imitates a transformation, and in his frenzy he acquires the attributes of an enraged animal.[13] This symbolic transmutation is supposedly an extended expression of more archaic beliefs, according to which ritual warriors were physically able to assume animal shapes. Such an interpretation, however, it is only tenuously supported by the existing sources. Old Norse literature was very fond of shape-shifting[14], and the "legendary sagas" (*fornaldarsögur,* literally "Tales of the Old Times") regularly feature characters who magically transform themselves into the most extraordinary animals. Yet despite the popularity of shape-changing, this ability is hardly ever ascribed to berserkers. It is possible that their behavior might be a faint echo of shape-changing beliefs, but their defining characteristics are their combat fury and their invulnerability rather than any physical animal transformation.[15]

There are exceptions, however: Egil Skallagrímsson, the slayer of Ljot the Pale in the example from *Egils Saga,* came from a berserker family himself. His grandfather, Kveldulf, was not only a berserker, but he was also known to be "shape strong" (Old Norse: *hamrammr*)[16], a term that usually indicates an ability to transform into an animal shape. Because his name translates as "evening wolf," it seems likely that the saga author imagined Kveldulf to assume a wolf's shape at night. He was known to be in a particularly bad mood during the evening, and this fretful behavior precedes his nightly transformation.

The most notable Old Norse character who combines traits of a berserker with those of a shape-changer is Böðvar Bjarki, one of the heroes of the late medieval *Saga of Hrólf Kraki*.[17] Böðvar Bjarki, whose name means "warlike little bear," is the greatest among the warriors in the retinue of Danish king Hrolf Kraki. In addition to his extraordinary prowess in combat, he is capable of sending forth his spirit in the shape of a mighty bear, and does so to great effect in the saga's climactic battle between Hrolf and his rebellious vassal, King Hjorvarth: "Then Hjorvarth and his men saw that a great bear advanced before king Hrolf's men, and ever nearest where the king was; he killed more men with his paws than five other of the king's champions; blows and missiles glanced off from him, and he felled down both men and horses of king Hjorvarth's army, and all that were near him he crunched to pieces with his teeth so that a murmur of fear arose in king Hjorvarth's host."[18]

One of King Hrolf's retainers, however, notices that Böðvar is nowhere to be seen. Indignant that their greatest hero is avoiding the battle, he searches for him, and finding Böðvar sitting motionless in his tent he reproaches him for his cowardice. Awoken from his trance, Böðvar agrees to join the battle but gloomily predicts that it will be to little avail: "I say thee forsooth, that now I can give less help to the king in many things, than before thou didst call me out hence."[19] As soon as Böðvar appears on the battlefield in person, the mighty bear is gone and the enemies gain the upper hand. Fighting in human shape, Böðvar is unable to turn the tide of the battle, and in the end he, his king, and the entire army are slain.

It seems likely that the apparition of the bear is to be understood as some kind of projection of the warrior's soul[20], similar to what modern psychologists would call an "out-of-body experience." This manifestation can only exist as long as Böðvar himself remains in trance—a supernatural phenomenon that the king's retainer misjudges, with tragic consequences. In summary, it can be stated that Böðvar Bjarki is not a shape-changing berserker, but he is the closest analogy to be found in Old Norse literature: The bear apparition possesses the classical berserker abilities[21]—it fights in a furious rage and is impervious to weapons and arrows—and although Böðvar does not transform physically, his extracorporeal bear shape is a closely related phenomenon.

As a renowned scholar of Old English and Old Norse literature, Tolkien was greatly inspired by Scandinavian sources. Numerous commentators have argued that the character Beorn is, essentially, a slightly domesticated version of an Old Norse berserker.[22] However, upon closer scrutiny the similarity is superficial, at best: Berserkers were invulnerable, furious warriors whose behavior shows faint traces of a belief in animal transformation. Beorn, on the other hand, is primarily and above all a skin-changer, a man-bear; in his case, shape-changing is the defining trait of his character. From that point of view, Beorn and the berserkers have little in common.

Scholars during the 1930s viewed berserkers differently. Tolkien's contemporaries emphasised the notion of shape-changing in their interpretation of the berserker phenomenon. They perceived the berserkers of the Icelandic sagas as descendants of older, archaic cults of masked warriors who, symbolically, assumed the shape and the characteristics of mighty predatory animals. The berserkers were the last remnants of these ecstatic warrior bands; they had degenerated into mere thugs and duellists and almost forgot about the ritual shape-changing that inspired their ancestors. Nowadays, this interpretation has few supporters: The idea of ecstatic Germanic warrior cults was thoroughly abused by Nazi ideologists — after all, a mysterious band of anti-rational elite warriors was pretty much the way the SS wanted to see themselves. But during the early 1930s, when Tolkien conceived *The Hobbit*, the Nazi misuse of this theory was not yet apparent, and the "ecstatic cult" interpretation was still considered state-of-the-art research.

Tolkien's characterization of Beorn's emotions and behaviors is unmistakably inspired by tales of Old Norse berserkers: During the evening, Beorn is moody and unkind, and he behaves rather aggressively. In the morning, on the other hand, he is far friendlier (*The Hobbit*, 122–23). He shares this trait with Kveldulf, "Evening-Wolf," the shape-changing berserker of Egil's Saga, who was known to be particularly unpleasant in the evening.[23]

Beorn's closest kinsman in Old Norse literature, however, is Böðvar Bjarki.[24] Both Böðvar and Beorn have their most epic moment in the concluding battle of their respective story, when they wreak havoc among their enemies in bear shape. In the Battle of the Five Armies, Beorn "tossed wolves and goblins from his path like straws and feathers" (*The Hobbit*, 275), just as Böðvar "felled down both men and horses of King Hjorvarth's army".[25] "[D]ismay fell on the Goblins" who had to face Beorn's wrath "and they fled in all directions," and, in the same vein, "a murmur of fear arose in king Hjorvarth's host." Both Beorn and Böðvar display the essential ability of all berserkers—their invulnerability to mundane weapons: "[N]othing could withstand [Beorn], and no weapon seemed to bite upon him." Similarly, "blows and missiles glanced off" from Böðvar's bear shape. The parallels are apparent, and it seems certain that Tolkien modeled Beorn's rampage on the last battle of Böðvar Bjarki. Tolkien knew the tale of Böðvar well; one of his students, Stella Mills, had translated *The Saga of Hrólf Kraki* and dedicated the edition to her teacher.[26]

Nevertheless, two major differences remain: Tolkien implies that Beorn had changed physically into a bear, while Böðvar's body, according to the saga, remained quiescent in his tent while his spirit savaged his enemies as a bear apparition. Consequently, Beorn prevails while his kinsman fails: Böðvar's trance is interrupted, which causes the bear to disappear and leads to Böðvar's defeat and death. Beorn, on the other hand, does not have to fear any meddlers and thus triumphs over the goblins.

Licked into Shape: Medieval Bestiaries and the Tale of the Bear's Son

The idea of a certain affinity between human and bear was not confined to the remote regions of medieval Scandinavia. For centuries, the educated elites of Europe believed that man and bear were somewhat akin[27]—in a sometimes rather discomforting way.

In the first century A.D., Pliny the Elder, the great Roman naturalist, gave a rather peculiar account of young bears: A bear cub, he claimed, is born as a shapeless and eyeless lump of flesh. The mother has to shape her offspring into its proper form by licking it.[28] Compared to other ideas in his *Natural History*, such an assumption is hardly extraordinary: Pliny, who has been described as "endearingly batty"[29] by a modern historian, also believed in a race of one-legged men who use their single enormous foot as a sunshade, and recommended treating a scorpion's bite by consuming the animal's ashes in a glass of wine. But although his opinions seem bizarre from a modern point of view, they were highly influential throughout the Middle Ages and for centuries after.

In medieval Europe, so-called bestiaries, illustrated collections discussing various animals, were enormously popular, second in importance only to the Bible. Particular attention was given to exotic and monstrous creatures, and the description of each animal was usually accompanied by a moral interpretation that explained its characteristics as an allegory of Christian beliefs.[30] Many motifs were taken from ancient authorities such as Pliny, Aristotle, or the *Physiologus*, an early Christian volume on animals. Bestiaries tend to be rather standardized; the selection of creatures discussed, the characteristics attributed to them, and even the sequence in which the animals are treated are often remarkably similar.

The bestiaries repeated Pliny's idea of the female bear licking her cubs into shape, and added another unusual feature to ursine reproduction: Bears do not mate like other animals; they behave like humans and embrace each other during sexual intercourse. A typical bestiary description of the bear reads as follows: "*Ursus* the Bear [. . .] is said to get her name because she sculptures her brood with her mouth (*ore*). For they say that these creatures produce a formless foetus, giving birth to something like a bit of pulp, and this the mother-bear arranges into the proper legs and arms by licking it. [. . .] They do not make love like other quadrupeds, but, being joined in mutual embraces, they copulate in the human way."[31] Bears were characterized as having ambiguous shape and also likened to humans—two factors that contributed the idea of human-bear shape-changing.

The conjecture that bears mate in a way *similar* to humans gave rise to the idea that bears could also mate *with* humans. The belief that bears are able to impregnate human females has a long tradition.[32] It seems that previous generations did not consider this thought as disturbing as we do now: Many notable heroes were believed to descend from a union between a bear and a human woman, and such a pedigree was undoubtedly seen as extraordinary but not as particularly scandalous. Folklorists have noted that the "Bear's Son" is a common motif in fairy tales all over Europe, from Spain to Russia, known, for example, as "*Bärenhansel*" in Germany or "*Jean de l'ours*" in France.[33] Lāčēplēsis, the national hero of Latvia, is also the progeny of a bear, but in a variation of the common motif, the bear in this instance is the hero's mother rather than the father. It's worth noting that Böðvar Bjarki, the previously mentioned saga hero, was the son of a man-bear, though in his case his father was originally a human being who had been enchanted by a witch. Comparable narratives have also been collected in non-European societies.

In most versions of the tale, a woman is abducted by a bear and kept captive in his cave. She gives birth to an extraordinary son, who usually possesses some features that prove his heritage—like hair covering his entire body, or the furry ears of a bear. In some of his more fanciful incarnations, the Bear's Son is a fully fledged hybrid, half-man and half-bear. When the boy is several years old, he helps his mother to escape from captivity, and in doing so, has to face and kill his ursine father. Usually, this deed marks the beginning of a remarkable career as a hero and adventurer.

The idea of human-bear procreation was not restricted to folklore, but can also be found in learned literature: William of Auvergne, the highly educated bishop of Paris in the thirteenth century, tells of a bear in Saxony that carried off a soldier's wife and kept her for years in his den. The bear fathered several children with her, and when she finally escaped, these children accompanied her in her flight. They earned a reputation as fierce soldiers and became known by the name *Orsini* (from Latin *ursus*, "bear").[34] Ursine ancestry was also associated with historical rulers and dynasties: The eleventh-century English Earl Siward of Northumbria allegedly descended from a bear[35]; the same motif can also be found in the writings of Scandinavian historiographers Saxo Grammaticus (twelfth century) and Olaus Magnus (sixteenth century), who trace the Danish royal house to a union between a bear and a woman.[36] In the eighteenth century, Enlightenment scholarship reinterpreted the "Bear's Son" tradition into a slightly more plausible version: The child was no longer the son of a bear; he was a human orphan who had been raised and nurtured by a she-bear. Philosophers and anthropologists were fascinated by reports of such "feral children" which, supposedly, offered them a unique opportunity to observe man in his most primitive stage, in a "state of nature."[37]

Whether half-bear or merely raised by bears, the fiercely heroic Bear's Sons of these stories came the closest to the Beorn whom Bilbo met and Gandalf knew so well. This semblance is certainly no coincidence: Tolkien was familiar with, and fascinated by, the folktales of the "Bear's Son".[38] In a short story from the 1940s entitled "Sellic Spell" [39], Tolkien wrote his own Bear's Son tale and envisioned an ursine origin for the hero of the Old English poem Beowulf, one of the main inspirations for The Hobbit.[40] "Sellic Spell" tells the story of a young boy who is found in the den of a great bear recently killed by some hunters. The child had evidently been fostered by the bear, and he has such a love for honey that he is eventually given the name "Bee-Wulf," Beowulf.[41]

In the initial manuscript of The Hobbit, the character that would later become Beorn was called Medwed.[42] "Medwed" is Russian for "honey-eater," an appropriate name for an ursine skin-changer. Tolkien borrowed the name from a book written by his friend and colleague R. W. Chambers, Professor of English at University College London. In his monograph "Beowulf: An Introduction to the Study of the Poem," which Tolkien appreciated greatly, Chambers had collected examples of Bear's Son stories, including the Russian folktale of "Ivashko Medvedko," "John Honey-Eater."[43]

When Tolkien later changed the name Medwed to Beorn, more appropriate to the Germanic setting of The Hobbit, he, again, chose a name from the Bear's Son tradition. In the medieval Vita Waldevi, the biography of a twelfth-century English saint, Earl Beorn Beresune is a valiant warrior of ursine ancestry: "The stories of the ancients tell us that Ursus (a certain nobleman whom the Lord, contrary to what normally happens in human procreation, allowed to be created from a white bear as a father and a noblewoman as a mother), begot Spratlingus; Spratlingus begot Ulsius; and Ulsius begot Beorn, who was nicknamed *Beresune*, that is, Bear's Son. This Beorn was Danish by race, a distinguished earl and famous soldier. As a sign, however, that due to part of his ancestry he was of a different species, nature had given him the ears of his father's line, namely those of a bear."[44]

The name "Beorn" is simply the Anglo-Saxon word for "bear," similar to Bjarki (Old Norse: "the little bear") and Beowulf (Old English: "the bee-wolf"—the one who lusts after bees and their honey, a literary circumlocution for a bear). But *beorn* is also a poetic designation for a warrior. Borrowing from the Bear's Son tradition, Tolkien had chosen a very appropriate name for his skin-changer—a name that implies his dual nature, both as a bear and a human warrior.[45]

Diabolic Fury: Witches and "Were-Bears" in the 16th and 17th Centuries

After the Middle Ages, the ambiguous relationship between human and bear gained an even more sinister quality. The sixteenth and seventeenth centuries marked the heyday of the European witch scare: Contemporary reports spoke of a diabolic conspiracy of enormous proportions that threatened to lure countless souls to eternal damnation. As a disciple of the devil, a murderer of children, and a sexual deviant, the witch was envisioned as an embodiment of evil, the quintessential criminal of the early modern period. Officials resorted to strict and often ruthless measures to overcome the alleged witch conspiracy, with torture and capital punishment being common. According to estimates, between 40,000 and 60,000 people were executed for witchcraft. Roughly 75 percent of the victims were women.

Animal transformations played an important role in the witch trials of the sixteenth and seventeenth centuries. Witches and warlocks supposedly took the shape of smaller animals such as cats or hares to commit thievery and to afflict their victims with spells, but they reportedly also transformed into larger and more dangerous creatures. A witch who intended to cause grievous bodily harm would, most commonly, assume the shape of a wolf—but bears were also a feasible alternative.[46] Such transformations were believed to be utterly devil-ish. Unlike Beorn's kind hospitality and brave service in the Battle of the Five Armies, a seventeenth-century person who assumed a bear's form was believed to be nothing more than an instrument of Satan.

In 1645, Mathias Perger, an itinerant peddler, was tried for witch-craft in the village of Rodeneck in South Tyrol. Under torture, Perger confessed to numerous crimes, including a pact with the devil, malev-olent sorcery, storm summoning, and the desecration of the host. In his wrongdoings, he was aided by a demon, Belial, who had assumed the shape of a seductive woman and had been his companion and lover for more than twenty years. According to the trial protocol, Belial had taught him to turn into a bear:

> In 1643 [...] Belial asked him if he wanted to become a bear. He could then eat meat to his heart's content. She was willing to provide him with a pelt that would give him the likeness of a bear. He agreed, and afterwards went to Lüsen, Afers and Villnöß in the shape of a bear. As a bear, he attacked many an ox, jumped on its back and bit it in the throat. Sometimes, he grabbed them at the horns and dragged and bit them until they were dead. Afterwards, he ate the best meat and put the rest in his pockets. [...] For almost nine weeks, he roamed as a bear and killed five or six oxen. Then he returned the skin to the beautiful woman.[47]

Based on his testimonial under torture, Perger was sentenced to death and burned at the stake. In Tyrolean folklore, he became legendary as one of the most infamous sorcerers of the Alpine val-leys. However, Perger's forays in bear shape were no unique occur-rence: In 1633, a woman in Pärnu in present-day Estonia confessed that she was able to turn into a bear while her fellow witches pre-ferred the traditional wolf shape.[48] Anne Bodenham, an elderly woman from Salisbury executed in 1653, could allegedly choose from a variety of animal shapes: Her repertoire reportedly included a bear and a mastiff, as well as a lion.[49] Witch-hunters in the Duchy of Lorraine reported several encounters with strange and even talking bears during the early seventeenth century; it is quite likely that they assumed these beings to be transformed sorcerers.[50] Bear transformations were also reported in North America: In 1661, a young woman in Plymouth Colony declared in public that her neighbor was a witch and had appeared to her in the shape of a bear. In this case, however, the magistrates turned against the accuser, who failed to produce evidence to support her claim and was found guilty of defamation.[51]

The relationship between witches and bears was, however, ambivalent[52]: According to popular belief, bears despised witches; they could sense if a person was guilty of sorcery and would try to avoid him or her. Tamed bears were sometimes used to determine the guilt of a suspect: If the bear refused to approach the defendant's house, it was seen as an indication that that person was indeed a witch. On the other hand, the devil himself reportedly appeared as a bear, as did the lesser demons that consorted with witches. In the thirteenth century, the previously mentioned bishop William of Auvergne explained that when demons intend to have sexual intercourse with mortal women and impregnate them, a bear's shape is the most suitable form for such fornication[53]—a theory undoubtedly based on the previously mentioned bestiary tradition that bears and humans are sexually compatible. A German ballad from the 1620s alludes to the same idea: In the story, the judges trick a witch into a confession by sending the hangman to visit her in the dungeon, clad in a bearskin. Fooled by the costume, the hapless witch believes that her demonic consort has come to save her and reveals her crimes to him.[54]

Judging from the trial of Mathias Perger and other seventeenth-century accounts of bear transformations, it seems that the "were-bear" was a variation of the more common werewolf motif. Taking the form of a predatory animal enabled a witch to attack people and livestock directly, even more devastating than the damage caused by malevolent sorcery. It was commonly believed that any animal transformation required a pact with the devil. In most cases, the accused confessed that they had been taught shape-changing by Satan, or that the Evil One provided them with an animal pelt or similar item that was a prerequisite for the magical transformation. Befitting their allegiance to the infernal powers, such "were-bears" appear in the sources as thoroughly evil individuals, killing and rampaging rather indiscriminately. In their chaotic and destructive attitude, they resemble medieval Norse berserkers—yet the aspect of shape-changing and transformation is far stronger emphasised.[55] When it comes to shape-shifting prowess, these wicked were-bears are certainly the closest analogy to Beorn in the European tradition.

But despite their similar abilities, a righteous warrior like Beorn could, at first glance, hardly be considered a kinsman to such villainous wretches. Tolkien's skin-changer, however, is an enigmatic being, and it takes quite a while until his good-natured character becomes apparent. Initially, neither Bilbo nor the readers know what to expect from Beorn. Gandalf seems worried that the hobbit or his dwarf companions might misbehave and arouse the skin-changer's wrath, and his ominous comments right before their encounter with Beorn are not exactly comforting. Beorn's gruff demeanor does little to ease his guests' anxiety.

Tolkien seems aware of the negative reputation of werewolves and were-bears, and toys with his readers' expectations: Could a shape-shifter be trusted? Would Beorn restrain his animalistic fury, or would he prove a far greater threat to our heroes than any goblin or Warg? It is hardly surprising that Bilbo has to spend an anxious night at Beorn's house, uncertain about the intentions of his ursine host: "There was a growling sound outside, and a noise as of some great animal scuffling at the door. Bilbo wondered what it was, and whether it could be Beorn in enchanted shape, and if he would come in as a bear and kill them. He dived under the blankets and hid his head, and fell asleep again in spite of his fears" (*The Hobbit*, 120–21).

Though Bilbo's fear was, in this case, unwarranted, he, like any denizen of Middle-earth, was well advised to be wary of skin-changers. Tolkien's world is populated by various shape-shifting beings, and many of them are as evil as their counterparts in sixteenth- and seventeenth-century accounts.[56] During the First Age, Sauron himself became known as the Lord of the Werewolves, residing at accursed Tol-in-Gaurhoth, the Isle of Werewolves. Accordingly, he assumed the shape of a wolf to do battle with Huan and Luthien, as recorded in *The Silmarillion*.[57] Some of the fell beasts survived into the Third

Age and continued to serve their master. In The Lord of the Rings, Gandalf mentions werewolves among the monstrous forces of Mordor.[58]

The long tradition of evil shape-shifters, in the European imagination as well as in Middle-earth, makes Beorn's virtuous nature, grim but just, appear even more outstanding than it would be otherwise. Without the stereotypical image of ferocious werewolves and were-bears that guides both Bilbo's and the readers' preconceptions, the encounter with mighty Beorn would probably turn out to be far less suspenseful and memorable.

Beorn and His Descendants

In his depiction of Beorn the skin-changer, J. R. R. Tolkien was able to draw on a rich literary tradition. Men and bears have a long common history in the European imagination, as shape-shifters, hybrids, and unlikely parents. By the time of Frodo's epic journey when the War of the Ring raged in Middle-earth, Beorn had passed away.[59] His offspring, the Beornings, were led by his son Grimbeorn the Old. "[I]t is said that for many generations the men of [Beorn's] line had the power of taking bear's shape, and some were grim man and bad, but most were in heart like Beorn, if less in size and strength" (*The Hobbit*, 279).[60] These few evil skin-changers, merely mentioned in passing, are the only beings of their kind in Tolkien's writing that resemble the antagonistic berserkers and diabolic "were-bears" of the medieval and early modern imagination.

Literary and folkloric traditions influenced the character of Beorn to a certain degree; yet, Tolkien interpreted the motif of the human-bear shape-shifter in an unprecedented fashion: As opposed to his medieval and early modern counterparts, Beorn is portrayed in a very positive way. The rough but good-natured and just Beorn has left his impact on modern fantasy literature, where man-bears are commonly depicted as benevolent creatures—from the "lawful good" were-bears of the *Dungeons & Dragons* role-playing franchise to Iorek Byrnison, the talking (although not shape-shifting) polar bear of Philip Pullman's *His Dark Materials trilogy*. As spiritual descendants of *The*

Hobbit's mighty skin-changer, they truly are "in heart like Beorn," and offer a sharp contrast to their vicious historical forebears.

Notes

1. All quotations from *The Hobbit* are taken from the 1997 edition by HarperCollins.

2. Tolkien himself was, initially, quite uncertain what kind of being Beorn actually was. The original manuscript of *The Hobbit* contains several fragmentary sentences on Beorn's nature, each crossed out by the author: "No one knows [> Most people disagree] > now knows whether he is an a magic bear with > a marvellous bear with magic > powers of magic, or a great man under an enchantment. 'Which is he?' said Bilbo who was becoming very interested: after all he had got to meet the 'person' before long. 'Neither' said the wizard 'He is a man [> an enchanter > a man.], one of <the> last of the old men who lived in these parts before the days of dragon. [...] He is an enchanter himself, and can be a bear if he wishes." Printed in John D. Rateliff, *The History of the Hobbit. Part One: Mr. Baggins* (London: HarperCollins, 2007), 247.

3. The character of Beorn has received considerable attention from Tolkien scholars: Cf. the chapter "Skin-Changing in More than One Sense: The Complexity of Beorn" in Marjorie Burns, *Perilous Realms. Celtic and Norse in Tolkien's middle-earth* (Toronto: University of Toronto Press, 2005), 30-43, based on the essay "J.R.R. Tolkien: The British and the Norse in Tension," *Pacific Coast Philology* 25 (1990), 49-59. See also Paul W. Lewis, "Beorn and Tom Bombadil: a tale of two heroes," *Mythlore* 25 (2007), 145-60; Jonathan A. Glenn, "To Translate a Hero: *The Hobbit as Beowulf Retold*," *Publications of the Arkansas Philological Association* 17 (1991), 13-34; Anders Stenström, "The Figure of Beorn," *Arda. Årsskrift för ardaforskning* 7 (1987), 44-83; Els Lapidaire, "Beorn, beren & berserkr," *Lembas. Tijdschrift van het Tolkien Genootschap "Unquendor"* 18 (1985), 22-23; Philip W. Helms and David L. Dettman, "Shape Changers in Tolkien's Middle-earth," in: *Wargs!*, ed. Philip W. Helms and David L. Dettman (Highland, Michigan: American Tolkien Society, 1978), 5-12.

4. Tolkien certainly allowed himself to be inspired by other sources as well when creating the character of Beorn. Bercilak de Hautdesert, for example, a character in the fourteenth-century poem *Sir Gawain and the Green Knight* which Tolkien himself translated to modern English, shares many traits with Beorn. Both are grim, stern men of imposing physique who dwell in the wilderness and act as hosts to the heroes. Cf. Burns, *Perilous Realms*, 34-35.

5. Snorri Sturluson, *Heimskringla. History of the Kings of Norway*, trans. Lee M. Hollander (Austin: University of Texas Press, 1964), 10.

6. Cf. Marjorie Burns, "Gandalf and Odin," in: *Tolkien's Legendarium. Essays on The History of Middle-earth*, ed. Verlyn Flieger and Carl F. Hostetter (Westport and London: Greenwood Press, 2000), 219-31. Tolkien himself referred to Gandalf as an "Odinic wanderer". See Humphrey Carpenter, ed., *Letters of J.R.R. Tolkien* (London: Allen & Unwin, 1981), 119.

7. Lee Milton Hollander, ed., *Old Norse Poems. The Most Important Non-Skaldic Verse Not Included in the Poetic Edda* (New York: Columbia University Press, 1936), 59.

8. Klaus von See, *Edda, Saga, Skaldendichtung. Aufsätze zur skandinavischen Literatur des Mittelalters* (Heidelberg: Carl Winter, 1981), 315.

9. Ibid., 313.

10. W. C. Green, ed., *The Story of Egil Skallagrimsson. Or, Egil's Saga* (Charleston: Forgotten Books, 2008), 177-80.

11. "Vatnsdœla saga," in: *Íslenzk fornrit. VIII. bindi*, ed. Einar Ólafur Sveinson (Reykjavík: Hið íslenzka fornritafélag, 1939), 97. Translation based on Stephan Grundy, "Shapeshifting and Berserkergang," *Disputatio: An International Transdisciplinary Journal of the Late Middle Ages* 3 (1998), 117.

12. Grundy, "Shapeshifting," 113-18.

13. Aðalheiður Guðmundsdóttir, "The Werewolf in Medieval Icelandic Literature," *Journal of English and Germanic Philology* 16 (2007), 281.

14. H. R. Ellis Davidson, "Shape-changing in the Old Norse Sagas," *Animals in Folklore*, ed. J. R. Porter and W. M. S. Russell (Ipswitch and Cambridge: Brewer, 1978), 126-42.

15. Cf. Grundy, "Shapeshifting," 116-17.

16. Green, *Story of Egil Skallagrimsson*, 15, 68-69. Cf. Grundy, "Shapeshifting," 108.

17. Cf. Michael P. McGlynn, "Bears, Boars and Other Socially Constructed Bodies in *Hrólfs saga kraka*," *Magic, Ritual and Witchcraft* 4 (2009), 152-75.

18. Stella M. Mills, trans., *The Saga of Hrolf Kraki* (Oxford: Blackwell, 1933), 83.

19. Ibid., 84.

20. According to Old Norse beliefs, the bear would be considered a *fylgia*. This is a very complex concept, difficult to express in modern terminology: A fylgia is a kind of spirit linked to a particular person. In some texts it seems to be part of that person, a projection or extra-corporeal manifestation of the individual's soul or being. Sometimes, however, it appears as a separate entity that accompanies and assists that person, similar to a guardian angel in catholic belief. Cf. McGlynn, "Bears, Boars, and Other Socially Constructed Bodies in *Hrólfs saga kraka*," 161-62; Grundy, "Shapeshifting," 111-12. The fylgia of another great saga hero, Gunnar of Hlíðarendi in *Njáls Saga*, was also observed in the shape of a bear. Cf. Davidson, "Shape-changing," 137.

21. McGlynn, "Bears, Boars, and Other Socially Constructed Bodies", 157, 163.

22. See, for example, Deborah Webster Rogers and Ivor A. Rogers, *J.R.R. Tolkien* (Boston: Twayne, 1980), 71; Timothy R. O'Neill: *The Individuated Hobbit: Jung, Tolkien, and the Archetypes of Middle-Earth* (Boston: Houghton Mifflin, 1979), 117; Stenström, "Figure of Beorn," 50.

23. Rudolf Simek, *Mittelerde. Tolkien und die germanische Mythologie* (München: Beck, 2005), 96.

24. Rateliff, *History*, 257-58.

25. Mills, *Saga of Hrolf Kraki*, 83.

26. Ibid., iii.

27. Unique among European predators, the bear's ability to walk upright gave it a certain human-like quality. Furthermore, the skinned carcass of a bear was said to resemble a human corpse. Cf. Will-Erich Peuckert, "Bär," *Handwörterbuch des deutschen Aberglaubens: Band I*, ed. Hanns Berchtold-Stäubli (Berlin and Leipzig: de Gruyter, 1927), 884.

28. Pliny, *Natural History*, book 8, 54.

29. Brian Cummings, "Pliny's Literate Elephant and the Idea of Animal Language in Renaissance Thought," *Renaissance Beasts: Of Animals, Humans and Other Wonderful Creatures*, ed. Erica Fudge (Urbana: University of Illinois Press, 2004), 177.

30. The eagle, for example, was believed to reject any of its young that are unable to stare unflinching into the sun. As such, it is an allegory of God who will reject the sinners who cannot bear His divine light. The pelican, which allegedly pierces its own breast with its beak to nourish its young with its blood is a representation of Christ who shed his blood for the redemption of humanity.

31. T. H. White, ed., *The Book of Beasts: Being a Translation from a Latin Bestiary of the Twelfth Century* (Madison: Parallel Press, 2002), 45-46.

32. Joyce E. Salisbury, *The Beast Within: Animals in the Middle Ages* (New York: Routledge, 1994), 83-84; Danielle Jacquart and Claude Thomasset, *Sexuality and Medicine in the Middle Ages* (Cambridge: Polity Press, 1988), 162-63.

33. Peuckert, "Bär," 886; Friedrich Panzer, *Studien zur germanischen Sagengeschichte: I. Beowulf* (München: C.H. Beck, 1910), 3-29; Maria Leach, ed., *Funk & Wagnalls Standard Dictionary of Folklore, Mythology, and Legend: Volume One* (New York: Funk & Wagnalls, 1949), 127; Stith Thompson, *Motif-Index of Folk-Literature: Volume One* (Copenhagen: Rosenkilde and Bagger, 1955), 461-66; Stanley L. Robe, "Wild Men and Spain's Brave New World," *The Wild Man Within: An Image in Western Thought from the Renaissance to Romanticism*, ed. Edward Dudley and Maximillian E. Novak (Pittsburgh: University of Pittsburgh Press, 1972), 40-41.

34. Guilielmus Alvernus, "De universo," *Guilielmi Alverni* [. . .] *opera omnia*, ed. Ioannes Dominicus Traianus (Venice: Zenari, 1591), 1009-10. Cf. Montague Summers, *The Werewolf in Lore and Legend* (Mineola: Dover Publications, 2003), 243. The name *Orsini* might be a reference to the famous Italian princely family of the same name, but this allusion is not stated explicitly.

35. J. Michael Stitt, *Beowulf and the Bear's Son: Epic, Saga, and Fairytale in Northern Germanic Tradition* (New York and London: Garland, 1992), 194; Axel Olrik, "Sivard den digre, en vikingesaga fra de danske I Nordengland," *Arkiv för nordisk filologi* 19 (1903), 199-200.

36. Thomas A. DuBois, "Diet and Deities: Contrastive Livelihoods and Animal Symbolism in Nordic Pre-Christian Religions," *More than Mythology: Narratives, Ritual Practices, and Regional Distribution in Pre-Christian Scandinavian Religions*, ed. Catharina Raudvere and Jens Peter Schjødt (Lund: Nordic Academic Press, 2012), 89; Carl-Martin Edsman, "The Story of the Bear Wife in Nordic Tradition," *Ethnos* 21 (1956), 50.

37. Maximillian E. Novak, "The Wild Man Comes to Tea," *The Wild Man Within: An Image in Western Thought from the Renaissance to Romanticism*, ed. Edward Dudley and Maximillian E. Novak (Pittsburgh: University of Pittsburgh Press, 1972), 186-97; E. Burnet Taylor, "Wild Men and Beast-Children," *Anthropological Review* 1 (1863), 27-28.

38. Cf. Stenström, "Figure of Beorn," 63.

39. J. R. R. Tolkien, "Sellic Spell," *Beowulf: A Translation and Commentary Together with Sellic Spell*, ed. Christopher Tolkien (London: HarperCollins, 2014), 358–84.

40. Bonniejean Christensen, "Tolkien's Creative Technique: *Beowulf* and *The Hobbit*," *Mythlore* 15 (1989), 4-10.

41. Douglas A. Anderson, "R. W. Chambers and *The Hobbit*," *Tolkien Studies* 3 (2006), 142.

42. Rateliff, *History*, 228-44. Cf. Anderson, "R. W. Chambers," 143.

43. R. W. Chambers, *Beowulf: An Introduction to the Study of the Poem with a Discussion of the Stories of Offa and Finn* (Cambridge: Cambridge University Press, 1932), 372-74.

44. "Vita et passio Waldevi comitis," *Chroniques Anglo-Normandes: Tome Second*, ed. Francisque Michel (Rouen, E. Frère, 1836), 104-05. Translation by Christine Rauer, *Beowulf and the Dragon: Parallels and Analogues* (Cambridge: D. S. Brewer, 2000), 163.

45. J. R. R. Tolkien, "On Translating Beowulf," *The Monsters and the Critics and Other Essays*, ed. Christopher Tolkien (London: Allen & Unwin, 1983), 54. See Simek, *Mittelerde*, 97; Burns, *Perilous Realms*, 37; Stenström, "Figure of Beorn," 46.

46. Cf. Peuckert, "Bär," 886, 890.

47. Ignaz Zingerle, *Barbara Pachlerin, die Sarnthaler Hexe, und Mathias Perger, der Lauterfresser: Zwei Hexenprozesse* (Innsbruck: Wagner'sche Buchhandlung, 1858), 40.

48. Maia Madar, "Estonia I: Werewolves and Poisoners," *Early Modern European Witchcraft: Centres and Peripheries*, ed. Bengt Ankarloo and Gustav Henningsen (Oxford: Clarendon Press, 1990), 271.

49. Malcolm Gaskill, "Witchcraft, Politics, and Memory in Seventeenth-Century England," *The Historical Journal* 50 (2007), 292.

50. Robin Briggs, "Dangerous Spirits: Shapeshifting, Apparitions, and Fantasy in Lorraine Witchcraft Trials," *Werewolves, Witches, and Wandering Spirits: Traditional Belief & Folklore in Early Modern Europe*, ed. Kathryn A. Edwards (Kirksville: Truman State University Press, 2002), 18.

51. Richard Godbeer, *The Devil's Dominion. Magic and Religion in Early New England* (Cambridge: Cambridge University Press, 1992), 153.

52. Peuckert, "Bär", 890.

53. Guilielmus Alvernus, "De universo," 1009. Cf. Michael Uebel, "The Foreigner Within: The Subject of Abjection in *Sir Gowther*," *Meeting the Foreign in the Middle Ages*, ed. Albrecht Classen (New York and London: Routledge, 2002), 98.

54 Montague Summers, *The History of Witchcraft and Demonology* (London: Routledge & Kegan Paul, 1973), 134.

55. Early modern scholars debated intensively how such an animal metamorphosis could be achieved. Most refused to believe that the devil could physically transform a witch into an animal—such a feat would have resembled an act of creation, and that was God's prerogative. The devil had to rely on deceit: He could shroud the witch in an illusion so that she appeared like a beast. Alternatively, he could commit the atrocities himself while the witch was sleeping, then send her a dream and make her believe that she had been a wolf or a bear and that she was responsible for the damage he had caused. As it seems, the Prince of Lies made quite an effort to deceive his own followers. But the illusionary nature of animal transformations did not lessen the witches' sin: They desired to be a bear or a wolf and indulge in the carnage, so, according to the opinion of the time, they were guilty, even if the devil had to perform all their evil deeds for them. Cf. Nicole Jaques-Lefèvre, "Such an Impure, Cruel and Savage Beast... Images of the Werewolf in Demonological Works," *Werewolves, Witches, and Wandering Spirits: Traditional Belief & Folklore in Early Modern Europe*, ed. Kathryn A. Edwards (Kirksville: Truman State University Press, 2002) 184-85; H. Sidky, *Witchcraft, Lycanthropy, Drugs, and Disease: An Anthropological Study of the European Witch-Hunts* (New York: Peter Lang, 1997), 218-20; Michael Siefener, *Hexerei im Spiegel der Rechtstheorie: Das crimen magiae in der Literatur von 1574 bis 1608* (Frankfurt am Main: Peter Lang, 1992), 145-53.

56. Helms and Dettman, "Shape Changers, 9-11."

57. J. R. R. Tolkien, *The Silmarillion* (London: Allen & Unwin, 1977), 156, 174-75.

58. J. R. R. Tolkien, *The Fellowship of the Ring, Being the First Part of The Lord of the Rings* (London: HarperCollins, 2002), 292.

59. Tolkien himself stated in a letter written in 1954: "Beorn is dead; see vol. I p. 241. He appeared in *The Hobbit*. It was then the year Third Age 2940 (Shire-reckoning 1340). We are now in the years 3018-19 (1418-19). Though a skin-changer and no doubt a bit of a magician, Beorn was a Man." Carpenter, *Letters*, 178.

60. Cf. Burns, *Perilous Realms*, 40.

CHAPTER 11

From Whence Came the Great Worms?:

History and Tolkien's Monsters

Jessica Monteith-Chachuat

"Suddenly in the woods beyond The Water a flame leapt up—
probably somebody lighting a wood-fire—and he thought of
plundering dragons settling on his quiet Hill and kindling it all to
flames. He shuddered; and very quickly he was plain Mr. Baggins
of Bag-End, Under-Hill, again."

— *The Hobbit*, 16

Fairy tales are not cozy stories: The worlds of fairies are populated
by monsters and monstrous people as well as heroes and her-
oines. *The Hobbit* was first conceived by J. R. R. Tolkien as a bed-

time story for his sons John, Michael, and Christopher, and included many fairy-tale elements drawn from history that would entertain and amuse children: elves, dwarves, and wizards, as well as Tolkien's own creation, the hobbits. Tolkien set them up against a host of monsters drawn from folklore and fairy tales: trolls, goblins, wolves, spiders, and even a fearsome dragon. In the stories he told his children, Gollum was uniquely Tolkien's creation, but is as monstrous in nature as any Warg, goblin, or medieval storybook foe.

The monsters in *The Hobbit* have their own personalities and lives, just as monsters did in historical mythology. Independent of and parallel to the five free races—elves, men, dwarves, Ents, and hobbits—are five monstrous races in *The Hobbit*: goblins, Wargs, dragons, spiders, and trolls. These monsters do not exist simply to hinder the progress of Bilbo and the dwarves; each of these groups has its own interests and agendas that only occasionally intersect with those of Bilbo and his friends. In some instances the monsters' actions determine the roles of the heroes: it is Smaug, lording over the Lonely Mountain, who determines the actions of Thorin's company, rather than vice versa. The magical creatures of *The Hobbit* are akin to the traditional monsters in folklore serving as a particular challenge, such as Grendel and his mother testing Beowulf. The monsters of Middle-earth also speak, think, plot, plan, and play, as seen, for example, in Gollum's riddle game with Bilbo. They are truly human as well as entirely monstrous, fitting neatly into the long tradition of folkloric sagas that Tolkien studied.

The monsters in *The Hobbit* demonstrate remarkably distinct personalities that set them apart from each other. The three trolls are presented as typical London East-End thugs, complete with comedic Cockney slang. The goblins have their own economy, cultural memory, hierarchical society, and even poetry. The goblins' accomplices, the wolves, also live in a culture with rigid social ranks, a complex language, and cutthroat politics. The Mirkwood spiders, like the larger and more terrifying Shelob that later battles Frodo and Sam, do not participate in the wider affairs of Middle-earth, yet they almost end the adventure of the heroes in Tolkien's stories. Finally, as the culmination of all monsters, Smaug the dragon is intelligent and perfectly capable of manipulating a situation to his own benefit. He is strong and old, and a worthy foe for any warrior. From the trolls to Smaug, *The Hobbit*'s monsters are distinctive, independent, and dangerous foes that stand in stark contrast to the heroes who fight them.

Tolkien knew that monsters were as important as heroes. The monsters of *The Hobbit* derive some of their history and characteristics from folklore and fairy tales, which Tolkien knew from his studies as Professor of Anglo-Saxon at Oxford. A dedicated student of Anglo-Saxon literature Tolkien was a recognized expert on the subject of dragons (he gave a keynote address on the subject at Oxford University[1]). In an essay written while he was working on *The Hobbit*, Tolkien argued that there were "many heroes but very few good dragons." The trolls, goblins, Wargs, and dragons of Middle-earth rely on traditions that Tolkien borrowed from historic folklore and fairy tales as well as his own inventions to become some of the most important characters in *The Hobbit*.

"Be Stone to You": The Lore of Trolls

The three trolls encountered by Thorin and company on the road to the Misty Mountains are unique in Tolkien's Middle-earth in comparison to *The Hobbit*'s other monsters. The other trolls Tolkien mentions, in the later Lord of the Rings series, are dumb brutes, mere pawns in Sauron's army. But not William, Bert, and Tom, who first capture Bilbo and then the rest of the dwarves. They still may not be smart, but they're crafty enough to catch the adventurers.

Here's how Tolkien describes them:

Three very large persons sitting round a very large fire of beech-logs. They were toasting mutton on long spits of wood, and licking the gravy off their fingers. There was a fine toothsome smell. Also there was a barrel of good drink at hand, and they were drinking out of jugs. But they were trolls. Obviously trolls. Even Bilbo, in spite of his sheltered life, could see that: from the great heavy faces of them, and their size, and the shape of their legs, not to mention their language, which was not drawing-room fashion at all, at all. (*The Hobbit*, 33)

The trolls speak a Cockney dialect of working-class Londoners very different from the language of Bilbo, the dwarves, or Gandalf. William terms Bilbo a "poor little blighter" and his fellow troll, Tom, a "booby" (*The Hobbit*, 35–39). But it takes more than working-class slang to make a troll, as Bilbo notes. In size and in appearance, not to mention appetite, Tolkien's trolls are monstrous.

William, Bert, and Tom are an interesting case study for Tolkien's use of folkloric elements in *The Hobbit*. These three trolls are much more akin to dwarves—not monsters—from medieval sagas with which Tolkien was familiar. For example, Tolkien's trolls turn to stone in the sunlight, a concept he created by drawing upon medieval legends of dwarves, who lived in caves and darkness. Tolkien took an interesting literary turn when he wrote the dwarves as allies to Men and Elves, rather than adversaries. Furthermore, Tolkien seems to have conceived of these three trolls as being entirely isolated from the larger events in Middle-earth, again like the dwarves in some medieval sagas. Regin, Sigurd's dwarvish foster father in the *Volsunga Saga*, is an example of an evil dwarf from folklore and fable, who operates in isolation to the larger goings-on in the kingdom. Regin plans to kill Sigurd for the treasure Sigurd has just won, but is killed in turn before he can act on his murderous intent[2]. Tolkien later suggested in *The Lord of the Rings* that trolls were the corrupted form of Ents, the majestic and mobile tree-creatures that guard the forests of Middle-earth.

Tolkien's trolls don't have a complex society, economy, or culture. The trolls seem to participate in the broader affairs of Middle-earth only as thieves, based on the fact that Thorin and Gandalf discover the swords Glamdring and Orcrist in the trolls' cave. The trolls are not allied with the more ominous goblins, nor do they make any mention of the Necromancer of Dol Guldur, Sauron's disguise as he lurks on the edge of Mirkwood. In fact, in the original draft of *The Hobbit*, Bert was of a mind to let little Bilbo go! In the final published versions of *The Hobbit*, they are not malicious: these three trolls are merely hungry. Interestingly, these are the only trolls we encounter at all in *The Hobbit*—none appear in the Battle of the Five Armies.

The three trolls are the first in a long series of monsters that Bilbo must overcome on his journey into the Wild. They are also the first real challenge that Bilbo faces, and his first opportunity to test his mettle and prove himself to the dwarves. He fails, of course, but therein lays the real purpose of the humorous Cockney-trolls – to demonstrate the perils of the Wild to Bilbo, and to act as the first antagonist, often encountered by the literary hero in Anglo-Saxon epic, against whom they first test their mettle, and fail. These are not real monsters like the monsters Bilbo encounters later in his journey. Despite their plans to eat the dwarves, these trolls are not much of a threat to Thorin and company—when they debate on how to cook their captives, they are easily confused by Gandalf's ruse of throwing his voice into the conversation:

> "No good roasting 'em now, it'd take all night," said a voice. Bert thought it was William's.
> "Don't start the argument all over again, Bill," he said, "or it *will* take all night."
> "Who's a'arguing?" said William, who thought it was Bert that had spoken. (*The Hobbit*, 38-39)

The trolls even seem very similar to Bilbo and the dwarves in some respects: They enjoy camaraderie and good food. At the same time, they clearly have a distinct language and civilization that exists entirely separately from Bilbo and the dwarves, and their monstrous plan to consume the captured dwarves is truly inhuman. Despite that, Bilbo and company quickly overcome the trolls, who serve as an easy introduction to the dangers posed by monsters that appear later in *The Hobbit*.

"Their Wicked Deeds": Goblins and Wargs as Fairy-Tale Monsters

The goblins and the Wargs, encountered next along the road into the Wild, are more akin to proper medieval monsters than the trolls. Although their culture is obviously very rich and musical, the goblins are not humorous like Tom, Bert, and William. They do not have a comical argument on how to dispose of the dwarves. The goblins are antagonists to be feared—they even pursue Thorin's company for a significant distance once they have escaped the tunnels in the Misty Mountains, and they play a significant role in the Battle of the Five Armies, marching en masse against Men and Elves. Tolkien credited George MacDonald, author of *The Princess and the Goblin*, a popular Victorian children's fantasy story, for the personalities of his goblins in *The Hobbit*. Tolkien's goblins are also influenced by Germanic literature, where goblins make an early appearance as Mares in the Ynglinga Saga as devious little hobgoblins who bring on nightmares.

Goblins already had a long history in Tolkien's world by the time of *The Hobbit*, having been introduced to Middle-earth as servants of Morgoth, the great villain of *The Silmarillion*. Tolkien rejected the idea of the goblins being created outright by Morgoth, opting instead for Aristotle's view that evil cannot create, but can only twist what has already been created. According to Tolkien's private notes, goblins are one and the same with the orcs encountered in *The Lord of the Rings*, whose name seems to derive from the Latin Orcus, meaning Hell.[3] This suggests that the goblins of *The Hobbit* are every bit as malicious as the orcs of *The Lord of the Rings*. Yet, like the trolls, Tolkien's goblins are often creative as well as destructive, as when they sing taunting songs while they prepare to burn Bilbo and his companions alive. The goblins of *The Hobbit* are not easily defeated: They are treacherous opponents in their own right. In fact, it is the goblins who return at the end of Bilbo's journey, at the Battle of the Five Armies, and not Smaug, the fearsome dragon.

The goblins in *The Hobbit* established their own economy, government, poetry, and social system. The Great Goblin rules their underground society with protection provided by his thuggish guards. They seem self-sufficient and owe no debt to the powerful Necromancer, Sauron in disguise, who inhabits the woods nearby. It is even suggested in *The Hobbit* that the goblins are not averse to working with some of the dwarves in order to achieve a common goal, because both races prefer subterranean spaces. "They did not hate dwarves especially, no more than they hated everybody and everything, and particularly the orderly and prosperous; in some parts wicked dwarves had even made alliances with them" (*The Hobbit*, 70). This stunningly well-adapted society hardly seems monstrous at all, yet goblins are the clearest example of what might be considered monstrous in popular understanding, because they are so close to the free races in skills and cultures while so set against them in their wars and their alliance with the Wargs.

The Wargs, fearsome, intelligent wolves who are allied with the goblins in *The Hobbit*, are another serious threat to the company. In *The Hobbit*, Wargs appear as mere wolves and not the hybrid creatures seen in *The Lord of the Rings*. But the wolves have a long history in Tolkien's world—in *The Silmarillion*, which Tolkien worked on when he wrote *The Hobbit*, Sauron is a werewolf and is accompanied by the great wolf Caurach, whose name means "the Red Maw." Caurach, the father of wolves, terrorizes his master's enemies and sits beneath Sauron's throne to devour men and elves. He and the other wolves of *The Silmarillion* are truly monstrous servants of Sauron. The wolves of *The Hobbit* are not as terrible as Caurach and Sauron, but they live close to the Necromancer's forest and participate in the Battle of the Five Armies alongside the goblins.

In 1967, J. R. R. Tolkien explained in a private letter that the name, warg, is derived from the Germanic *wearg*, literally meaning both outlaw and wolf.[4] This double meaning was well known in medieval England, where, according to the thirteenth-century legal scholar Henry Bracton, an outlaw who fled from justice must "bear the wolf's head and in consequence perish without judicial inquiry."[5] In *The Hobbit*, Wargs inhabit the fields and woods, traditional dominions of medieval outlaws. With their own language, hierarchy, and an independent alliance with the goblins, Wargs are so human-like they could almost be considered werewolves. Werewolves in medieval French and English literature were ". . . ferocious beast(s) which, when possessed by this madness, devour(ed) men, cause(d) great damage, and dwell(ed) in vast forests."[6] The fear of werewolves during that time period was very real, and though the wolves in *The Hobbit* manage to escape from Gandalf's fiery pinecones relatively unscathed, a man or woman accused of being a werewolf in the Middle Ages would have been tortured and burnt alive. It's no big intellectual or imaginative leap from Wargs to werewolves, as Sauron had the ability to change his shape into that of a wolf and lived for a time during the First Age on the Isle of Werewolves.

Even if they are not werewolves, the Wargs are still very monstrous to Thorin and company: Only Gandalf understands their language, and his knowledge doesn't make the Wargs seem more approachable to the wizard or the dwarves. From the Wargs' refuge in the tall trees, Gandalf hears their plans to renew their alliance with the goblins and kill the woodsmen and their families who have been settling near their forest. Bilbo and the dwarves are a surprise to the Wargs when they arrive, but not an opportunity the Wargs will ignore: "So the Wargs had no intention of going away and letting the people up the trees escape, at any rate not until morning. And long before that, they said, goblin soldiers would be coming down from the mountains; and goblins can climb trees, or cut them down" (*The Hobbit*, 95). Because Tolkien's Wargs are so human-like, they are more villainous than the wolves of history and legend.

Tolkien's goblins and Wargs terrorize Bilbo and his companions in the traditional folkloric manner. Fairy tales and folkloric epics involving wolves and werewolves abound in European tradition long before the Roman foundation myth had the city's founder, Romulus, suckled by a she-wolf. Tolkien's Wargs draw on the memory of monstrous wolves in Anglo-Saxon and Latin literature, and the contradictory interpretations of biological wolves. The Wargs in *The Hobbit* are also much like the wolf in *Little Red Riding Hood*: intelligent rogues out for their own good. The Wargs comprehend that what they are doing is against the forces of good represented by Bilbo, Thorin, Gandalf, and the rest of their company. They're smart and possessed of the very real terror of sharp teeth and hungry mouths. Even when Gandalf rains down fire against them, they are relentlessly monstrous:

> All round the clearing of the Wargs fire was leaping. But the wolf-guards did not leave the trees. Maddened and angry they were leaping and howling round the trunks, and cursing the dwarves in their horrible language, with their tongues hanging out, and their eyes shining as red and fierce as the flames. (*The Hobbit*, 97)

"Lazy Lob and Crazy Cob": Medieval Fears and the Mirkwood Spiders

The Mirkwood spiders are presumably the offspring, or at least the relations of, Shelob, the terrifying spider that would fight Frodo and Sam in *The Return of the King*, which in turn was the descendent of Ungoliant, a being of primordial chaos or night. The spiders that Bilbo encounters, and eventually slays, in Mirkwood do not have quite such an impressive role as Shelob or Ungoliant, but it is against the spiders that Bilbo first draws blood with Sting (in fact, it is against the spiders that Sting is christened by an excited Bilbo), and is left to rescue his companions. This a major step for Bilbo as an adventurer and a great leap forward from the situation in the Misty Mountains when Bilbo might have been alone, but was only responsible for his own well-being. Against the spiders, Bilbo must protect both himself and the dwarves. It seems doubtful that Tolkien based his spiders on actual arachnids, as spiders have neither stingers nor beaks.[7] Whether or not Tolkien was aware or the anatomy of real spiders, these features made the Mirkwood spiders a more threatening, or monstrous, presence.

The Mirkwood spiders are the first monsters encountered in *The Hobbit* that Bilbo is forced to deal with alone. For the purposes of *The Hobbit*, the spiders are every bit as important as Grendel, the monstrous half-man faced and defeated by Beowulf at the outset of the epic Beowulf, and the mighty Dragon that ends the hero's life.[8]

Some folkloric and medieval stories about spiders were tragic, like the tale of Arachne in the Classical Greek tradition, who challenged Athena to a weaving contest and won but was rewarded with being transformed into a spider. Other medieval ideas of spiders were negative. The fifteenth-century French king Louis XI was sometimes called "The Spider King" due to his plots and double-dealings. Bilbo's opponents were rather more straightforward, if far more horrific. But they are not too big for little Bilbo; he has the capability to defeat them.

The spiders of Mirkwood are fairly isolated from the affairs of the wider world—like the trolls, they do not appear in the Battle of the Five Armies. By slaying the Mirkwood spiders in the story, Bilbo is joining a very select group of heroes who achieved victory against these most alien of monsters: Earendil the Mariner, Beren, and Samwise (who did not actually kill Shelob, but fought her to a standstill). The monstrous spiders of Mirkwood are the particular bane of the Wood-elves whose realm they infest. They are also abhorred by Beorn the shape-shifter, and even Gandalf warns the dwarves against them. And yet the spiders, like the trolls, goblins, and Wargs, have their own language and social organization. They are monstrous because they have reason and forethought, but they still eat humans, dwarves, and hobbits. The spiders are not as clever as the goblins and the Wargs, however; they are easily duped by Bilbo and enraged by his silly songs. This is unfortunate because Ungoliant and Shelob are so deeply monstrous, despite Shelob having no voice of her own. The Mirkwood spiders had the potential to be hazardous to the company of dwarves and to therefore act as truly monstrous adversaries, but such an approach by Tolkien would have not been in keeping with the tone of the book. Instead he took advantage of the spiders in later works, when they could adequately be compared to even greater monsters like Sauron and Glaurung. The Mirkwood spiders are Bilbo's first successful foray as a warrior in his own right: They have terrorized his friends and left him with no choice but to attack. From his conquest, Bilbo gains respect and a small amount of glory. However, Bilbo still has to face the greatest monster in *The Hobbit*—the dragon.

Fear the dragon: a medieval siege
weapon inspired more terror when
disguised as the legendary monster.

Here Be Dragons: Smaug and His Legendary Kin

Smaug is the product of the dragon fascination held by Tolkien since
he was a boy, and also of the medieval lore he knew better than anyone else, thanks to his studies in Anglo-Saxon literature.[9] Dragons
have a long history of involvement in folklore and fairy tales, including Fafnir, the dwarf of Icelandic sagas whose greed for treasure transformed him into a dragon guarding his hoard, and the dragon who
battled St. George. Dragons also appear in Japanese, Chinese, and
even African folklore and mythology.[10] Medieval European associated dragons with comets and meteors. Both fiery and unpredictable
objects that raced across the sky.

 Smaug's monstrosity is due in part to mystery, in which he is
shrouded for so much of the story. The dwarves, for example, describe
the outright destruction of their kingdom to Bilbo, but they do not

describe the dragon. But the lore of dragons speaks for itself: They are large, scaly, flying creatures that are immensely destructive. We do not hear from or directly encounter Smaug until Bilbo is already inside the mountain. Bilbo is afraid of Smaug long before he ever lays eyes on the dragon, and rightly so. In a scene deleted from an early draft of the story, known as the Pryftean fragment, Bilbo even dreams of the dragon laying waste to the fields of Hobbiton as he listens to the dwarves' music.[11] First, Bilbo sees the glow of Smaug, and then the red-gold dragon's fiery air and sheer size take his breath away: "Smaug lay, with wings folded like an immeasurable bat, turned partly on one side, so that the hobbit could see his underparts and his long pale belly crusted with gems and fragments of gold from his long lying on his costly bed" (*The Hobbit*, 198). Although the dragon is still vastly intimidating, Bilbo's meeting with him cuts the monster down to size—Bilbo's survey of Smaug's belly provides the secret to the monster's downfall: a weak spot in his chest armor. As soon as Smaug can be seen, described, and therefore defeated, he loses some of his monstrosity.

Like all of Tolkien's monsters, Smaug speaks and has a sophisticated understanding of the world around him, even engaging in a riddle contest with Bilbo the Barrel-Rider, as the hobbit calls himself in conversation with the sneering dragon. This is part of what makes Smaug particularly monstrous—Bilbo himself is lured into a false sense of safety by the idle words of the dragon—that is, until he has the hair on the back of his heels singed off! Smaug's monstrosity even rubs off on some of those who would act against him—namely, the dwarves and the Master of Lake-town. Not only does Smaug accuse the dwarves of trying to cheat Bilbo out of his reward, but once they are in full possession of the treasure, they become dragon-like themselves in the fervor to protect the gold they eventually win. The Master of Lake-town receives a share of the treasure, but will starve to death in the wastelands trying to protect his riches. Smaug's complete understanding of "normal" behavior, and his disregard for it, makes him a monster. Furthermore, his size and strength make him a monster worthy of a heroic epic.

Although we are told by Smaug himself that he has "laid low the warriors of old" (*The Hobbit*, 207), we do not get a demonstration of his full monstrous power until he begins the search for the dwarves in earnest, and commences his final attack on Lake-town. All of this is Smaug's own doing; he is the only dragon unaffiliated with any master in Tolkien's world. In *The Silmarillion*, Glaurung, the Father of Dragons, wreaked destruction on behalf of Melkor, commanding battalions of goblins against the elves. In *The Lord of the Rings*, Gandalf speculated what damage Smaug might have done had he survived — including destroying Rivendell — although the independent dragon actually might never have roused himself from the Lonely Mountain on Sauron's behalf.

Dragons are the most persistent monsters in Middle-earth. Tolkien, who lectured on *Beowulf*'s dragon just a few years prior to *The Hobbit*'s release and had also given a lecture on the topic at Oxford's Natural History Museum, considered dragons as a worthy challenge for a great hero. With the dragon in *The Hobbit*, Tolkien borrowed from Beowulf, a medieval epic that Tolkien believed stood "amid but above the petty wars of princes, and surpass[ed] the dates and limits of historical periods, however important"[12]. Bilbo, however, was no great hero but rather a personification of the "everyman," and so not fit to do battle with a dragon. Smaug's death, therefore, was brought about by Bard, a man of Dale with old royal blood and a special arrow; the hero of this encounter, if not of the story.

"He was Gollum": The Monster in All of Us

Gollum, who plays such a small role in *The Hobbit*, and who might have been forgotten entirely had it not been for his "precious" Ring, is a monster unlike any other in Middle-earth. In fact, we find out in *The Lord of the Rings* that he was once a hobbit of Stoorish origin. Gollum is not a monster in the traditional sense, not like dragons and trolls are monsters: Gollum's nature is monstrous, but he did not start out in life that way. Because of the warped power of the One Ring, Gollum evolves into a monstrous creature suited for living in complete darkness. He is transformed by the power of the Ring into "a small slimy creature . . . as dark as darkness, except for two big round pale eyes in his thin face" (*The Hobbit*, 67). The transformation of Gollum is similar to the Classical era transformations of Lycan and Nebuchadnezzar, both punished by God for blasphemy (and in Lycan's case, cannibalism) and turned into beasts. Gollum is the mirror held up to Bilbo, or a future vision of what Bilbo might become if he allows the Ring to rule him. This concept of the beast in the everyman is a theme frequently found in werewolf stories of the medieval period. Gerald of Wales wrote in the twelfth century about an entire Irish village's population that was transformed into werewolves by a saint as punishment for unspecified crimes. He could only identify the two wolves he encountered on the road as werewolves because they were able to pull back their wolf-skins to reveal human bodies underneath.[13] In a very real sense, Gollum wears the wolf-skin that could be meant for Bilbo.

Like the hobbits, Gollum does not have a direct counterpart in Icelandic literature, but he can be compared to Milton's Satan in *Paradise Lost*[14] who, after his fall from Grace, was ever seeking that which he had lost, much like Gollum was ever seeking the Ring. Gollum can also be compared to the creature Grendel in *Beowulf*: Both are monsters who have learned to live in quiet, dark, and lonely places, but who are violent when roused by the hero. Gollum and Grendel are both minor characters in a story that is much larger than their individual problems, and yet they are pivotal to the development of the narrative as well as to that of the hero himself. One of the most important similarities between Grendel and Gollum is that both are invisible. Although Grendel is never described in any detail by the author of *Beowulf*, Tolkien describes Gollum as having the ability to become invisible when wearing the Ring. After Bilbo steals the Ring from him, Gollum disappears completely from the narrative. The idea of the invisible monster, like Gollum, is a very old theme that did not originate with *The Hobbit* but was featured in works as early as Malory's *Le Morte d'Arthur*.[15] In *The Hobbit*, Gollum does not even have a proper name.

That Gollum reappears in *The Lord of the Rings* is a testament to the appeal of the monster in all of us. There is a thrill associated with seeing the wicked side of ourselves, and in seeing a small hero overcome his own darker half to triumph at the end of the day. Bilbo's mighty "leap in the dark" (*The Hobbit*, 86) that wins him freedom from

Gollum's cave is more than just a leap into the light, away from the dank, dark tunnels that Gollum loves; Bilbo is leaving Gollum, his monstrous counterpart, behind. But he is taking a small token of his own deeply rooted monstrosity away from the Misty Mountains: the One Ring.

"The Wild Was Still the Wild": Monsters and Their Legacy

Bilbo's journey home at the end of the story isn't an easy task. "He had many hardships and adventures before he got back. The Wild was still the Wild, and there were many other things in it in those days besides goblins . . ." (*The Hobbit*, 267). The monsters in *The Hobbit*—from the truly frightening variety such as Smaug, the Mirkwood spiders, and Gollum to the comedic trolls and singsong goblins—invigorate Tolkien's narrative with the richness of folklore. Tolkien's monsters are drawn from traditions in medieval history, literature, and popular imagination that he respected and understood.

In the wilderness, Bilbo faces and overcomes monsters, from trolls to dragons, that aren't as wild as he might expect. In fact, like the monsters of medieval myth and folklore, they seem more akin to the Free Races—talkative, sociable, and sometimes frighteningly clever—while at the same time their monstrous appetites threaten the very existence of Bilbo and his friends. Bilbo, who begins his journey living cozily in Hobbiton, tucked away from the Wild and the dangers of northern Middle-earth, exemplifies the model of civilized man, growing up and measuring his growth by how far he has come from the wilderness.[16] But how far is that, in the end? *The Hobbit* draws on epic traditions that warned adventurers of the elemental danger of dragons, wild beasts, and other, more human-like monsters, always lurking on the edge of civilization.

Notes

1. John D. Rateliff, *The History of the Hobbit: Return to Bag-End* (London: Harper Collins, 2007), 527.

2. See J. R. R. Tolkien, *The Legend of Sigurd & Gudrun* (New York: Houghton Mifflin Harcourt, 2009) for a more in-depth study.

3. John D. Rateliff, *The History of the Hobbit: Mr. Baggins* (London: HarperCollins, 2007), 217.

4. Ibid., 217.

5. Paul Dalton and John C. Appleby, *Outlaws in Medieval and Early Modern England: Crime, Government and Society*, c. 1066-c.1600 (Farnham, UK: Ashgate, 2009), 41.

6. *The Lais of Marie de France*, trans. Glyn S. Burgess and Keith Busby (Toronto: Penguin Books, 2003), 68.

7. Rateliff, *The History of the Hobbit: Mr. Baggins*, 331.

8. Tolkien, "Beowulf: The Monsters and the Critics," *Proceedings of the British Academy* 22 (1936), 245–95.

9. Tolkien's experiences are discussed and analyzed in Randel Helms, *Tolkien's World* (London: Granada, 1978).

10. Stith Thompson, *The Folktale* (New York: Holt Rinehart and Winston, 1946), 25–30.

11. Rateliff, *The History of the Hobbit: Return to Bag-End*, 531.

12. Tolkien, "Beowulf: The Monsters and the Critics." *Proceedings of the British Academy*, 22 (1936) 277.

13. Gerald of Wales, *The History and Topography of Ireland* (Harmondsworth, UK: Penguin, 1983) 71–72.

14. Helms, 37.

15. Rateliff, *The History of the Hobbit: Mr. Baggins*, 183.

16. Barry Holstun Lopez, *Of Wolves and Men* (New York: Scribner, 1979), 141.

CHAPTER 12

"Until the Dragon Comes":

Literature, Language, and
The Hobbit

Martha Driver

"There he lay, a vast red-golden dragon, fast asleep; a thrumming came from his jaws and nostrils, and wisps of smoke, but his fires were low in slumber. Beneath him, under all his limbs and his huge coiled tail, and about him on all side stretching away across the unseen floors, lay countless piles of precious things, gold wrought and unwrought, gems and jewels, and silver-red-stained in the ruddy light."

—*The Hobbit*, 198

The *Hobbit*, like the later *Lord of the Rings* series, is a form of fan fiction, a continuation and elaboration of themes first seen in the

Anglo-Saxon and later medieval works John Ronald Reuel Tolkien loved, taught, and translated. Tolkien's engagement with the primary sources, whether *Beowulf*, Icelandic sagas, or the Finnish *Kalevala*, as well as Old Norse, Germanic, Anglo-Saxon, and Middle English linguistics and literature, prepared him as an artist, stocking his imagination with powerful language, imagery, and characters.

The *Hobbit*, or *There and Back Again*, was published by George Allen & Unwin on September 21, 1937, illustrated by the author and with a dust jacket of his own design. The medievalist reader acquainted with eth, thorn, and yogh, letter forms frequently found in medieval literature, will be able to decipher the runes on the book jacket and on Thror's map fairly readily. Readers' familiarity with medieval literature helps them to recognize in the heroic character of Beorn one re-creation of the Anglo-Saxon hero Beowulf. *Sir Gawain and the Green Knight*, written in the fourteenth century, is another medieval source that Tolkien, a Rawlinson and Bosworth Professor of Anglo-Saxon at Oxford and a fellow of Pembroke College, translated for modern-day readers; like *The Hobbit* (and *Beowulf*), it concerns the testing of the hero. The Arkenstone, the centerpiece of Smaug's hoard, not only derives from the dragon hoard as described in *Beowulf*, but also has links to *Sir Orfeo*, a work that Tolkien edited and translated into modern English. The otherworldly fairies of *Sir Orfeo* provide one parallel for the Elves of the Woodland Realm, who, like them, hunt and feast in the woods. Likewise, the dragon Smaug is wittily interpolated from the fearsome dragons of old yet retains many of their traits: he is lethal, greedy, and guards the gold hoard. More lethal still, perhaps, is dragon sickness, the compulsive illness that affects both men and dwarves so that they become miserly, irrational, and violent.

What did dragons mean to Tolkien? Writing in his famous essay "*Beowulf*: The Monsters and the Critics," Tolkien identifies the dragon with the death of the individual and ultimately the destruction of the world (a central theme of "The Wanderer," a medieval elegy that survives in the Exeter Book, a manuscript copied sometime in the tenth century). This chapter explores the ways in which Tolkien crafts his literary art from older fictions, particularly the medieval stories that he studied at Oxford, making them new for modern readers in his tales of Middle-earth.

Beowulf and the Importance of Believing

In "On Fairy-Stories," an essay originally published in 1947, Tolkien explains that a writer of fiction "makes a Secondary World which your mind can enter. Inside it, what he relates is 'true'; it accords with the laws of that world. You therefore believe it, while you are, as it were, inside. The moment disbelief arises, the spell is broken; the magic, or rather art, has failed."[1] In many cases, Tolkien's creation of fictional characters or other worlds is drawn from *Beowulf*, an early medieval text Tolkien translated and edited, and the beauty and power of that poem permeates his fictions and criticism. Beorn, the shape-shifting bear-man who provides safe haven for Bilbo and his fellows, for example, is a re-creation of *Beowulf*. Douglas A. Anderson comments that Tolkien draws on literary criticism written about Beowulf in this part of his story: "The Beorn episode is suffused with imagery inspired by critical thought on Beowulf: from the Germanic-styled hall in which Beorn entertains his visitors, to the leisurely descriptions of clover, bees, hives, and bee-pastures all surrounding his hall—this imagery circles around elements associated with the derivation of the name Beowulf from 'Bee-wolf,'" a compound term, or kenning, a form often used in Old English and Old Norse, in this case meaning bear.[2]

Tolkien's description of Beorn was particularly inspired by how he and his fellow medievalists understood the *Beowulf* poem. He was much taken with the critical work on *Beowulf* of his personal friend, Raymond Wilson Chambers, the Quain Professor of English at University College London. Writing on stories with the common theme of the "Bear's Son" and their possible links with the superhero Beowulf, Chambers remarked upon one very close parallel, the character "Ivashko Medvedko, 'John Honeyeater' or 'Bear.'"[3] In Tolkien's handwritten manuscript of The Hobbit, Beorn was originally named Medwed (Russian for "honey-eater"). Tom Shippey points out that Tolkien's character Beorn also "has a very close analogue in Böthvarr Bjarki (= 'little bear'), a hero from the Norse *Saga of Hrólfr Kraki*."[4]

In the 1933 *Hobbit* typescript, Tolkien changed the character's name from Medwed to Beorn, a word which originally meant "bear" in Anglo-Saxon.[5] Tolkien's drawing of Beorn's Hall that appears in chapter 7 of *The Hobbit*, "Queer Lodgings," is modeled directly on archeological evidence of Anglo-Saxon halls, familiar again from *Beowulf*. Tolkien's picture evokes early twentieth-century reconstructions of a timbered Viking hall with a central fireplace and a hole in the roof to let out the smoke. Tolkien's drafts of this drawing may have been based "on a drawing by his colleague, the medievalist E. V. Gordon, printed in Gordon's 1927 *Introduction to Old Norse*."[6] Tolkien may also have seen a similar hall illustrated by James Guthrie as the frontispiece to *The Riding to Lithend* by Gordon Bottomley, published in 1909.[7] The full imagining of Beorn from his physical description to Tolkien's drawing of his hall derives from medieval sources, modern recreations of medieval sources, and scholarly criticism, demonstrating the range of materials Tolkien had at hand in making fantasy that is entirely believable and completely alive as a "Secondary World."

The Green Knight and Testing the Hero

Another medieval work to which Tolkien alludes in *The Hobbit* is *Sir Gawain and the Green Knight*, a story that concerns the testing of the hero. The saying attributed in *The Hobbit* to Bilbo's father, "Third time pays for all!" is taken directly from this fourteenth-century poem, which Tolkien both edited and translated. In *The Hobbit*, as the dwarves debate what to do before the door leading to the dragon's cave, Bilbo addresses Thorin and says "'third time pays for all' as my father used to say" (*The Hobbit*, 267). The expression occurs in the lines spoken to Sir Gawain by his mysterious host in the Middle English version of *Sir Gawain and the Green Knight*, edited by Tolkien and E. V. Gordon, first published in 1925.[8] The passage was translated by Tolkien as "For I have tested thee twice, and trusty I find thee. / Now 'third time pays for all,' bethink thee tomorrow!"[9] Bilbo repeats this expression a bit later to gird his loins for confrontation with the dragon: "'While there's life there's hope!' as my father used to say, and 'Third time pays for all.' I am going down the tunnel once again. I have been that way twice, when I knew there was a dragon at the other end, so I will risk a third visit when I am no longer sure" (*The Hobbit*, 290). In a letter, Tolkien explained that this phrase is employed "when a third try is needed to rectify two poor efforts, or when a third occurrence may surpass the others and finally prove a man's worth, or a thing's" (*The Hobbit*, 290, n. 1).[10]

Although this describes Bilbo perfectly on his third visit to Smaug's cave, Sir Gawain, the medieval hero, fails his third test, which is the most subtle and challenging. In the fourteenth-century poem, Gawain passes the first two tests by resisting the temptations presented by the host's wife, and for two evenings, he is able exchange his daily winnings with those of the host, as previously agreed upon. On the third, while Gawain just barely escapes the wife's romantic advances, he accepts a green girdle from her when he is told it has magical powers and then conceals it, breaking his bargain with the host. So the third trial, in Gawain's case, is the toughest, yet he fails it. Similarly, in Beowulf's monster fights, Beowulf as an old man is defeated in his third battle, against the dragon, a more formidable monster than Grendel and his mother, whom Beowulf as a young hero dispatches fairly rapidly in the first part of the poem. Bilbo, on the other hand, passes his third monster test with a fair amount of ease. In *The Hobbit*, Tolkien provides a more optimistic resolution to medieval notions of testing, though in the case of Beowulf, even undertaking the third, impossible challenge proves the mettle of the hero.

"Sparks of White Radiance": From *Sir Orfeo* to the Arkenstone

Lighted stones are mentioned early on in *The Hobbit*, in "An Unexpected Party." The song sung by the dwarves cites their work in the mines and their making of swords and jewelry from the metals: "on crowns they hung / The dragon-fire, in twisted wire / They meshed the light of moon and sun" (*The Hobbit*, 44). Like these gems, the Arkenstone, the Heart of the Mountain in The Hobbit and the greatest treasure of the dwarves that has become part of Smaug's dragon hoard, seems to have been influenced by medieval sources. The name "Arkenstone" derives from "eorclanstān" (or precious stone), an Anglo-Saxon term used in *Beowulf* to describe the neck-ring worn by Hygelac, the lord and uncle of Beowulf, in his final battle against the Frisians: "He wore that neck-ring, precious stone." (*The Hobbit*, 293, n. 1).[11] The Arkenstone gem shines "of its own inner light" like the lighted treasure found by Wiglaf in the dragon hoard after Beowulf is mortally wounded in his fight against the beast:

> Also he saw a banner of gold hanging
> high over the hoard, the greatest of hand-wonders,
> woven by skillful hands;
> from it, shone a light so that he might
> see the ground.[12]

Stones lit from within also appear in the fairyland of *Sir Orfeo*, a medieval retelling of the story of Orpheus and Eurydice in which the classical Underworld becomes a frightening fairyland. In this fourteenth-century story, Orfeo is a king and harper who leaves his kingdom and becomes a pilgrim to seek his wife, Heurodis, who has been taken by the fairy king. Carl F. Hostetter identifies Tolkien as the editor of an anonymous edition of the Middle English version of this poem from the Auchinleck manuscript, which was copied in London in the 1330s, and has published Tolkien's edition in a recent article.[13] Printed in 1944 by the Academic Copying Office in Oxford, there are five surviving copies of this edition with several annotated in Tolkien's hand. Tolkien also translated *Sir Orfeo* into modern English. In *Sir Orfeo*, the fairy king wears a crown that of itself shines brightly like the sun, or, as Tolkien translated: "But of one single gem 'twas hewn / That shone as bright as sun at noon."[14] Fairyland in *Sir Orfeo* is perpetually lit by gems so that it never grows dark. Tolkien's translation retains the rhyme scheme and is close to the original:

> And all that land was ever light,
> For when it came to dusk of night
> From precious stones there issued soon
> A light as bright as sun at noon.[15]

Similar to the gems that light the fairy world in *Sir Orfeo*, the Arkenstone "took all the light that fell upon it and changed it into ten thousand sparks of white radiance shot with glints of the rainbow" (*The Hobbit*, 293), and is probably shown at the very top of the pile of treasure in Tolkien's illustration "Conversation with Smaug," one of his original illustrations that was first published in the second

Tolkien's own illustration of Bilbo's "Conversation with Smaug"

impression of the 1937 English edition of *The Hobbit,* accompanied by the caption: "O Smaug the Chiefest and Greatest of Calamities"[16] (Plate 1, Conversation with Smaug; *Hobbit,* 277, marginal note). When Bilbo reveals the Arkenstone to Bard and the Elvenking, Tolkien describes it as full of light as "if a globe had been filled with moonlight and hung before them in a net woven of the glint of frosty stars" (*The Hobbit,* 331). *Sir Orfeo* also provided some of Tolkien's inspiration for the elves in *The Hobbit,* both the gentler Elves of Rivendell and the Elves of the Woodland Realm whose king holds Bilbo and the dwarves prisoner, though the fairy king in *Sir Orfeo* is more menacing and less kindly than the elves Tolkien presents.[17] So, too, is the dragon, Smaug, being a friendlier descendant (though just as lethal) of the dragons in medieval stories.

"Of Dragons Direst": The Medieval Myths Behind Smaug

In "On Fairy-Stories," Tolkien wrote about his childhood interest in medieval literature, commenting that "best of all [was] the nameless North of Sigurd of the Völsungs, and the prince of all dragons. . . . The dragon had the trade-mark *Of Faërie* written plain upon him. In whatever world he had his being it was an Other-world," an imaginary place with, as we have seen previously, its own interior logic. Writing to the poet W. H. Auden, Tolkien commented that his first story, written at around the age of seven, concerned a dragon, and he says further in "On Fairy-Stories" that "I desired dragons with a profound desire" and that "the world that contained even the imagination of Fáfnir was richer and more beautiful."[18] Sigurd Fafnisbani (or killer of the dragon or serpent Fáfnir) is mentioned throughout the Icelandic sagas.[19] In *The Legend of Sigurd and Gudrún,* an adaptation of the Old Norse sagas (specifically *The Poetic Edda* and the prose *Völsunga Saga*), translated by Tolkien in the early 1930s, there are several references to dragons. In *Upphaf* (or Beginning), the poem foreshadows the coming of the end of the world, describing the familiar story of the wolf Fenrir who will kill Ódin at the time of Ragnarok, or Apocalypse, while "The deep Dragon / Shall be the doom of Thór— / Shall all be ended, / Shall Earthperish?"[20]

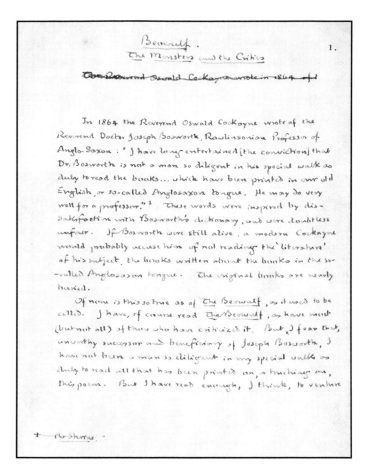

J.R.R. Tolkien's handwritten manuscript of
"Beowulf: The Monsters and the Critics"

In Norse myth (and in Christian apocalyptic writing), dragons survive until the end of time. In the Sigurd story, Regin, the foster father of Sigurd, describes the dragon hoard as containing "Gold more glorious / Than greatest king's" and challenges Sigurd to achieve both "Wealth and worship," or honor, by slaying the dragon.[21] The hero, Sigurd, is well aware that Fáfnir is "Of dragons direst," and perhaps for that very reason undertakes the challenge.[22] In *Beowulf*, when a similar story is recounted in the feasting hall, the dragon-slayer is called "Sigemund," who in Norse mythology is the father of Sigurd but who otherwise has nothing directly to do with dragons. Tolkien, however, thought there must be some link between Beowulf's dragon and Sigurd's, commenting, "It is highly unlikely—however different in detail—that there should be no connexion between Sigemund's wyrm [dragon] and Fáfnir."[23]

In "Smaug Flies Around the Mountain" J.R.R. Tolkien depicted the dragon's threat.

The dragons in *Beowulf* and in the story of Sigurd are similarly described, though Tolkien seems to have preferred the fuller characterization of Fáfnir. Writing to Naomi Mitchison in 1949, Tolkien says: "I find 'dragons' a fascinating product of imagination. But I don't think the *Beowulf* one is frightfully good. . . . Fáfnir in the late Norse versions of the Sigurd-story is better; and Smaug and his conversation obviously is in debt there."[24] Though the *Beowulf* dragon is just as adept at guarding his treasure and, as a fire-breathing, scaly, poisonous monster, shares many of the same physical characteristics with

Fáfnir and later Smaug, and also, like them, destroys buildings with his flames (including Beowulf's own hall), he is silent. He is given some "vivid touches of the right kind—as Þa se wyrm onwoc, wroth waes geniwad; stonc aefter stane, 2285—in which this dragon is real worm, with a bestial life and thought of his own, but the conception, none the less draconitas rather than draco," as Tolkien informed his hearers in his famous scholarly lecture, "Beowulf: The Monsters and the Critics," which then became the best-known scholarly essay on Beowulf to date.[25] (Plate 2, Tolkien's autograph, "Beowulf: The Monsters and the Critics") The Old English passage simply describes the awakening of the dragon, the renewal of his wrath, and his slithering along the rock, though he is, according to Tolkien, more a personification of evil, of draconitas or dragon-ness, than a fully realized dragon.

But personification or not, the one trespass that galvanizes Beowulf's dragon into action after hundreds of years of somnolence also furnished material for Tolkien. In the Beowulf poem, a slave awakens the dragon's wrath by stealing a cup from the dragon's closely guarded treasure hoard—armor, wealth, and weapons buried by the Last Survivor of a lost tribe 300 years before—in order to pay wergild (a fine for a crime) to his master. Readers of The Hobbit will immediately recognize similarities between Tolkien's description of Smaug's hoard ("coats of mail, helms and axes, swords and spears hanging; and there in rows stood great jars and vessels filled with a wealth that could not be guessed") and Bilbo's parallel theft of "a great two-handled cup, as heavy as he could carry," as Smaug briefly stirs in his slumber (The Hobbit, 270–71). When asked whether he had lifted the cup-stealing episode from Beowulf, Tolkien rather ingenuously and jokingly replied in a letter to the editor of the Observer:

> Beowulf is among my most valued sources; though it was not consciously present to the mind in the process of writing, in which the episode of the theft arose naturally (and almost inevitably) from the circumstances. It is difficult to think of any other way of conducting the story at that point. I fancy the author of Beowulf would say much the same.

In his opening to the same letter, Tolkien even identifies himself with dragons: "I am as susceptible as a dragon to flattery, and would gladly show off my diamond waistcoat," an allusion to Smaug's "belly crusted with gems and fragments of gold" (*The Hobbit*, 270).[26]

In *The Hobbit*, the dragon is mentioned right in the first chapter, in the song of the dwarfs: "The dragon's ire more fierce than fire / Laid low their towers and houses frail" (Plate 3, Smaug flies around the Mountain). And the dwarves end by singing: "We must away, ere break of day / To win our harps and gold from him!" (*The Hobbit*, 44–45). In the same chapter, Thorin describes to Bilbo the main characteristics of dragons: They "steal gold and jewels, you know, from men and elves and dwarves" and "they guard their plunder as long as they live (which is practically for ever, unless they are killed), and never enjoy a brass ring of it. Indeed they hardly know a good bit of work from a bad, though they usually have a good notion of the current market value" (*The Hobbit*, 55). While the Beowulf poet says briefly that the area where the dragon lives is a stone hollow marked by dragon's fiery breath, Tolkien describes the dragon's lair as "undoubtedly hot" (*The Hobbit*, 270) and further develops the idea of the dragon's destruction of the whole vicinity by naming it the Desolation of the Dragon. The area Smaug inhabits is "bleak and barren," with no bushes or trees, just "broken and blackened stumps to speak of ones vanished" (*The Hobbit*, 257); for Tolkien, "areas become wastelands because dragons live there."[27]

Thorin then mentions that "most specially greedy, strong and wicked worm called Smaug," who has held the treasure trove for 171 years before *The Hobbit* opens (*The Hobbit*, 55; 55, n. 47).[28] This description of finding and guarding the hoard, too, seems partially drawn from *Beowulf*, where the dragon comes with delight upon the buried treasure and weaponry of a dead tribe and guards it for 300 years without knowing its true value: "The ancient night-ravager found the hoard-joy standing open. . . . he is none the better for it".[29] Thorin tells Bilbo that Smaug appeared "in a spout of flame," killed the dwarves, and took "all their wealth for himself. Probably, for that is the dragons' way, he has piled it all up in a great heap far inside, and sleeps on it for a bed" (*The Hobbit*, 56), an elaboration upon the dragon's activities as described by the *Beowulf* poet.

While Beowulf's nameless dragon seems content to drowse out his years on his hoard without much human interaction until he is alerted to the loss of his cup, Smaug carries off people, "especially maidens, to eat, until Dale was ruined, and all the people dead or gone" (*The Hobbit*, 56); Smaug, in other words, initially behaves in the time-honored way of fairy-tale dragons, his actions calling to mind the story of St. George's rescue of the beautiful maiden from a destructive, murderous, fire-breathing dragon. But like the dragon in *Beowulf*, Smaug, too, feels great rage at Bilbo's theft of his cup:

> Thieves! Fire! Murder! Such a thing had not happened since first he came to the Mountain! His rage passes description— the sort of rage that is only seen when rich folk that have more than they can enjoy suddenly lose something that they have long had but have never before used or wanted. His fire belched forth. (*Hobbit*, 272–73)

This again is an expansion of the notion found originally in *Beowulf* that dragons guard treasure without understanding its worth, while it compares Smaug to a wealthy person who does not value all he has. When Bilbo puts on his invisibility ring and visits the dragon, Smaug scents him and pays him a backhanded compliment ("You have nice manners for a thief and a liar"), and Bilbo speaks to him in riddles, as "No dragon can resist the fascination of riddling talk" (*The Hobbit*, 279).

Riddles were a famous form of Anglo-Saxon entertainment, and the oldest ones in English, over ninety of them, may be read in the Exeter Book, a manuscript dating from the tenth century. The chat between Bilbo and Smaug has been influenced, as Tom Shippey points out, by the riddling in "an Eddic poem *Fáfnismál*, in which Sigurthr [Sigemund] and Fáfnir talk while the dragon dies from the wound the hero has given him. Like Bilbo, Sigurthr refuses to tell the dragon his name but replies riddlingly (for fear of being cursed)."[30] We also learn that Smaug has one penetrable spot, his left breast (*The*

Hobbit, 283), again similar to both the *Beowulf* dragon and Fáfnir, whose vulnerable parts are beneath or below.

"The Monsters Do Not Depart": The Enduring Dangers of Dragon Sickness

Even after they are defeated, dragons remain dangerous, as their poisonous greed has a malevolent afterlife. In *The Legend of Sigurd and Gudrún*, Tolkien's adaptation of the prose *Völsunga Saga*, Fáfnir warns Sigurd about the charm on the hoard: "my guarded gold / Gleams with evil, / Bale it bringeth / To both my foes." To the dying dragon, Sigurd then reaffirms the mortality of all creatures: "Life each must leave / On his latest day, / Yet gold gladly / Will grasp the living!" an elliptical passage that suggests that while all men will eventually die, they will gladly possess gold while on earth.[31] There is a further implication that gold will literally grasp them, reflecting the idea that grasping is a property inherent in the gold itself. Fáfnir then says "this gold is glamoured. / Grasp not! Flee thou!" attesting to the charm or enchantment placed upon the gold hoard.[32] Though Fáfnir tells him the gold is cursed, Sigurd ignores this, believing this "merely the device of greed to protect the gold even though its guardian be slain. . . . Yet the curse began to work swiftly."[33] Similarly, the dragon's hoard in *Beowulf* has been wound in a spell, one reason it is reburied with Beowulf after he wins it from the dragon for his people:

> Then that huge heritage,
> gold of men of old, was wound
> in a spell, so that no one of men might
> touch the ring-hall.[34]

Here again, the *Völsunga Saga* and *Beowulf* provide sources for lethal dragon hoards with poisoned treasure. The dragon sickness in *The Hobbit*, which comes from encountering gold guarded by dragons, is a form of coveting and greed that afflicts men, elves, and hobbits: "The quality is that of possession, possessiveness. A dragon like Smaug embodies possessiveness vividly in his great, but useless, hoard," and the disease can be passed on.[35] After Smaug is slain, the people of the Lake-town Esgaroth become obsessed with the unguarded treasure: "Men spoke of the recompense for all their harm that they would soon get from it, and wealth over and to spare with which to buy rich things from the South" (*The Hobbit*, 311). The dwarves are afflicted with coveting, and even Bilbo does "not reckon with the power that gold has upon which a dragon has long brooded, nor with dwarvish hearts." (*The Hobbit*, 323).

The Master of Lake-town, who takes his gold into the wilderness and loses the company of men, is one of a long line of characters who are destroyed by greed when they become misers, descended from the bad kings or lords in Anglo-Saxon and older literature. In *Beowulf*, for example, Heremod is presented as one model not to follow, a miserly king who "lived without joy" (l. 1720) and who turns on his own people and is ultimately betrayed and killed by an enemy tribe. So, too, the Old Master who appropriates for himself the gold given him to help the people of Lake-town comes to "a bad end"; he "fell under the dragon-sickness, and took most of the gold and fled with it, and died of starvation in the Waste, deserted by his companions" (*The Hobbit*, 362). The hoard also engenders greed in the dwarves and incites the ferocious battle with the goblins near the end of the story, causing strife and warfare.

The themes of greed, enmity, and destruction also appear in another Anglo-Saxon poem from the *Exeter Book* called "The Wanderer," in which the end of the world is predicted to come after long warfare: "All this earthly habitation shall be emptied."[36] Against this inevitable doom stands only the hero, whom Tolkien celebrates in "The Monsters and the Critics," a man who can stand against certain death and who cares more for his fame, or reputation, than life itself. Discussing Sigurd, Tolkien says, "the prince of the heroes of the North, supremely memorable—*hans nafn mun uppi meðan veröldin stendr* [his name shall last while the world lasts]—was a dragon-slayer."[37] In *Beowulf*, Tolkien says, the author shows "forth the permanent value of that pietas which treasures the memory of man's struggles in the dark past, man fallen and not yet saved, disgraced but not dethroned."[38]

Tolkien describes the dragon-slayers Beowulf and Sigurd as "more significant than a standard hero, a man faced with a foe more evil than any human enemy of house or realm," as they are also "incarnate in time, walking in heroic history, and treading the named lands of the North."[39] Fictional characters are placed in named historical settings, creating identification with time and place; they are heroes who inspire the hearers of their tales to take on whatever challenges life presented, especially the greatest of these: their own mortality. In his lecture, Tolkien imagines the stories' original audience living "in a little circle of light about their halls, men with courage as their stay

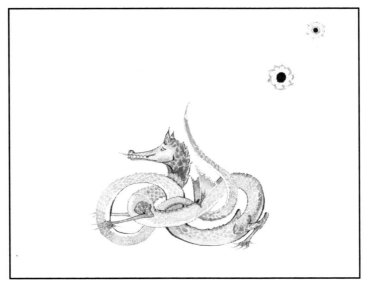

Tolkien's medieval inspiration shows in his watercolor of
a "Coiled Dragon"

went forward to that battle with the hostile world and the offspring of the dark which ends for all, even the kings and champions, in defeat." Against that certain ending which all must face, there is only courage. Yet even though heroes die, "the monsters do not depart."[40] The power of *Beowulf*, Tolkien concludes, derives from its "peculiar solemnity," its language, which retains "essential kinship with our own," and its poetic voice that "must ever call with a profound appeal—until the dragon comes."[41] *Beowulf* and the Northern sagas end tragically and magnificently, the denouement of the plot a confrontation between a mighty dragon and a mighty hero; the hero falls, but his bravery transcends inevitable defeat.

"Very Happy to the End of His Days": Tolkien's Modern Take on the Medieval

The Hobbit, however, ends happily. At the beginning of the final chapter, the elves sing a triumphant song: "The dragon is withered, / His bones are now crumbled; / His armour is shivered, / His splendor is humbled!" (*The Hobbit*, 355). The hero Bilbo returns to the Hall at Bag-End, and readers are told "he remained very happy to the end of his days" (*The Hobbit*, 361). Though his medieval sources are often solemn, Tolkien's own work is marked by playfulness, even effervescence, in *The Hobbit* and elsewhere.

Two years after he presented "*Beowulf*: The Monsters and the Critics" to the British Academy on November 25, 1936, Tolkien talked on the theme of dragons as one of a series of Christmas lectures for children at the University Museum, Oxford, using slides of various drawings he had made himself. In the latter lecture, perhaps drawing again on *Beowulf*, in which the dragon is said to be fifty feet long, Tolkien explained that "A respectable dragon should be 20 ft or more," and that there are two types, creeping and winged.[42] Among the slides of his drawings of dragons that Tolkien showed the children was a coiled dragon (Plate 4, Coiled Dragon), which he described as: "a nice little worm in an early stage of growth, a newly hatched dragonet, which was pretty (as young things so often are)."[43] In Tolkien's imagining, even baby dragons have their charms. Appropriating details from medieval stories, Tolkien alchemically transforms aspects of the medieval texts he loved, edited, and translated. Drawing on Anglo-Saxon works, Old Norse and Icelandic sagas, *Sir Orfeo*, and *Sir Gawain and the Green Knight*, among other sources, Tolkien creates a fully realized Other-World in *The Hobbit*, complete with maps and illustrations and inhabited by characters, monsters, and even gems inspired by medieval models.

Notes

1. J. R. R. Tolkien, "On Fairy-Stories," in *The Monsters and the Critics and Other Essays*, ed. Christopher Tolkien (Boston: Houghton Mifflin, 1984), 109–61, 132. All references to *The Hobbit* are taken from Douglas A. Anderson, *The Annotated Hobbit: Revised and Annotated Edition* (Boston: Houghton Mifflin, 2002), and are subsequently abbreviated as *The Hobbit* in the text.

2. Douglas A. Anderson, "R. W. Chambers and *The Hobbit*," in *Tolkien Studies: An Annual Scholarly Review* 3 (Morgantown: West Virginia University Press, 2006), 137–47, 142. Tolkien's translation of *Beowulf* was found in the Bodleian Library in 2003 and is being edited for publication by Michael Drout (forthcoming from Arizona State University Press).

3. Raymond Wilson Chambers, *Beowulf: An Introduction to the Study of the Poem with a Discussion of the Stories of Offa and Finn*, 2nd ed. (Cambridge, UK: Cambridge University Press, 1932), 372.

4. Tom Shippey, *The Road to Middle-Earth: Revised and Expanded Edition* (Boston: Houghton Mifflin, 2003), 80.

5. Rawlinson and Bosworth Professor of Anglo-Saxon at Oxford and a fellow of Pembroke College

6. Wayne G. Hammond and Christina Scull, *J. R. R. Tolkien: Artist and Illustrator* (Boston: Houghton Mifflin 1995), 124, n. 28. They further comment, 150–51, "This connection was first suggested by Prof. J. S. Ryan in 'Two Oxford Scholars: Perceptions of the Traditional Germanic Hall,'" *Minas Tirith Evening-Star* 19, no. 1 (Spring 1990), 8–11."

7. Hammond and Scull, *J. R. R. Tolkien*, 124. Bottomley's one-act play, set in Iceland, was published by the Pear Tree Press in Flansham, Sussex, 1909.

8. "*For I haf fraysted þe twys, and faythful I fynde þe. / Now 'þrid tyme þrowe best' þenk on þe morne.*" J. R. R. Tolkien and E. V. Gordon, eds., *Sir Gawain and the Green Knight* (Oxford: Clarendon Press, 1925), ll. 1679–1680.

9. J. R. R. Tolkien, trans., *Sir Gawain and the Green Knight, Pearl, and Sir Orfeo* (New York: Ballantine, 1975), 66.

10. Anderson, *The Annotated Hobbit*, 267–68, n. 1, cites Jared Lobdell, "A Medieval Proverb in *The Lord of the Rings*," *American Notes and Queries Supplement* 1 (1978), 330–31, quoting a letter from Tolkien to Lobdell dated July 31, 1964: "It is an old alliterative saying using the word *throw*: time, period (unrelated to the verb *throw*); sc. this third occasion is the best time—the time for special effort and/or luck."

11. "*He þā fraetwe waeg, / eorclan-stānas*" ll. 1207–1208. The text of *Beowulf* is taken from Frederick Klaeber, ed., *Beowulf and The Fight at Finnsburg*, 3rd ed. (Boston: D. C. Heath, 1950). The translation is my own but relies to some extent on E. Talbot Donaldson, trans., *Beowulf: The Donaldson Translation, Backgrounds and Sources, Criticism*, ed. Joseph F. Tuso (New York: Norton, 1975). All subsequent references to *Klaeber's Beowulf* are cited in the text by line numbers. See also J. R. R. Tolkien, "On Translating Beowulf," in *The Monsters and the Critics and Other Essays*, ed. Christopher Tolkien (Boston: Houghton Mifflin, 1984), 49–71

12. *Swylce he siomian geseah segn eallgylden/ heah ofer horde, hondwundra mæst,/ gelocen leoðocræftum; of ðam leoma stod,/ þæt he þone grundwong ongitan meahte,/ wræte giondwlitan.* (*Beowulf*, 2767–2771)

13. Carl F. Hostetter, "Sir Orfeo: A Middle English Version by J. R. R. Tolkien," *Tolkien Studies: An Annual Scholarly Review* 1 (Morgantown: West Virginia University Press, 2004), 85–124, 93. All subsequent references to Tolkien's Middle English edition of "Sir Orfeo" published in Hostetter's essay are cited in the text by line numbers.

14. "Ac it was al on precious ston, / As briȝte so the sonne it schon" (ll. 151–152) Tolkien, *Gawain, Pearl, and Sir Orfeo*, 137.

15. "Al that lond was euer liȝt, / For when it was the therke niȝt, / The riche stones liȝte gonne, / As briȝt as doth at none sonne." (ll. 349–352) Ibid., 142.

16. Of the five color paintings for *The Hobbit*, this was one of four that Tolkien painted over a few weeks of university vacation in mid-July 1937 ("Introduction," *Hobbit*, 14). According to *J. R. R. Tolkien: Life and Legend. An Exhibition to Commemorate the Centenary of the Birth of J. R. R. Tolkien (1892–1973)* (Oxford: Bodleian Library, 1973), 95, Tolkien always intended that *The Hobbit* would be illustrated, and "His published black and white *Hobbit* pictures, as well as a number of preliminary versions, seem to have been made all in one great concentration of effort during the holidays of December 1936 and early January 1937."

17. Stuart D. Lee and Elizabeth Solopova, *The Keys of Middle-Earth: Discovering Medieval Literature through the Fiction of J. R. R. Tolkien* (New York: Palgrave Macmillan, 2005), 123, 126–27. See also Tom Shippey, *The Road to Middle-Earth* (London: Allen and Unwin, 1982; rev. ed. HarperCollins, 2003), 63–64. The differentiation between elves in Tolkien's fiction may derive from Norse mythology. According to Tolkien's lecture notes, "The Light Elves dwell in a glorious place called Álfheimer (Elf-home, Elf-world), but the Dark Elves 'live down in the earth, and they are unlike the Light Elves in appearance, but much more unlike in nature. The Light Elves are fairer to look upon than the sun, but the Dark Elves are blacker than pitch.'" (quoted in J. R. R. Tolkien, *The Legend of Sigurd & Gudrún*, ed. Christopher Tolkien (New York: Houghton Mifflin, 2009), 359. The Wood-elves appear in the chapters "Flies and Spiders" and "Barrels out of Bond.")

18. Tolkien, "On Fairy-Stories," 109–61, 135. Humphrey Carpenter, ed., with Christopher Tolkien, *The Letters of J. R. R. Tolkien* (London: George Allen & Unwin, 1981; Boston: Houghton Mifflin, 1981, rev. ed. 2000), item 163, 211–17, 214.

19. There are even early comic references to Sigurd the dragon-slayer. In George Clark, trans., "The Tale of the Sarcastic Halli," in *The Sagas of Icelanders*, ed. Ornolfur Thorsson, trans. Katrina C. Attwood, George Clark, et al. (New York: Penguin, 2000), 694–712, 696, King Harald Sigurdarson of Norway asks a scop, or bard, to make a poem on the spot about a quarrel between a tanner and a blacksmith, but "to make them into altogether different people than they really are. Make one of them into Sigurd Fafnisbani (Killer of the Serpent Fafnir) and the other into Fafnir, but nevertheless identify each other's trade." In "The Tale of Thorstein Shiver," trans. Anthony Maxwell, 713–16, a demon tells Thorstein that Sigurd Fafnisbani endures the torments of hell best of all because he both kindles the oven and serves as the kindling.

20. Tolkien, *Legend of Sigurd & Gudrún*, 63. See also Tom Shippey, "Virgin's Ring: How Tolkien Set Out to Hit Readers 'in the Eye' and Fill a Famous Gap in the Legend of Brynhild," *TLS*, May 8, 2009, 3–4.

21. Tolkien, *Legend of Sigurd & Gudrún*, 101.

22. Ibid., 101.

23. Tolkien's lecture notes quoted in Tolkien, *Legend of Sigurd & Gudrún*, 355.

24. Carpenter, *Letters*, no. 122, 134.

25. Tolkien, "*Beowulf*: The Monsters and the Critics," in *The Monsters and the Critics and Other Essays*, ed. Christopher Tolkien (Boston: Houghton Mifflin, 1984), 5–48, 17. The Anglo-Saxon quoted by Tolkien may be translated: "Then the worm awoke, wrath was renewed; he moved along the rock." In Klaeber, *Beowulf*, these are lines 2287–2288.

26. Carpenter, *Letters*, no. 25, 30–32, 31, 30. In a subsequent letter to his publisher, Stanley Unwin, no. 26, 32–35, Tolkien commented that he had not intended that the whole of the letter to the editor be published in the newspaper.

27. John D. Rateliff, *The History of the Hobbit. Part Two: Return to Bag-End* (Boston: Houghton Mifflin, 2007), 484.

28. "Smaug descended on Erebor . . . one hundred and seventy-one years before the time in which *The Hobbit* is set."

29. "*Hordwynne fond / eald uhtsceaða opene standan. . . . ne byð him wihte ðy sel*" (*Beowulf*, ll. 2270–2271, 2277).

30. Shippey, *Road to Middle-Earth*, 90.

31. Tolkien, *Legend of Sigurd & Gudrún*, 110.

32. Ibid., 110, 209.

33. Ibid., 99.

34. "*þonne wæs þæt yrfe, eacencræftig, / iumonna gold galdre bewunden, / þæt ðam hringsele hrinan ne moste / gumena ænig.*" (*Beowulf*, ll. 3051–3054)

35. Colin Duriez, *The J. R. R. Tolkien Handbook: A Concise Guide to His Life, Writings, and the World of Middle-Earth* (Grand Rapids, MI: Baker Books), 72–73, 73.

36. This line is quoted from memory. "The Wanderer" further includes the famous *ubi sunt* (where are they?) passage, a lament for lost heroes and a lost way of life that is incorporated by Tolkien into the example given by Aragorn of the songs of the Riders: "Where now the horse and the rider?" Cited in Tom Shippey, *J. R. R. Tolkien, Author of the Century* (Boston: Houghton Mifflin, 2001), 97.

37. Tolkien, "*Beowulf*: The Monsters and the Critics," 16.

38. Ibid., 23.

39. Ibid., 17.

40. Ibid., 18.

41. Ibid., 33.

42. *Tolkien: Life and Legend*, 53.

43. Hammond and Scull, *J.R.R. Tolkien*, 53. See also *J. R. R. Tolkien: Life and Legend*, 52, 53; as a caption for his drawing "Coiled Dragon," Tolkien added a quotation from *Beowulf*: "*hringboga[n] heorte gefysed*" (the heart of the coiling beast was stirred), l. 2561; Carpenter, *Letters*, no. 25.

Plates (By permission of the Tolkien Trust and the Bodleian Library, Oxford)

Plate 1

Conversation with Smaug. Pencil, black ink, colored ink, watercolor, white body color (Tolkien Drawings, fol. 30).

Plate 2

Tolkien's autograph, "Beowulf: The Monsters and the Critics" (Tolkien 1, fol. 1).

Plate 3

Smaug Flies Around the Mountain. Pen and ink (Tolkien Drawings 89, fol. 24).

Plate 4

Coiled Dragon. Pencil and watercolor (Tolkien Drawings 87, fol. 37).

The White Council

(Contributors)

Kristen M. Burkholder is at present a librarian at Oklahoma City University, and is also an erstwhile medieval historian with an especial interest in food. She first read *The Hobbit* at the age of eight, thinks that everyone should eat second breakfasts (and elevenses, and tea, and . . .), and would love to try one of Beorn's honey cakes.

Stefan Donecker studied history and Scandinavian studies in Vienna and Umeå, Sweden, and received his Ph.D. from the European University Institute in Florence in 2010. Currently, he is a postdoctoral researcher at the Institute for Medieval Research of the Austrian Academy of Sciences in Vienna, specializing in the intellectual history of the 16th and 17th centuries. Accordingly, some of his closest friends are scholars who have been dead for roughly 400 years, which makes him the only academic necromancer on the White Council. He has researched extensively on werewolves and shape-changers and has been described as "hairy" by witnesses.

Martha Driver is a Distinguished Professor of English and Women's Studies at Pace University and has published extensively on many topics, particularly medieval manuscripts and early print books. She is considering taking her next research leave in the archives of Minas Tirith, where she is certain to find some wonderful manuscripts to study.

Christina Fawcett teaches English Literature and Cultural Studies at the University of Winnipeg in Canada. Her Ph.D., from the University of Glasgow, discusses the morally representational figure of the monster in Tolkien's fiction. She has been imagining journeys in Middle-earth since the age of three, after her father read her *The Hobbit* as a bedtime story.

Colin Gibbons completed his Master's Degree in History at Laurentian University, where he researched the Viking invasion of England under Ívarr the Boneless as well as other medieval topics. Having received a Bachelor of Education from Lakehead University, Colin now teaches on the southern shores of Georgian Bay, where in the summer he sometimes hears a noise like a hurricane coming from the north, causing the pines to creak and crack in the hot dry wind.

Janice Liedl is an Associate Professor of History at Laurentian University in Canada who specializes in English history since the time of Henry VIII. After a workweek spent teaching, reading criminal trial records, and working her way through musty manuscripts, she longs for a peaceful retreat amongst the elves of Rivendell.

Bram Mathew studied at the University of Manchester and Laurentian University and specializes in Vikingism and other reconstructions of the Old North. After a day of reading through the print culture of 19th-century Britain, he dreams of blowing elaborate smoke rings with Bilbo Baggins while relaxing in the idyllic countryside of Bag End.

Aven McMaster teaches Classical Studies at Thorneloe University at Laurentian in Canada and works mainly on Latin poetry and Roman social history. She is always looking for ways to sneak her lifelong love of fantasy literature into her classes and research, so she's very grateful for Tolkien's fascination with ancient civilizations.

Laura Mitchell wrote her doctoral dissertation on magic in 15th-century England at the University of Toronto's Centre for Medieval Studies and has taught at the University of Saskatchewan. She can currently be found writing about magic at The Recipes Project (http://recipes.hypotheses.org/). Laura grew up reading the works of Tolkien, and if she ever got her hands on a magic ring like Bilbo's, she would definitely use it to play tricks on people.

Jessica Monteith-Chachuat is pursuing her doctorate at the University of Reading. She specializes in hunting down the monsters found in obscure medieval texts and writing lengthy commentary on the folklore of werewolves and witches. She is excited that the White Council offers opportunities for practical application of her hard-won knowledge.

Leila K. Norako specializes in Middle English romance and Crusades literature. She began her residence as a postdoctoral fellow in Stanford's "Thinking Matters" Program in the fall of 2014. When she isn't pouring over medieval texts, she enjoys heading off on adventures with her husband and daughter.

Nancy Reagin is a Professor of History and Women's & Gender Studies (joint appointment) at Pace University in New York, where she chairs the Department of Women's & Gender Studies. She holds a doctorate in history from Johns Hopkins University and has sundry publications in modern German and European women's history. She hopes to take her next vacation at Rivendell.

Marcus Schulzke is a Post-Doctoral Research Fellow in the School of Politics and International Studies at the University of Leeds; he holds a Ph.D. in Political Science from the University at Albany, SUNY. His research interests include contemporary political theory, applied ethics, and issues of political violence. He is currently finishing a dissertation about how soldiers make ethical decisions during war — a project that fortunately only involves interviews with human soldiers and not with any dwarves or goblins.

Mark Sundaram teaches English at Laurentian University in Canada and specializes in Anglo-Saxon and Norse language and literature. He enjoys exploring the endless knot of connections between language, thought, culture, history, literature, and just about everything else.

Index

Worthy Folk of Middle-earth

Page numbers in *italics* refer to illustrations.

CPSIA information can be obtained at www.ICGtesting.com
Printed in the USA
BVOW05s0236251114

376639BV00006B/208/P